Another Way of Believing

A Brethren Theology

Dale W. Brown

Paul Grout, illustrator

Another Way of Believing: A Brethren Theology
Dale W. Brown

Copyright 2005 Dale W. Brown.
Published by Brethren Press®, 1451 Dundee Avenue, Elgin, IL 60120. Brethren Press is a program of the Church of the Brethren General Board.

All rights reserved. No portion of this book may be reproduced in any form or by any process or technique without the written consent of the publisher, except for brief quotations embodied in critical articles or reviews.

Illustrator: Paul Grout

Library of Congress Control Number: 2005926644
ISBN: 0-87178-064-x

09 08 07   5 4 3 2

Printed in the United States of America

This book is one of several Brethren Press publications displaying the mark of the 300th anniversary of the Brethren (1708-2008). It represents the theme "Surrendered to God, Transformed by Christ, Empowered by the Spirit."

Contents

Foreword v
Tom Kinzie, editor

Preface: How Brethren Do Theology ix

1 Another Way of Believing 1

2 Faith of Believers 13

3 Christ Existing as Community 31

4 Original Blessedness or Original Sin? 49

5 Jesus the Christ 61

6 Living in the Spirit 75

7 Brethren and the Bible 95

8 Sacraments or Ordinances 109

9 Baptism, Love Feast, Anointing 119

10 New Testament Symbols 139

11 Unity and Dissension 155

12 Tossed To and Fro by Winds of Doctrine 171

13 Heritage of Peace 191

14 Whither Brethren? 217

Bibliography 235

Index 241

Foreword

In one of her books, Esther de Waal quotes a wonderful Jewish proverb:

On the Day of Judgment God will ask only one question:
Did you enjoy my world?

Joy is such an integral part of a God-centered life that we might only note its importance when it is gone. In its absence the world seems flat. There is no dimension to things. It is as if a certain spaciousness in which beauty and generosity flourish is no longer there. Even the things that might ordinarily be delighted in seem empty. And what to do when joy is gone?

There is a saying from the early desert tradition that gives a clue to the way joy is recovered and maintained.

> *A certain brother came to Abba Poeman and said: "What ought I*
> *to do, Father? I am in great sadness."*
> *The elder said to him: "Never despise anybody, never speak evil of*
> *anyone, and the Lord will give you peace."*

The joy that is in Dale's book owes much, I think, to his refusal to judge anyone. Perhaps no one's joy for Brethren folk and heritage exceeds Dale's. He would prefer to be called Brother Dale, and so he is to many, many people.

Dale holds within himself—within his heart—some of the great tensions, even polarities, of the Brethren experience, both historical and as the church is now. I mean by that that Dale seems to be as perfectly at home with a young radical filled with dismay at the sorry shape of the world as he is with the older, gentle deaconess savoring homemade ice cream, singing the well-known hymns, and wondering what all the fuss is about.

I have conjectured on how many folks are in Dale's e-mail and snail mail address lists. We could surely find there BRFers, BPFers, former BAMers, Brethrenphiles, and the formerly Brethren, Old Orders, evangelicals, fervent Anabaptists and charismatics, feminists, liberals, fundamentalists, and that whole group of folks who just show up Sunday after Sunday and prefer to be called "none of the above." We would then need to add folks from the larger church: Quakers, Mennonites, mainline Protestants, the Catholic and the Orthodox. And also there would be folks from what has been called the unknown church: unbelievers, the uncertain, and all manner of folk from non-Christian spiritualities . . . Well, the list of his friends will be long, because the heart is large.

Dale's love, generosity, openness, and fairness are quite evident throughout this book. It is as if all of us above were gathered in a meetinghouse (and it would have to be a meetinghouse!) sitting, waiting as Brother Dale finished reading the scriptures, closed the revered tome, and started preaching. I was twenty-one or two when I first heard Dale preach. There were a few of us in my home church, waiting to hear a word amid the pain and sorrow we carried during those days of the war in Vietnam. We were waiting on a word from our tradition that we knew was there but hadn't heard, or heard clearly enough, from the pulpit before then.

Dale did preach that word and with real power. I remember tears coming to my eyes (and I was not alone), tears of relief that there was a home for us after all in the Church of the Brethren. I have always thought since then that the line between Dale's preaching and teaching is a thin one and that this is part of Dale's strength. You will notice this slim distinction in many parts of this book, and you will be happy for it.

Dale's preaching and teaching voice is insistent that the gospel calls us to lives dedicated to the good news of peace and justice. He is quite clear about this. For this is what it means to follow Jesus. But Dale also says clearly that we are also to be in Jesus. Dale's sermon that is this book says both things to us, that the church (both Brethren and non-Brethren manifestations of church) must find a way that both follows and lives in Jesus. These together are the way of the gospel—the path of peace and justice, yes, and every step of this way an expression of the love of God we experience in Jesus.

Dale's joy and generosity is in his naming of the various expressions of how Brethren have tried to be both followers and lovers of Jesus. In all of this, we find symbols that have meant so much, the stories that are cherished, the shared failures, heroism that has amazed, the arguments never quite finished, and the remarkable tenacity of the bond that has held so many disparate impulses (and sometimes some mighty cranky folks) together. All of this you will find in Dale's sermon/story of how Brethren think about, share, and live out their faith.

This book, then, is teaching and preaching about the major ways Brethren do theology together. Don't be too worried. There is little technical jargon, and what is there is gently explained. For Brethren, doing theology and living out the faith are very similar. It turns out that what Brethren do intuitively is right: Brethren do theology best when singing, when washing one another's feet, when witnessing to the truth, when staying connected in the midst of contentious issues. Brethren do theology with their feet, by how they live.

Someone once said, "Joy is the echo of God's love within us." So, I invite you to this book that is filled with much joy. Here is much wonderful heartfelt theologizing and storytelling. It is a story Dale tells with love.

Tom Kinzie, editor
February 2005

Preface

The communal heritage of the Brethren dictates that no one person is able to give definitive interpretations of our beliefs and practices. Old portraits of elders, deacons, ministers, and spouses sitting on front pews and behind the preachers' table offer a paradigm of convictions shaped by many. Throughout our history, it has been easier to name Brethren leaders than *the* Brethren leader. The noncreedal legacy of Pietism adds to the problem of knowing and expressing what we believe. Anti-theological biases and anti-intellectualism have both encouraged the virtue of simplicity and undermined the commandment to love God with all our minds. In rejecting the pursuit of theological consensus, many have echoed the motto "It's not what you believe but how you live that counts."

Since for many Brethren the word *theology* elicits negative connotations, it may be necessary to state its meaning. From it roots the word simply means interpretations, meditations, statements, or study of God. In spite of prejudices that many of us share, every generation has nurtured those who explore our roots and interpret anew our faith heritage. Many have sensed that how we live is often based on what we believe. Our context makes it more difficult to determine our beliefs than it is for other denominational scholars who treasure creeds, catechisms, and a single theologian such as Luther whose writings remain quite normative. Yet Brethren have experienced a variety of ways to "do theology."

One approach is to peruse the primary sources. This imitates the first Brethren who relied on "authentic sources" for their first baptisms. Among others they read Gottfried Arnold's *The True Picture of the First Christians in Life and Faith* (1696). Scholars in the twentieth century recovered a wealth of other anabaptist and pietist sources in German and English translations. These efforts have facilitated a better understanding of the beliefs and practices of the early movement. Brethren Press has published four source books: the first two by Donald F. Durnbaugh, *European Origins of the Brethren* (1958) and *The Brethren in Colonial America* (1967); the last two by Roger E. Sappington, *The Brethren in the New Nation* (1976) and *The Brethren in Industrial America* (1985). Each of the source books has a theological section identified as publications, ordinances and beliefs, or devotional writings. Fortunately,

Dale Stoffer's masterful and thorough dissertation on the *Background and Development of Brethren Doctrines, 1650-1987,* was published in the Brethren Encyclopedia Monograph Series. Unfortunately, for Church of the Brethren scholars, in Part V Stoffer needed to focus exclusively on the development of his progressive strand, the Brethren Church, which came after his thorough and fair interpretations of the divisions of 1881-1883.

Another way to do theology is to examine the minutes of Annual Meetings or Conferences. It has been fortunate that a people who espouse no creed but the New Testament come together regularly in order to renew their covenant. In this way Brethren strive to resolve differences in the family ethos of the big meeting. Ideally, the Holy Spirit leads the body to a greater sense of unity in the bond of peace. Often a committee representing different opinions is chosen to produce a document that is debated, revised, adopted, or rejected by the delegate body. The intent is to formulate decisions that embody New Testament teachings and the mind of Christ.

Henry Kurtz, editor of the *Gospel Visitor,* forerunner to *Messenger,* our denominational magazine, published a *Brethren's Encyclopedia* in 1867. In it he organized minutes alphabetically by topics that deal with the life and thought of the Brethren. His added notes reveal his own insights and views about the consensus he found in the minutes. The same random and intentional search for doctrinal topics can be appropriated from three (soon to be four) volumes of *The Brethren Encyclopedia.* In the historical libraries and archives of our church headquarters, colleges, and seminary, it is possible to do the same by perusing clusters of old periodicals from the mid-nineteenth century to the present. Likewise, a mixture of popular and more substantive theological articles is available in *Brethren Life and Thought,* a periodical published first in 1955.

Throughout our history, modest and more major efforts of Brethren writers approach what in scholarly circles is named *systematic theology.* The bibliography will include a more complete listing. Here we refer to some influential authors of the eighteenth and nineteenth centuries. We have *The Complete Writings of Alexander Mack,* edited by William Eberly. The source books contain major theological writings of Alexander Mack, Jr., and excerpts from influential Brethren such as Christopher Sauer, Jr., Michael Frantz, Peter Nead, Henry Kurtz, John Kline, James Quinter, R. H. Miller, D. L. Miller, and J. H. Moore. The last three also nurtured theological understandings in the nineteenth century. From the twentieth century, we add names such as Edward Frantz, D. W. Kurtz, S. S. Blough, C. C. Ellis, William Beahm, Donald F. Durnbaugh, Emmert Bittinger, Wayne Zunkel, William G. Willoughby, Roger Sappington, and Vernard Eller. It would be remiss to neglect the theological influence of hymn writers such as William Beery and Kenneth Morse. More numerous influential interpreters of our faith may be unnamed role models: relatives, camp leaders, teachers, college administrators, musicians, evangelists, peacemakers, beloved elders, and pastors.

This reality leads to another way of believing, which constitutes a major way that Brethren absorb theology. In scholarly circles it is defined as *narrative theology*. Though a popular theological current, it has been with Brethren from their beginnings. Basic convictions are derived from a lived theology.

Beliefs are molded when revelatory stories out of our heritage are existentially remembered, when biblical stories and songs we love shape our story, and when stories of saints in our tradition empower our beings and define our faith. Narrative theology filters through James Lehman's fascinating portraits in *The Old Brethren*. In classes, I recommended the book as delightful reading. I judged it an excellent way to saturate students with the ethos, the *zeitgeist*, of our people. I was surprised how those not acquainted with our heritage were attracted to the foibles and lifestyles of these peculiar pioneers. A Lutheran student exclaimed: "What I appreciate about your heritage are your fascinating characters. I thought we had one with Luther, but he does not hold a candle to yours."

James Wm. McClendon more formally defined this narrative perspective in his *Systematic Theology*. McClendon was of Baptist background and theology professor at the Episcopal Church Divinity School of the Pacific and the Graduate Theology Union, Berkeley, when he and his wife moved to Pasadena and joined the Church of the Brethren. Nancey Murphy McClendon was called to a professorship in philosophy at Fuller Theological Seminary, and James was appointed Distinguished Scholar in Residence at Fuller. He continued to write his *Systematic Theology* and finished it shortly before his death. He intentionally wrote for a cluster of Baptist traditions, including the Brethren. Instead of the conventional order of doing theology, he titled his first volume *Ethics* instead of *Doctrine,* the title of his second volume. He believed that one best derives doctrine from a knowledge of the commitments, practices, stories, and ethics that shape the common life of the people. This other way of doing theology recognizes that in these traditions doctrine and ethics are so interwoven that the seam between the two is difficult to find.

Personal Professions, Confessions, and Biases

I have learned that one can be more fair and objective by acknowledging basic biases. I love my Brethren heritage. The best things in life permeated my pilgrimage as my modest parental and congregational roots expanded to the larger Brethren milieu. Biblical newness of life came through youth camps, workcamps, and exemplary lives of students and faculty at McPherson College and Bethany Seminary. I experienced another way of living through the lives of saintly parishioners when I was a pastor, through networks of relationships on conference committees, in my involvement with peace activists, and through the gracious hospitality of congregations.

Another side of me resonates with a sentiment expressed in a student paper: "I love our heritage, but I hate the Church of the Brethren." Such erupted when the student felt little support for his resistance to the draft, a position he claimed from his heritage. With him I often wish that Brethren were less accommodating to our culture and more faithful to the best of our heritage. I realize that others desire the same for me. Unlike the above sentiment, my love abides with brothers and sisters through discouraging times and through times of new awakenings of incarnations of the Spirit's presence through our efforts to continue the work of Jesus.

I enjoy probing the origins of our doctrines and practices. I like what I find. Being Brethren, however, does not mean we worship our heritage. We do not need to choose between being Brethren and being a Christian. Instead, we believe our heritage helps us to interpret what it means to be Christian. For this reason I strive to remain Christ-centered and biblically faithful in interpreting our beliefs. We study our past to discern who God wants us to be today and to envision and participate in the biblical vision of the kingdom coming. Our efforts to learn, lament, or rejoice how we have changed should lead us to allow the Spirit to inspire new applications of our heritage for today.

Though I desire greater doctrinal clarity and unity of faith, I join McClendon in understanding that a different way of living means a different way of believing. For Brethren, New Testament emphases lead to a theology that is relational more than propositional. The two greatest commandments chosen by our Lord refer to our loves and relationships more than propositions that we should believe. The Gospel of John names Jesus as truth. We learn that right relationships with God, Jesus, others, and God's good creation define truth more than dogmatic propositions, which nevertheless can be helpful. This may seem counter to much that is named theology. Yet an emphasis on loving relationships with God, Jesus, and others as the source of doctrines is in itself a theological statement.

I am ecumenical in the sense that I have gained much from a lifetime of discerning the beliefs of other Christians and religions. We often experience that we have much in common. We discover in these endeavors that our different way of believing constitutes in part our theological uniqueness. Some seem to be more interested in being evangelical or liberal Protestants than being Brethren. To this primary identity they add a few Brethren distinctives. My experience has been that there are often some basic theological differences with most fundamentalists, evangelicals, liberals, and other Protestants. How else can we explain differences on issues like the priesthood of all believers, capital punishment, rejection of oaths, relationship to the state, the "theologianhood" of all believers, love of enemies, and judgments about the things that make for peace? In spite of these differences, I believe in cooperating with others in areas of common mission.

In summary, I hope my writing participates in some way in the recovery of our Brethren vision. I acknowledge that such recovery has benefitted greatly from the work of my colleague, Donald F. Durnbaugh.

I remain aware how presumptuous it seems for any one person to articulate theological themes for the Brethren. Yet I confess that I have not worked in isolation. I dedicate this book to four decades of students from whom I have learned, while at the same time in our being together we have engendered new understandings and appreciation for our heritage in a class entitled Brethren in Theological Perspectives.

I also dedicate this book to my parents. Their lifestyle and priorities imparted to me what it means to be Brethren. And I would be remiss not to include Lois, my companion of nearly sixty years, whose inclusive grace in living for others has embodied our heritage more concretely than I.

D. W. B.

Chapter 1

Another Way of Believing
Noncreedalism and nonconformity

We are meant to hold firmly to the truth in love and to grow up in every way into Christ, the Head.
—Ephesians 4:15, J. B. Phillips translation

It was our final class discussion. Non-Brethren members were asked to honestly respond to our heritage. A Lutheran woman was the first to reply: "There are many things I admire, but your refusal to formulate creeds seems like you want to have religion without any clothes."

Benjamin Franklin Meets Michael Wohlfahrt

A founding father of our nation, Benjamin Franklin could be labeled a secular humanist if living today. He absorbed the skepticism of his English philosopher friend, David Hume. An apocryphal story by Wesleyan scholars relates that the free-thinking Franklin was so moved by George Whitefield's preaching that he placed a coin in the offering. Franklin seemed to enjoy his relationships with the sects. As a competitor to the Sauer press, he accepted printing jobs from the Ephrata community. In his *Autobiography*, Franklin recalls a conversation with Michael Wohlfahrt, a leader in the cloisters (115-16). Wohlfahrt complained about the "abominable," unfair charges of zealots of other persuasions. Franklin explained that such had always been the case with new sects and advised him "to publish articles of their belief and the rules of their discipline." Wohlfahrt responded that such had been proposed and rejected for this reason:

> When we were first drawn together as a society, it had pleased God to enlighten our minds so far as to see that some doctrines which were once esteemed truths, were errors, and that others which we had esteemed errors, were real truths. From time to time He has been pleased to afford us farther light, and our principles have been improving, and our errors diminishing. Now we are not sure that we are arrived at the end of this progression, at the perfection of spiritual or theological knowledge; and we fear that if we should once print our confession of faith, we should feel ourselves as if bound and confin'd by it, and perhaps be unwilling to receive farther improvement, and our successors, still more so as conceiving what we their elders and founders had done to be something sacred, never to be departed from.

Franklin's style likely pervaded the recording of the conversation. Yet his response to a follower of Conrad Beissel articulated views held by the German Baptist Brethren. No doubt, they relished this compliment and clever analogy of their famous contemporary:

> This modesty of a sect is perhaps a singular instance in the history of mankind, every other sect supposing itself in possession of all truth, and that those who differ are so far in the wrong like a man traveling in foggy weather, those at some distance before him on the road he sees wrapped up in the fog, as well as those behind him, and also the people in the fields on each side. But near him all appears clear, tho' in truth he is as much in the fog as any of them.

Symbolical (Creedal) Books of Lutheranism

The setting for Franklin's story begins with Martin Luther. Luther maintained that his was a reformation of doctrine, not life. The emphasis on right doctrine led to a legacy of many doctrinal disputes. In efforts to restore unity, theologians began to appropriate rationalistic elements of the scholastic method that Luther had rejected. In defense of orthodox theology, scholars sought to produce an exact formal expression in regard to controversial issues.

Their efforts culminated in publishing the creedal or *Symbolical Books* of Lutheranism in 1580 (Jacobs 472). The collection begins with the ancient Apostles', Nicene, and Athanasian Creeds followed by Lutheran symbols, the chief being the Augsburg Confession and Luther's catechisms. The *Formula of Concord*, which had endeavored to settle numerous controversies, was added. It had been circulated among theologians for revision and correction. This book of books was then circulated for signatures and approval of over eight thousand pastors and teachers, three electors, twenty-one princes, twenty-two counts, and thirty-five cities.

Pietist Evaluations of the Creeds

These *Symbolical Books* prevailed as the major source of theology of Lutheran scholasticism throughout the seventeenth century. A few reformers either ignored or questioned an inflexible orthodoxy. The influence of Johann Arndt's *True Christianity* (1605) and the mystical writings of Jacob Boehme created the milieu for the Pietist Reformation in the last decades of the century. Arndt has often been called the father or grandfather of Pietism. Boehme has been considered a seminal source of Radical Pietism. Major questioning of the creeds appeared within pietist movements in both Reformed and Lutheran traditions. This was but one factor in the genesis of what is often named the churchly pietist movement that surfaced in 1675 when Philip Jacob Spener introduced a book of sermons by Arndt with his *Pia Desideria* (Pious Wishes for the Church).

Both Spener and August Hermann Francke, the most visible leaders of the Pietist Reformation, agreed with the creeds. But they articulated a hermeneutical problem. They believed their orthodox opponents elevated the *Symbolical Books* to the level of Scripture. They felt that the Bible was used to confirm the creeds instead of being regarded as the source and judge of these theological confessions of faith. In contemporary language, dogma replaced exegesis. The focus of the pietist conventicles was to study the Bible to nurture devotional life and receive guidance for daily living. They opposed an "intellectual Pelagianism" in which works of understanding replaced good works and the Holy Spirit became an intellectual process of being acquainted with the truth.

The study of theology overshadowed all subjects in the university. The same mood dominated the preparatory schools. The following exaggerated caricature of the effect on a pupil of lectures on dogmatics was possibly derived from expressions of Protestant scholasticism:

> *This filled Anton's head with a good deal of useless lumber, but he learnt how to make divisions and subdivisions, and to go to work systematically. His note-books grew bigger and bigger and in less than a year he possessed a complete system of dogma, combined with passages from the Bible to prove it, and a complete polemic against heathens, Turks, Jews, Greeks, Papists, Calvinists. He was able to talk like a book about transubstantiation in the sacrament, about the five steps of the exaltation and humiliation of Christ, about the chief proofs of the existence of God urged against free-thinkers. And he did actually speak like a book on all these things.* (Moritz, *Anton Reiser* 98)

In the aftermath of the Thirty Years' War (1618-1648), the spirit of hatred between the three legal traditions continued. Roman Catholics, Calvinists, and Lutherans felt threatened. The rhetoric of attack permeated the life of Christians. Sermons were crafted to highlight the theological heresies of others. Paul's "no" in Ephesians 4:14 was to the many winds of doctrine that were tempting the early Christians. Spener's "no" was to a rigid, persecuting orthodoxy. Rejecting homiletical polemics against other Christians, Spener advocated speaking the truth in love, even to Roman Catholics. His wish list for reformation included another way of dealing with theological controversies, namely, with heartfelt and persuasive love (97-99). This fourth proposal for the reformation of church constitutes unique appeals for tolerance in his context.

Early Brethren Context of Persecution

Before the first baptisms in the Eder River, the early Brethren absorbed the spirit and views of a variety of Pietists. Whereas it is difficult to understand Amish, Mennonite, and Hutterian communities apart from the persecution of their Anabaptist forebears, my thesis is that it is difficult to understand the Brethren without understanding their rejection of coercive creedal orthodoxy. The people named by others as re-baptizers, the Anabaptists, were tied up and burned at stake. Tongues were cut out, and eyes were often punched out. Women were put in sacks and thrown in rivers. The *Martyrs Mirror*, a huge book of the stories of their faithful ancestors, is found in numerous homes of contemporary believers. It is unfortunate that *Pia Desideria* seldom is treasured on the shelves of Brethren homes.

However, stories of the first Brethren are not void of experiences of persecution. It is true that their persecution does not measure up to the numbers and suffering of earlier Anabaptists. This may help explain why the Brethren have accommodated more easily to the culture of their "worldly" neighbors. We do have details of the galley slave experience of Christian Liebe and the prison accounts of the Solingen Brethren (Durnbaugh, *European Origins* 234-80) who baffled their captors with Gandhian-like responses. Armed guards who escorted them often went home considering it unnecessary to watch over such peace-loving and cheerful people. This elicits an amusing story. The guards of the Solingen Brethren met a captain of a militia who needed many soldiers to guard and capture thieves and dangerous criminals. Upon learning about the Solingen Brethren, the captain replied to the guards of the Brethren: "You want to seize the good people, and I the bad. Who will finally be left?" (Durnbaugh, *European Origins* 243).

When we read the nearly four-year account of the Solingen Brethren's imprisonment, we might judge that it would have been preferable to be burned live at the stake. For they slept in dungeonlike places with lice, fleas, and rats. Forced labor was often more than they could bear. At times, they were sick almost to death. Once, cursed with scurvy, their gums grew over their teeth.

The experience of these men offers one of the best windows for viewing first Brethren attitudes about creeds. Though hated because of their convictions and mocked by fellow prisoners for their virtues, the six Brethren were often showered with the love and visits of kindred brothers and sisters in Christ. They were also visited frequently by official representatives of the only legal Christian religions granted by the Treaty of Westphalia in 1648. On occasion the religious leaders seemed sincere in attempting to convince them to abandon their new doctrine and choose one of three legal churches. The men responded that their so-called new doctrine was in reality the old doctrine in Scriptures that "Jesus taught and commanded us to do" (Durnbaugh, *European Origins* 244).

Responding to a Roman Catholic visitor, they questioned him on how many things in his tradition could be found in the Bible (248). A Lutheran preacher sought to persuade them to join any one of the three. In failing to convince them, he gave up and stayed away. It was during a visit of six Reformed preachers that the Brethren responded to the Heidelberg catechism. This was regarded to be the confession of faith of traditions that identified with the theology of John Calvin. Similar to Spener's evaluation of the Lutheran creeds, they affirmed they could agree with most propositions of the catechism. But they could not accept infant baptism, swearing of oaths, and the sixtieth question on justification by faith alone (249-50). In their willingness to suffer in giving priority to the teachings of Jesus over confessions of faith, their statements verify agreement with views of both churchly and Radical Pietists, who questioned or rejected the creeds.

Brethren Responses to the Chicago Quadrilateral

A more contemporary story reveals how the noncreedal stance has continued to prevail. The background for the story begins within the ecumenical movement. Anglican bishops from many countries meet periodically. Episcopal, a synonym for bishop, is the name of the American branch of the Church of England. This name and the meetings of bishops signify a tradition that bestows authority to its bishops. In meetings at Chicago in 1886 and in Lambeth in 1888, the bishops defined what is necessary to be the church. They gave form to what has been known as the Chicago or Lambeth Quadrilateral. The formula has been openly or implicitly influential in ecumenical discussions.

According to the Quadrilateral, the first requirement is to have the Bible. This poses no problem for most Christian traditions. Discernment for inclusion becomes more difficult when some Christians regard another book to have equal authority. Another mark is to have at least two sacraments, namely, baptism and eucharist (or communion), even though this may seem to eliminate Quakers who reject outward forms. A third basic requirement is to confirm the historic ministry often referred to as the apostolic succession. The emphasis is on the continuity of the lineage of bishops in history. Valid ordinations insure that bishops are in the procession from Peter. This requirement has engendered the most discussion and problems especially in church union determinations. The fourth mark is to adopt the apostolic creeds.

In the 1970s and 1980s, the World Council of Churches initiated gatherings for discussion and responses to BEM, an acronym that refers to basic components of the Chicago Quadrilateral, namely Baptism, Eucharist, and Ministry. The study assembled theological statements from evangelicals, Orthodox voices, Roman Catholics, confessional and mainline Protestants. The discussion assumed the general authority given to the Bible. The project was well received. Faith and Order commissions of the World and National Council of Churches began to plan for the fourth component, the Apostolic

Faith. For most participants of the larger bodies, this meant that the study would center on the status and substance of the creeds.

Many wondered how Brethren, Baptists, Disciples, and other noncreedal traditions would relate to a study that focuses primarily on the creeds. Melanie May and Lauree Hersch Meyer, the Brethren representatives to Faith and Order meetings, observed that many were perplexed in sensing that they could relate to each other as brothers and sisters in Christ, but were unable to recognize each other's church. Some believed they should define boundaries exactly in creeds or confessions of faith. Others opted for additional ways to define the apostolic faith. Peace church representatives proposed another way.

In light of the fact that the apostolic creeds were formulated in ecumenical councils in early decades of the fourth century, Melanie and Lauree requested that Faith and Order members consider the apostolic faith of the first three centuries. For the anabaptist tradition, the faith of the early Christians embraces the relationship of Christians to the world, to one another, even to their enemies. This implied a radical revision. Consideration of the pacifism of the early church had always been referred to Life and Work sections of the ecumenical movement. The anabaptist proposal meant that a theology of peace and justice also belonged to Faith and Order discussions.

This request is similar to an overlooked insight about the Apostles Creed. It is acclaimed in worship by millions of Christians and appears in the worship section of our *Hymnal: A Worship Book*, published in 1992. Yet believers in the anabaptist traditions point out that the ancient creeds move from the birth stories to the crucifixion accounts in the four Gospels and skip over portions of the New Testament that focus on the life and teachings of Jesus, basic ingredients in the formation of the Brethren faith.

Grass Roots and the Brethren's Card

Our noncreedal tradition poses a major problem for members who long for statements that define our faith clearly. Unlike Christians who have memorized portions of their catechism, it is difficult for Brethren to answer questions about what we believe. Some of our pat answers, such as "we are something like the Mennonites and Quakers," are neither satisfactory to inquisitor or responder. For people whose personalities require more definition than we often seem to provide, it is relevant to ask how we structure our faith.

One influential solution to the problem was a widespread use of the "Brethren's Card," which was first published by Brethren's Book and Tract Work around 1887. It is not certain how many revisions there were. The last

The Brethren's Card

Be it known unto all men,

That there is a people who, as little children (Luke 18: 17), accept the Word of the New Testament as a message from heaven (Heb. 1: 1, 2), and teach it in full (2 Tim. 4: 1, 2; Matt. 28: 20).

They baptize believers by trine immersion (Matt. 28: 19), with a forward action (Rom. 6: 5), and for the remission of sins (Acts 2: 38), and lay hands on those baptized, asking upon them the gift of God's Spirit (Acts 19: 5, 6).

They follow the command and example of washing one another's feet (John 13: 4, 17).

They take the Lord's Supper at night (John 13: 30), at one and the same time, tarrying one for another (1 Cor. 11: 33, 34).

They greet one another with a holy kiss (Acts 20: 37; Rom. 16: 16).

They take the communion at night, after supper, as did the Lord (Mark 14: 17, 23).

They teach all the doctrines of Christ, peace (Heb. 12: 14), love (1 Cor. 13), unity (Eph. 4), both faith and works (James 2: 17, 20).

They labor for nonconformity to the world in its vain and wicked customs (Rom. 12: 2).

They advocate nonswearing (Matt. 5: 34, 37), anti-secretism (2 Cor. 6: 14, 17), opposition to war (John 18: 36), doing good unto all men (Matt. 5: 44, 46).

They anoint and lay hands on the sick (James 5: 14, 15).

They give the Bread of Life, the message of the common salvation unto all men without money or price (Matt. 10: 8).

Dear reader, for the above we contend earnestly, and you, with all men, are entreated to hear, to examine and accept it as the word, which began to be spoken by the Lord, and the faith once delivered to the saints (Jude 3).

The above principles are briefly explained in tract form and will be sent with a catalogue of the publications of the Committee free, to anyone by addressing the General Mission Board, Elgin, Illinois.

An early version of the Brethren's Card circulated in the late 1800s and early 1900s.

The Church of the Brethren
Formerly Called Dunkers

1. This body of Christians originated early in the eighteenth century, the church being a natural outgrowth of the Pietistic movement following the Reformation.

2. Firmly accepts and teaches the fundamental evangelical doctrines of the inspiration of the Bible, the personality of the Holy Spirit, the virgin birth, the deity of Christ, the sin-pardoning value of his atonement, his resurrection from the tomb, ascension and personal and visible return, and the resurrection, both of the just and unjust (John 5: 28, 29; 1 Thess. 4: 13-18).

3. Observes the following New Testament rites: Baptism of penitent believers by trine immersion for the remission of sins (Matt. 28: 19; Acts 2: 38); feet-washing (John 13: 1-20; 1 Tim. 5: 10); love feast (Luke 22: 20; John 13: 4; 1 Cor. 11: 17-34; Jude 12); communion (Matt. 26: 26-30); the Christian salutation (Rom. 16: 16; Acts 20: 37); proper appearance in worship (1 Cor. 11: 2-16); the anointing for healing in the name of the Lord (James 5: 13-18; Mark 6: 13); laying on of hands (Acts 8: 17; 19: 6; 1 Tim. 4: 14). These rites are representative of spiritual facts which obtain in the lives of true believers, and as such are essential factors in the development of the Christian life.

4. Emphasizes daily devotion for the individual, and family worship for the home (Eph. 6: 18-20; Philpp. 4: 8, 9); stewardship of time, talents and money (Matt. 25: 14-30); taking care of the fatherless, widows, poor, sick and aged (Acts 6: 1-7).

5. Opposes on Scriptural grounds: War and the taking of human life (Matt. 5: 21-26, 43, 44; Rom. 12: 19-21; Isa. 53: 7-12); violence in personal and industrial controversy (Matt. 7: 12; Rom. 13: 8-10); intemperance in all things (Titus 2: 2; Gal. 5: 19-26; Eph. 5: 18); going to law, especially against our Christian brethren (1 Cor. 6: 1-9); divorce and remarriage except for the one Scriptural reason (Matt. 19: 9); every form of oath (Matt. 5: 33-37; James 5: 12); membership in secret, oath-bound societies (2 Cor. 6: 14-18); games of chance and sinful amusements (1 Thess. 5: 22; 1 Pet. 2: 11; Rom. 12: 17); extravagant and immodest dress (1 Tim. 2: 8-10; 1 Peter 3: 1-6).

6. Labors earnestly, in harmony with the Great Commission, for the evangelization of the world, for the conversion of men to Jesus Christ, and for the realization of the life of Jesus Christ in every believer (Matt. 28: 18-20; Mark 16: 15, 16; 2 Cor. 3: 18).

7. Maintains the New Testament as its only creed, in harmony with which the above brief doctrinal statement is made.

The last revision of the Brethren's Card was approved by Annual Conference in 1923.

revision came from the request of Annual Conference delegates in 1922. In 1923 the card was approved by Conference with the understanding that it was not an official creed. The decision also allowed the card to be circulated publicly. For several years it continued to appear in each issue of the *Gospel Messenger*. The longevity of the revisions of this card demonstrates how difficult it is for a people to exist without some statement of faith.

It may serve historical and theological interests to compare the revision in use in 1903 with the Conference revision of 1923. In examining the two cards, you will observe that the 1923 card reflects the influence of the popular fundamentalist movement that emerged around the turn of the century. This card accepts and teaches eight fundamental evangelical doctrines followed by excellent lists of ordinances and practices. The earlier card poses a remarkably different list of doctrines: "They [the people called Brethren] teach all the doctrines of Christ, peace (Heb. 12:14), love (1 Cor. 13), unity (Eph. 4), both faith and works (James 2:17, 20)." This comparison may illustrate how both conservatives and liberals have been influenced by other winds of doctrine. Both cards, however, agree concerning the status of the New Testament. The earlier modest statement stated, "That there is a people who, as little children (Luke 18:17), accept the Word of the New Testament as a message from heaven (Heb. 1:1, 2), and teach it in full (2 Tim. 4:1, 2; Matt. 28:20)."

Contemporary Liberal Views

In interpreting the slogan "We have no creed but the New Testament," some liberals in the twentieth and twenty-first centuries have been tempted to drop the last phrase and emphasize that we have no creed, period. They have been influenced by currents of philosophical idealism that define truth with a capital T, which our rational minds can know, but never completely. As science has improved our standard of living, many assume that understanding of moral truths would improve so as to realize greater manifestations of the kingdom of God.

Consistent with views that reforming the church needs to happen in each generation, the Reformed tradition advised: "Let us be open to new light as it breaks forth from the Word." Both conservatives and liberals in our denomination like this saying. Yet many of us often neglect the last phrase—"as it breaks forth from the Word."

Personal Views

Most of my vacillating responses surfaced as I listened to delegates respond to the queries brought to the Portland Conference in 1992. The agenda revealed that Brethren do deal with theological issues. The first query came from the Atlantic Northeast District. It sought a study to "define the essential nature of the Church of the Brethren, that without which we would no longer be the Church of the Brethren." As a teacher of theology, I thought it would be good for our people, who are generally anti-theological, to attempt to do this. But eloquent speeches persuaded Brethren to return the query. Several testified they were attracted to the church because the Brethren claimed no creed but the New Testament.

The same district was concerned about manifestations of religious pluralism and our relationships with other world religions. This query requested Conference to formulate "a clear and concise statement declaring Jesus Christ to be Savior of the world and head of the church." Having rejected one query, the Conference seemed friendly to this one. However, a sister rose and moved that we declare Jesus to be the Son of God. This quickly was accepted. In a typical debriefing session afterwards, one person said, "Why didn't I rise and make a motion that we declare Jesus is the Prince of Peace?" Another added: "Why not a motion to declare Jesus to be the Son of Man?" a phrase used frequently by biblical writers. In musing on the reactions to the second query, I felt that our noncreedal stance may be better than I have judged. If the New Testament is our creed, we can agree with various christological titles. There will be some of us who will center more on one than the others. There will be brothers and sisters who will emphasize other New Testament teachings about Jesus. We will tolerate differing views, consistent or not with differing views of the Gospel writers.

At the same time, I left that Conference believing that it might be helpful for us to be a bit more like the Mennonites, who are not as afraid of confessions of faith, or like the Bohemian Brethren who periodically reviewed and changed their statements of faith. Another and perhaps more helpful way to deal with this issue is found in a statement in pietist circles. As John Wesley distinguished basic beliefs from what he regarded as human opinions, the love theology of this popular aphorism in pietist circles might be helpful (Spener, *Consilia Theologia Latina* 794):

in non necessarii libertas	in things not necessary, liberty
in necessarii veritas (unitas)	in necessary things, truth [or unity]
in omnibus caritas	in all things, love

Spener wished to reduce dogma to essentials and allow more liberty for nonessentials. Though he spoke of apostolic simplicity, we know the difficulties related to naming what is necessary and what is not necessary in defining our beliefs. Yet, I believe Brethren attempt more often than not to seek common ground. Alexander Mack [leader of the first 8 Brethren] affirmed a Christ-centeredness and obedience to the Jesus way. Could we find common ground in the love theology of the two commandments Jesus proclaimed to be the greatest, namely love of God and our neighbor? We might add the historic vows we make in the baptismal waters. Can we think of important issues that are not worth dividing us, such as the furniture of heaven, the temperature of hell, or even more important theological and ethical issues? Hopefully, I will keep in mind this desire in proposing rather than mandating what I have discerned is most important for Brethren. For now might we begin to seek common ground in the unifying doctrines suggested in the early Brethren's Card: "We seek all the doctrines of Christ—peace, love, unity, both faith and works." Or, we can affirm the recent identity line with doctrinal overtones: "Continuing the work of Jesus. Peacefully. Simply. Together."

Chapter 2

Faith of Believers
Pietism and Anabaptism

But sanctify the Lord God in your hearts: and be ready always to give an answer to every man that asketh you a reason of the hope that is in you with meekness and fear.
—1 Peter 3:15 KJV

At Bethany Theological Seminary, a director of an evangelical youth movement enrolled in an evening Bonhoeffer seminar. The off-campus minister had never encountered Brethren. Her journal disclosed that the class aroused her curiosity. In a small group setting, she asked, "What do the Brethren believe?" She received an equivocal answer: "You can believe anything you want to and still be Brethren." She was not impressed. The professor was not pleased. The story evokes basic questions: Do the Brethren believe anything? If they do, what is it?

Anti-Intellectual and Anti-Theological Biases

Simple faith nurtured by nonprofessional leaders has been congenial to anti-intellectual stances that judge worldly learning to be subversive to Christian faith. Anti-intellectualism has permeated our heritage of simplicity and practical religion. My mother's eighth grade education was refined with gifted intelligence. Nevertheless, she was wary of higher education. In each step of my academic quest, she expressed deep concern that my faith might be destroyed. She breathed a sigh of relief when I made it through college. Her fears were somewhat soothed when I became a pastor following seminary. But it was too much when I announced I was entering graduate school. In talking with another mother over the backyard fence, my mother lamented that some, like her neighbor, could not keep their children in school, while her problem was getting them out. These concerns were not in vain. Throughout my studies, my faith was empowered in knowing she was praying for me.

When I observed attractive, dedicated students entering seminary, I realized that my mother's fears lingered in me. I wondered whether such enthusiastic commitment would blossom or wither in academia! Admonishing the Corinthians, Paul cautioned that we can understand all mysteries and all knowledge and yet this amounts to nothing without love. A brilliant mind can be used for evil or for good. We are not saved by reason. We are saved by faith. But faith seeks understanding. The greatest commandment offers the answer to both my mother's fears and unregenerate intelligence. It commands us to love God with our total beings, soul, heart, strength, *and* minds (Luke 10:27).

An often quoted statement by D. L. Miller represents anti-theological strands in Brethren history. "In the subtleties of speculative theology the church takes but little interest. She is chiefly concerned in giving willing and cheerful obedience to the plain, simple commandments of Jesus Christ." Our heritage has focused more on living than thinking. A popular motto has been: "It's not what you believe but how you live that counts."

It is difficult to maintain, however, that the heritage has been void of doctrinal interests. There is evidence that the early Brethren desired to join belief and life, word and deed. Alexander Mack, Sr., in writing about the Mennonites, claimed that the early Brethren were in complete agreement with them in doctrine. Better known is the prophecy about his spiritual descendants: " . . . as their faith is, so shall be their outcome" (Durnbaugh, *European Origins* 343). During decades of prejudicial sentiments against formal education, the title *Theological Writings* appeared in the collection of works of Peter Nead, a prolific nineteenth-century Brethren author. His writings remain meaningful to the Old German Baptist Brethren, who often quote the King James Version of the instruction of Peter. "[Christians should be] ready always to give an answer to every man that asketh about their faith. And this should be with meekness and fear [reverently]" (1 Pet. 3:15).

Others have attempted to correct an excessive anti-theological bias. In the mid-twentieth century, Edward Frantz wrote in *Basic Belief*, "To say that it is what you do that counts, not what you believe, overlooks the simple fact that what you do depends on what you believe" (95). Similarly, the often repeated saying that Christians should live their faith rather than talk about it overlooks the reality that talking is a part of living. There is a theological circle here: belief gives shape to life and life experiences shape belief. When we assert that theology derived from the New Testament is relational more than propositional, we are, nevertheless, making a theological statement with theological presuppositions.

Early Sources of Brethren Theology

Whether Brethren believe in doing theology and how they engage in theological discourse will continue to influence our life and thought. An obvious problem in claiming the New Testament as our creed is its length. This long creed is subject to a variety of interpretations. In needing to deal with the resultant pluralism in ways that build up the body of Christ, this problem may foster openness to the presence of the Spirit. The lengthy creed of Gospel narratives, history, epistles, and biblical visions of hope offers opportunities to be open to new light as it breaks forth from the Word.

Consistent with the noncreedal legacy, Brethren historians have not limited the source of theology to the New Testament. They have searched for biblical interpretations of beliefs in the writings and context of the early movement. Positively, we believe our forebears appropriated the best from several traditions. Negatively, such eclecticism has suggested throughout history that Brethren are often tossed "to and fro" by "every wind of doctrine" (Eph. 4:14).

Without claiming direct lineage, Floyd Mallott, long-time popular historian at Bethany Seminary, noticed the kinship of early Brethren with a stream of medieval Catholic piety. Bernard of Clairvaux (1090-1153), a dominant thinker of the twelfth century, added to affirmations of the divinity of Christ an emphasis that Jesus is our brother, teacher, and example. For this monastic leader, the most striking traits of Jesus were humility and love. This led him to earnestly advocate feetwashing as a sacrament of the church. Bernard's writings embody a Jesus mysticism. Unlike speculative mysticism, which focuses on the union of human with the divine essence, this devotion stresses a relationship of will and affection of the believer with Jesus and God. Such is expressed in a hymn by Bernard, "Jesus, the very thought of thee with sweetness fills my breast" (No. 588, *Hymnal, A Worship Book*). His writings represent a practical mysticism that involves a love for the things that Jesus loved and an identity with his way. A fuller discussion, however, would reveal that Bernard also promoted a crusade. This would decrease our enthusiasm in naming him our spiritual church father.

What Bernard taught was lived by Francis of Assisi (ca. 1182-1226). Rejecting both military service and his father's wealth, Francis devoted his life to living like Jesus. This medieval pacifist became an itinerant preacher who identified with the poor and traveled to make peace where there was conflict. His mystical love of God's creation avoided nature worship at the same time his intimate relationship with creatures has provided a Christian basis for ecological concerns. He loved people and fondly addressed "brother sun, sister earth, lady poverty, brother fox." Francis's society of brothers modeled another kind of monastic order of friars instead of monks, who were sent out to preach and minister among the people. Mallott's hunch has been affirmed by Brethren who admire the Catholic Worker movement that identifies with the legacy of Francis of Assisi. Brethren service programs send members to Catholic Worker farms and houses.

Peter Waldo, a rich merchant of southern France, experienced a radical conversion in 1173. He gave all his goods to the poor and began preaching to the people. Unlike the Franciscan order, which received official approval a few years later, the pope rejected Waldo's request for giving official status to those who had joined him. The church banned him from preaching and regarded him and his followers as heretics. Believing that one must obey God instead of men, Peter and his "order" named themselves "the Poor in Spirit." They constituted an active underground movement. Adopting the New Testament as the sole rule of belief and life, they focused on the Sermon on the Mount. Barefooted and clad in simple robes, they rejected oaths and the shedding of blood and defended lay preaching by men and women. This persecuted group was often identified as a radical free church before the Reformation. Known as the Waldensians, the community later joined the Reformed churches. In recent history their radical anabaptist-type roots have been discovered anew.

Mallott proposed that wherever Bernardine-Franciscan-Waldensian emphases have appeared, there exists a Christian lifestyle that is ethical, humanitarian, democratic, nonconformist, and characterized by a devotion to the character and teachings of Jesus (*Studies in Brethren History* 17-20).

Similar conjectures of theological influences were made by nineteenth- and twentieth-century historians who regarded Brethren to be in the apostolic succession of New Testament groups. They adopted Peter Waldo as an ancestor. When they learned that a Waldensian bishop had ordained ministers of the Bohemian Brethren, this strengthened their belief in an unbroken link of free churches. The Bohemian Brethren burst forth when John Huss, who was promised safe conduct to testify at the great Council of Constance in 1415, was burned at the stake. Huss had claimed Christ, not the pope, to be the head of the church and that the New Testament was its law. He advocated offering the cup to the laity in the Lord's Supper. Movements in Bohemia that identified with the popular martyr were often cited as a bridge to sixteenth-century movements that scholars refer to as the Radical Reformation.

The Socinian or Unitarian wing of the Radical Reformation in Poland later became known as the Polish Brethren. Because they rejected doctrines of God's triune nature and Christ's deity, emphasizing human freedom and reasoned faith, they were expelled in 1660 from Poland and traveled to the Netherlands. The refugees soon established close relationships with the Collegiants, a societal offshoot from the Dutch Arminian Party of the Dutch Reformed Church. The Polish Brethren introduced their baptismal practice of immersing adults in a single forward action. The Collegiants later adopted this mode of baptism. In a visit to Schwarzenau, the Dutch Collegiants may have encouraged and influenced those who were considering immersion baptisms in forming a new community.

The same Collegiants introduced the early Brethren to the writings of Jeremias Felbinger, who had been a co-pastor of a Polish Brethren congregation. His *Christian Manual*, which was written after he had relinquished some of his unitarian views, was published with the writings of Alexander Mack, Sr., in 1799 and 1822. The Polish Brethren were called *Dompelaars*, meaning dippers or Baptists. This name was bequeathed to the early Brethren in Germany and the Netherlands. From several variations, the name was anglicized on the American frontier where Dunkers became the common name to identify German Baptist Brethren.

The relationships of Brethren to the Collegiants is better documented than connections with the Polish Brethren. The Collegiants were part of the milieu that linked the Brethren to the Dutch Mennonites. Both groups helped the "needy Schwarzenauers." Collegiant money helped release the imprisoned Solingen Brethren. They also provided resources to help the Brethren make the trip to America. (For fuller accounts of these groups, see Don Durnbaugh's "The Descent of Dissent: Some Interpretations of Brethren Origins," *Brethren Life and Thought*, Spring 1974, 125-33; also William Willoughby, *The Beliefs of the Early Brethren* 1706-35, 47-51.)

It may not be possible to derive many theological motifs from these relationships. If not the sole source of immersion baptism, the practices of the Polish and Dutch sectarians, no doubt, strengthened the convictions of the early Brethren concerning the mode and meaning of believers baptism. Yet the three-dips departure from the one-dip mode of their sectarian friends dramatically demonstrated their affirmation of the trinity. Lacking knowledge of influences of more specific beliefs, these relationships represent friendships with radical sectarians, who shared their common experience of being refugees. Doctrinal disagreement did not keep them from identifying with others who were on the fringes of society. The first generation of Brethren identified with others in counter-culture movements who like themselves had been persecuted because they committed civil disobedience in refusing to baptize infants and thereby formed separated movements of believers.

Brethren indebtedness to the Protestant Reformation is much more extensive. Most early members had been baptized as infants in either Lutheran or Reformed Churches. Rather than repudiating basic Reformation doctrines, Anabaptists, Pietists, and Brethren sought to carry these beliefs to their logical conclusions. For example, Brethren believed with other Pietists that the reformation of doctrine by the reformers needed to lead to a reformation of life. Examples of both agreements and disagreements with classical Protestantism will be discussed in subsequent chapters dealing with specific doctrines and practices.

Pietism and Anabaptism

For the most part, students of Brethren origins have derived theological roots from the anabaptist movement of the sixteenth-century Radical Reformation and seventeenth-century pietist reform activity in the Lutheran and Reformed Churches. However, both the noncreedal stance and the eclectic nature of the beginnings of our formation make it difficult to neatly define our theological roots. Unlike Mennonites, Brethren are not as exclusively anabaptist. Unlike the Evangelical Covenant Church, Brethren are not as predominantly pietist. Rather, Brethren historiography has struggled to discern how much of this and how much of that historical stream have affected our life and thought.

For this reason a seal with the initials "A M" has threatened to become a Brethren icon for understanding theological sources. Discovered in documents preserved by the Germantown, Pennsylvania, congregation, the seal was used on a deed in 1753 for a land transaction involving Christopher and Catherine Sharpnack Sauer. It is possible that Alexander Mack and others performed legal services for one another because of Paul's teaching against going to law (1 Cor. 6:1-8). This constitutes our meager knowledge. Vernard

Eller has introduced the pedagogical value of this seal. The seal depicts a heart imposed on a cross with a vine laden with grapes springing from the heart. The cross, Eller proposed, represents the continuity of Brethrenism with ecumenical Christianity. The heart is a symbol of Pietism. The fruit of the vine suggests the ethical commandments legacy of Anabaptism. Emphases on one or the other basic sources of our heritage have shifted from generation to generation. There is a strong consensus, however, that Radical Pietism provided the matrix for birthing the Brethren more than churchly Pietism. Likewise, the first baptisms represented strong influences of anabaptist views of the church and disciplined discipleship to the Jesus way. Some reason that the first baptisms meant that the first members rejected Pietism in embracing anabaptist views of the church. Others argue that, even in so doing, the eight Brethren retained much from their life with Radical Pietists.

Eller observed a dialectical corrective between the two influences. When radical pietist tendencies slide too far into mystical subjectivism, they are disciplined by anabaptist demands for obedience to a more objective scriptural norm as discerned by the community of faith. Conversely, when anabaptist tendencies slide off into legalistic biblical literalism or works-righteousness, they are corrected by faith and grace themes, which emphasize that relationships with God and others are personal, not legal. Though fundamental motifs of Anabaptism and Pietism often seem to be in contradictory tension, we need to affirm both to understand the essence of our tradition. If we appropriate this double heritage with a degree of modesty, we may be embracing the heart of our tradition.

Carl Bowman, in his outstanding sociological study, *Brethren Society*, adds a helpful nuance. He maintains that the two movements are "mutually reinforcing." For example, he proposes "that the Pietist emphasis on the presence of the Spirit may inspire increased Anabaptist-shaped obedience" (46-50). With Eller he believes both streams are necessary to interpret and embody the heritage. Yet, Eller focuses on the resulting tension while Bowman stresses the complementary nature of anabaptist and pietist motifs. With Bowman, I have long believed that our heritage is strongest when similar beliefs have been inherited from both historical streams. However, tensions have emerged whenever one of the traditions is neglected. These have produced polarities between factions. Or is it possible that inevitable tensions serve as helpful correctives to opposing factions? Both affinities *and* tensions of the two movements have served as resources for our lived faith.

The names reveal much about their context and beginnings. Anabaptist literally means "one who rebaptizes." The first anabaptist congregation was born in 1525 when Conrad Grebel, Felix Manz, and other young followers of Ulrich Zwingli became disillusioned when they realized that the Reformation at Zurich, Switzerland, was not being implemented to its logical conclusion. The Town Council overruled reforms derived from the study of the Bible. The Swiss Brethren movement began when those who rejected Zwingli's adherence to the state church gathered in nearby Zollikon. They disregarded the order of the Town Council that all children must be baptized within eight days of their birth. The young men baptized each other on January 21, 1525. This has been regarded as the birth of the anabaptist movement.

In the following June, a peculiar procession of men, women, and children wearing willow twigs or ropes departed from the farms of Zollikon. They proceeded through Zurich crying, "Woe, Woe! Woe to Zurich!" They called the inhabitants and the Council to repentance. Following Jonah's example, they gave the city forty days of grace. The Town Council of Zurich, along with Roman Catholic and Lutheran governments, soon declared the penalty of death for "rebaptizers" according to a decree of the Justinian code in AD 529. The so named Anabaptists did not accept the name, declaring believers baptism to be their first baptism. Their infant baptism lacked the biblical call to "believe and be baptized." The movement spread. The Justinian decree provided the legal basis for the persecution and death of thousands of so-called Anabaptists.

As with Anabaptism, Quakerism, and Methodism, Pietism was an uncomplimentary nickname given by those who ridiculed or despised the movement. The word may have come from Spener's *Pia Desideria*, which concretely set forth his pious desires to reform the corrupt conditions of his church. This initiated the birth of the second reformation in the Lutheran Church in Germany. These proposals occurred in 1675, one hundred and fifty years after the baptisms of the first anabaptist community. Or the pietist label might have come from devotional conventicles named *collegia pietatis* ("study classes in piety"), which were suggested by Spener in 1669 following a sermon dealing with false righteousness. Spener described his critics: "Those who feared through such holiness to have their own deeds put to shame began to call in mockery, 'Pietists!' " Spener advised the groups to bear in patience the growing criticism. He hoped that "no one among us . . . or our friends has at any time used this name for themselves."

The name gained its greatest reputation from an outbreak of disputes at the University of Leipzig. August Hermann Francke had been a leading participant in a *collegium philobiblicum*, a conventicle formed for the purpose of entering more deeply into edifying exegesis. The numbers and enthusiasm of students and citizens grew so much that the authorities forbade such assemblies in an electoral edict in 1690. At a funeral for one of the "awakened" students, one of Francke's faculty opponents gave evidence of his displeasure: "Our mission as professors is to make students more learned and not more pious." In response, a professor of poetry, Joachim Feller, fervently defined Pietism in a poem: "The name of the Pietists is now known all over town. Who is a Pietist? He who studies the Word of God and accordingly leads a holy life. This would be good for every Christian."

The root word *piety* connotes both positive and negative expressions. A pious person can be marked favorably in worship and conduct, or pious can refer to one whose actions are marked by self-conscious virtue, conspicuous religiosity, or hypocrisy. The same ambiguity can be associated with Pietism, the name given to the historical reformation movement. Pietism has been critiqued for it simplistic division of people as regenerate or lost, extreme subjectivism, and preoccupation with private virtues. Yet Pietism has been commended for the recovery of an emphasis on regeneration as a supplement to the doctrine of justification and for its missionary efforts, ecumenism, and charitable institutions.

Philip Jacob Spener (1635-1705) has been called the father of Pietism and second only to Luther in shaping German Protestantism. Throughout several pastorates in influential parishes, he authored many theological tomes and guided the movement through extensive correspondence with both friends and foes.

Unlike the more irenic, mild-mannered Spener, August Hermann Francke (1663-1727) has been known as the controversial, organizing genius of the movement. After he was fired from teaching at Leipzig, he was appointed to a parish at Erfurt where he experienced the success of large crowds. Through his influence with the court of Brandenburg, Spener was able to have Franke appointed as the dominant leader in the new University of Halle. During thirty-six years, he served as pastor, theologian, professor, and founder of many philanthropic institutions. Through prayers, contributions, and divinity students who absorbed practical theology as tutors, teachers, house parents, and laborers, Francke established a poor school that soon evolved into a famous orphanage, a school for upper-class students, a Latin school, a chemical laboratory, a bookstore, a home for indigent widows, a home for itinerant beggars, a Bible institute for the printing and distribution of Bibles, a laundry, a farm, and even a brewery. As a result, Halle Pietism has been heralded as the cradle of social service ministries, foreign missions, and worldwide philanthropic activities.

In spite of the growing influence of Pietism within Lutheran and Reformed churches, some Pietists became even more alienated from the state churches. In the movement, they obviously did not identify each other with names like churchly or Radical Pietists. But Radical Pietism evolved as a label later historians gave to those who had greater despair about the church and greater appropriation of medieval and Protestant mystical writings. Theologically many identified with the mystical writings of a shoemaker, Jacob Boehme (1575-1624).

This circle included Gottfried Arnold, a professor and pastor who witnessed inside and outside church institutions. He had considerable influence on the beliefs and practices of the early Brethren. Mack and others refer to his works. His writing with the greatest appeal to the Brethren was *True Portrayal of the Early Christians According to Their Lived Faith and Holy Lives (Wahre Abbildung der Ersten Christen Im Glauben und Leben:* Gottlieb Friedeburgs Buchhandlung, 1696). He is better known for the three-volume *Impartial Church and Heretic History* of several thousand pages. These tomes embrace his thesis that heretics constituted the true church through the centuries, thus the title: *Kirchen und Ketzer Histories, I, II, III, Band,* 1740-1742. Arnold has been regarded as the foremost church historian of the seventeenth century and the first major scholar to interpret Anabaptists through their writings rather than from sources authored by their enemies.

The Radical Pietist who personally influenced Mack was Ernest Christopher Hochmann. From a prominent family, the free-spirited Hochmann became a traveling preacher who challenged his listeners to shake the burden of institutional Christianity from their backs and walk freely as children of God. Regarded as a fanatic, Hochmann was frequently imprisoned. In a castle dungeon at Detmond, he defended his views by writing a confession of faith. This *Confession* was widely circulated. Later it was published several times by the Brethren (found in M. G. Brumbaugh's *History of the Brethren* 75-88, in German and English).

Anabaptist and Pietist Themes

Since both pietist and anabaptist strands persist in Brethren theology as it is lived, it may be prudent to briefly interpret enduring themes through comparative analyses. Later chapters will consider more specifically these themes along with perspectives from other traditions in order to discern what may be relevant and right for today.

Believers Church. This name does not imply that other Christians are nonbelievers. It refers to the rejection of infant baptism by Anabaptists who believed membership in the body of Christ to be a voluntary decision of faith before baptism. In the sixteenth century, this involved more than a personal decision. It meant rejection of what has been named Constantinianism, from the emperor in the fourth century who granted tolerance for Christians in the Edict of Milan in AD 313. Constantine realized he needed Christianity to unify the different people of the empire. He sponsored large councils to settle disputes such as the nature of Christ and the date of Easter. The councils addressed many issues facing the early church. For example, the Apostles and Nicene Creeds were adopted. When the Nicene party won the day, a law of the Roman Empire was passed that anyone who did not believe in the Trinity should be put to death. In contrast to the minority and persecuted status of Christians in the first three centuries, from the fourth century onward there existed a church-state synthesis known as *corpus christianum*. The powers in both Eastern and Western empires required all infants to be baptized. Heretics often were tortured and killed.

In the sixteenth century, the death penalty was revived for Anabaptists because their baptismal views were believed to be subversive. After centuries of enforcing allegiance to Christendom, it was difficult to imagine that a civil society could survive without everyone being Christian in the prescribed manner. Believers baptism thus signified advocacy for religious liberty and the separation of church and state, positions espoused today by many other traditions.

A century and a half later, Pietists in Lutheran and Reformed Churches strived to reform what they regarded to be a fallen church through small groups, changed hearts, revival of catechetical instruction, Bible study with devotional literature, and preaching that proclaimed a new life in Christ.

Pietist traditions, including those that retain infant baptism, have maintained that reformation of the church is the fruit of reformation of lives in adult experiences of new birth and conversion. Radical Pietists extended this sentiment in believing that transformation of lives and culture would best be served by repudiating all institutional structures.

Eight sisters and brothers at Schwarzenau magnified their illegality when the Bible study group baptized each other in the Eder River. By this action they deviated from their radical prejudices. From their pietist milieu, they resembled Anabaptists. Before long, some were calling them *neubaptists* (New Baptists). The Church of the Brethren was born in this act of civil disobedience.

Primitivism, Restitutionism. These words name the resolution of historic movements to restore the primitive church of the first three centuries. From New Testament epistles, Anabaptist communities, and Gottfried Arnold's writings, Brethren embodied the desire to pattern their practices and beliefs after the early church. The minority, persecuted, egalitarian patterns of the first Christians fit the early Brethren context and experience. The Corinthian correspondence dampens claims of perfection for the first communities of faith. Yet the pacifism and style of Christians of the first three centuries were vastly different from the identity of church and society of the post-Constantinian establishment. Pietists of all kinds shared this vision with the earlier Anabaptists. Because Lutheran and Reformed theologies acknowledged the presence of sin in the church, Pietists, including the Brethren, may not have been as confident of achieving perfection as the more disciplined Mennonites. Nevertheless, similar visions of imitating the apostolic church provide another motif that supports views that these two strands are mutually reinforcing.

Communal Ecclesiology. Anabaptist views of the church assume that one cannot come to God apart from a brother or sister. The community constitutes an essential element in one's spiritual pilgrimage. The church is a fellowship more than an institution. The prayers of Pietists may proportionally include more I and me expressions than the plural pronouns of Anabaptists. Yet Pietism's concern for the individual is different from many versions of contemporary individualism. Unlike a prevalent narcissism with an excessive preoccupation with the self, pietist individualism originally focused on the sacredness and value of each and every person. The emphasis on personal conversion was interwoven with a passion for reformation of the church. In spite of falling short of their ideal, anabaptist and pietist congregations generally have been blessed by manifestations of sharing and caring communities, such as mutual aid and barn raising for neighbors. This emphasis has been one that has been strengthened by the intersection of anabaptist and pietist motifs.

Spiritualism. More than the ecclesiology of Anabaptism and mainstream Pietism, radical pietist views inclined toward invisible or anarchical views of the church. *Spiritualism* is a word that connotes a variety of phenomena such as communicating with departed love ones. When applied to Radical Pietism, however, the word expresses prejudices against outward forms, structures, and organizations. Hochmann, who remained a friend of the Brethren, shared their rejection of infant baptism in espousing a believers conversion of the heart. When his Schwarzenau friends sought his advice for their first baptisms, Hochmann agreed that it was all right for them. However, he believed outward baptism was not necessary and that it would be wrong to require it of everyone. Radical pietist views of material symbols were similar to Quaker rejections of outward forms. The latter believed in spiritual communions without physical symbols. Quakers feared that possible idolatry of bread and wine could undermine devotion to the sacramental nature of all of life.

Radical Separatists, however, retained strong communal convictions outside the walls of the institutional church. As illegal refugees, they were motivated by necessity and the New Testament to organize communities of goods and relationships consistent with their Christian principles. In subsequent centuries their legacy continued in movements such as the English Philadelphian Society led by Jane Lead and several American communal groups. Ephrata Cloisters in Pennsylvania modeled an example of one such community. It was founded by Conrad Beissel who, in departing from the Brethren, attracted many members due to his charisma, mystical theology, and radical pietist beliefs.

The first members to emigrate to America may have carried a streak of spiritualism in their veins. It was four years before they gathered for their first love feast and baptisms. As a house church movement for more than a century, the meetings in homes deviated from their neighbors' more rigid observance of the sabbath on Sunday. In recent decades our denominational agencies have been aware of the varying degrees of anti-institutionalism among the Brethren.

Theology of Love. The more I read sources of Brethren theology, the more it is impossible to neglect the centrality of a theology of love. The pietist spirituality of love permeates the writings of Michael Frantz, John Kline, and Anna Mow. This motif becomes visual in practices of the holy kiss or hug and holy communion. It is present in the caring ministries of service and the familial nature of the Annual Conference. For many the theology of the Brethren can be derived from the two greatest commandments. Our love of God cannot be separated from our love of one another. In his epistles the Apostle Paul proclaims that the entire law can be summed up in one word, love. In naming love the greatest theological motif, Paul's love chapter (1 Cor. 13) becomes basic to any Brethren sacred canon within the canon. The favorite Johannine epistles have led Brethren to discern God's love flowing through the love of believers.

> *God is love. . . . There is no fear in love, but perfect love casts out fear; for fear has to do with punishment, and whoever fears has not reached perfection in love. We love because he first loved us. Those who say, "I love God," and hate their brothers and sisters, are liars; for those who do not love a brother or sister whom they have seen, cannot love God whom they have seen.* (1 John 4:16b-21)

Love theology has been a gift of our pietist heritage. More than any other attribute, Pietists and Brethren believe that God is love. Likewise, the theme has been derived from stories of anabaptist martyrs. Voluminous testimonies in the *Martyrs Mirror* reveal a faithfulness to the teaching of Jesus in the Sermon on the Mount: "You have heard that it was said, 'You shall love your neighbor and hate your enemy.' But I say to you, Love your enemies and pray for those who persecute you" (Matt. 5:43-44). An etching from the huge book pictures Dirk Willems turning around to rescue his captor who was struggling in broken ice. The enemy whose life he saved escorted Dirk to his fate of being burned at the stake (1569). The etching remains an icon in Amish, Mennonite, and Hutterite culture. Future references to *universal restoration* may serve as a case study of an early application of the theology of love. Additional expressions of this theme will bear on interpretations of the *theology of the cross* and *nonresistance*. A sense of reality for the necessity of tough love can be discussed in relation to church discipline.

Anabaptist Discipleship and Pietist Justification, Regeneration, and Sanctification. In addition to modeling the church as a fellowship of believers, *Nachfolge* (literally, following after Jesus) is the most impelling motif bequeathed to the Brethren by Anabaptists. No one can know Christ apart from following Jesus in all of life. As justification by faith served as the fundamental motif of the Protestant Reformation, discipleship was basic to the Radical Reformation. Obedience has been an important word, especially when applied to the teachings of Jesus clearly given in the Sermon on the Mount. A visiting group asked an Hutterian elder how their people know whether they are going to heaven. "We do not worry about this," he responded. "We are glad to leave this decision to God. We want to learn how we can be faithful to the Jesus way." A Brethren might respond with Jesus language: "Our emphasis should be on what we can do for Jesus and his way more than on what Jesus can do for me." Many Brethren and other strands of Pietism, however, will not neglect the good news involved in the latter.

Basic themes of Pietism inspire many discipleship responses with other biblical words and symbols, such as a judicial metaphor, justification, to interpret how we can get right with God. With Luther they became aware that God's righteousness is grace rather than judgment. Thus, we are saved not by our goodness, but by God's loving forgiveness through faith. Pietists and Methodists accepted this. However, they added biblical teachings that we are not only accepted, but we can also be transformed. The God who is good enough to forgive us is powerful enough to change us. This was derived from biblical texts about the new birth, a biological metaphor—regeneration, speaking theologically. Both the consciousness of forgiveness and the new birth are related to sanctification, the gradual growth of grace and holiness in the life of the believer. Spener preached many sermons on the new birth; however, he preached even more sermons on the new life, the walk of newness of life (Rom. 6:4). John Wesley affirmed that Luther spoke better than anyone about justification but seemed to be completely ignorant of sanctification.

Anabaptist and pietist nurturing have fostered a unity of faith and life. Having the dual heritage of ethical traditions, Brethren seem to be destined to be involved in a wide range of ethical issues. Whereas Anabaptism leads us to be active in witness for peace and justice in the Spirit and the ways of Jesus, pietist teachings would have us embody the fruit of the Spirit, namely, love, joy, peace, patience, kindness, generosity, faithfulness, gentleness, and self-control (Gal. 5:22). Theologically, Brethren heritage may join the emphases on obeying the commandments of Jesus with a sense of empowerment of the Holy Spirit.

Personal Generalizations

The long-held motifs of *nonresistance to evil*, inherited to a greater extent from anabaptist theology, and *nonviolent resistance to evil,* a later motif that is more congenial to the pacifism of Radical Pietism, will be treated in a future chapter. However, like other issues, I discern these themes to divide us, to be in tension. But I also affirm both as being necessary ingredients for our peace church tradition. In our witness I believe them to be mutually reinforcing, even though our members, who hold one or both of these positions, probably constitute a minority of our total membership. Nevertheless, Conference delegates have repeatedly affirmed our historic peace position by near consensus majorities. This kind of stability, preserved in different aspects of our heritage, has perhaps served to keep us together.

Through the generations we have been in dialogue with and influenced by mystical devotees, communal groups, great awakenings, revivalism, universalism, premillenialism, modernism, liberalism, fundamentalism, neo-orthodoxy, charismatic movements, the social gospel, death of God advocates, liberation theologies, narrative theology, the religious right, spirituality, and postmodern trends. Positively, this may signify the warmth of our openness to others. Negatively, it may be a result of our too easy acculturation with beliefs alien to our biblical heritage. In addition, our unity has been threatened through polarized positions around ethical decisions dealing with simplicity, divorce, abortion, alcohol, racism, sexism, civil disobedience, and homosexuality, among other issues that can be found throughout Annual Conference minutes. It is surprising that we have not experienced more schisms. However, our heritage has also provided the inspiration, gatherings, and structures to renew our covenant through efforts to maintain unity of the Spirit in the bond of peace. This brings me to these generalizations.

Sectarian and Ecumenical

Through Bible study the founders decided to establish a church after the pattern of the New Testament whereby the order of Matthew 18:15-17 could be carried out. Having rejected infant baptism, they understood themselves to be without baptism. The first baptisms by three immersions created a sectarian *Gemienschaft* (community or communion). Through the years this community has been known as a peculiar people, for many years with plain, uniform dress and continuing degrees of nonconformity to a violent, materialistic, and secular culture.

The first baptism of Alexander Mack occurred with fasting and drawing a lot. The men and women wanted the one doing the first baptism to remain anonymous, lest the church be named after any of the first eight. They did not record or tell others the day or month of the baptisms. Such humility and fear of making too much out of their beginnings may be related to the noncreedal intention to be open to new light as it is discerned through study of the Word. Early Brethren in America refused to agree with Zinzendorf's proposal for what seemed to them to be too similar to a state church. Still, they did join in gatherings and cooperated with other Christians in publications and the use of buildings (such can be documented in Stephen Longenecker's *Piety and Tolerance*).

In recent history Brethren have opposed any proposals for organic union with others, while at the same time we have engaged in mission and service ministries and held membership in local, state, and the National and World Councils of Churches. Our rootedness in affirming the Jesus way makes us sectarian. Our love of neighbor, enemy, and God's good creation requires us to be ecumenical.

Conservative and Liberal

It is often said and felt that our identity as Brethren is neither conservative nor liberal. Another way of defining this is to affirm that in some ways we remain conservative and in other ways we appear to be liberal. Some have observed that plain Brethren elders in Lancaster County enjoyed listening on their radios to "Fuller's Old Fashioned Revival Hour." Moreover, the same elders greatly appreciated the sermons of Harry Emerson Fosdick, who was labeled a modernist by fundamentalists. They appreciated the evangelistic and evangelical tone of Fuller's sermon and song. Yet they agreed with Fosdick's emphasis on the teachings of Jesus and the kingdom of God. Here I note my own experience. When I sing "Amazing Grace," I know I am a conservative. When I sing Fosdick's prayer, "Cure thy children's warring madness. . . . Grant us courage lest we miss thy kingdom's goal," I am aware that I will be labeled a liberal. Rather than seeking an identity of conservative, liberal, or evangelical, I prefer to be labeled by words from our heritage.

Particularity and Pluralism

Loyalty to denominations is diminishing. When shopping for a church, many people choose a church based on their personal needs more than on their traditional beliefs and loyalties. In spite of all our faults, I love my heritage and its people. I realize our members are often cliquish, self-righteous, and judgmental. Yet, at our best, what better spiritual home than to be a member of a body whose purpose is to help us to be faithful members of the body of Christ? For many of us, such a heritage is preferable to giving primary allegiance to such things as a lodge, a celebrity, a politician or political party, a corporation, a football or basketball team. Even when our allegiances give priority to a loving nuclear family or small intimate group, we need an extended family of people who want to live according to the spirit and way of Jesus.

In reality, we live in a pluralistic environment saturated with many options for fellowship, relationships, lifestyles, and religious expressions. Is it possible that Brethren exist for such a time as this? I suggest that we neither glorify nor demonize our pluralistic society. In light of New Testament commandments to love even our enemies and God's creation, we can open our hearts so as to live the prayer of St. Francis. Where there is hatred we can sow love; where there is injury, pardon; where there is doubt, faith; where there is despair, hope; where there is darkness, light; and where there is sadness, joy.

The third theological conference of the 1960s was planned to bring the polarities of the church together for dialogue and greater unity. If you were known as a typical middle-of-the-road Brethren, you probably would not have been invited. After three days a brother from a sister denomination, who had been invited to be an observer, emoted: "You Church of the Brethren people differ so much on many issues and doctrines. But when you come together, you are really glad to see each other. In our gatherings that expect us to agree on basic doctrines, it is different. When we come together, we are usually not that glad to see one another." This story reveals both our vulnerability and something that is basic to our tradition.

What keeps us together? Can it be what brought us together in the first place: a need to freely assemble and separate from intolerance, doctrinal strangulation, and the cultural state religion of redemptive violence? We have inherited a deep abiding faith that we are the church, the people of God, the body of Christ. Believing this, there are no forces that can presume (or that have the power) to call us from our nonconformity to obey other than the way and teachings of Jesus Christ.

Chapter Three

Christ Existing as Community
The power and attraction of communal ecclesiology

How very good and pleasant it is when kindred live together in unity!
—Psalm 133:1

In the chapter on community in *Life Together,* Dietrich Bonhoeffer adds a refrain to this psalm for Christians: Unity exists "when kindred live together through Christ" (47). In Bonhoeffer's doctoral dissertation, *The Communion of Saints,* his favorite identity line for the church is "Christ existing as community." This incorporates what Brethren profess. *Community* is a word that has been overworked and stretched beyond reality by Brethren. Nevertheless, community is the word that defines the church for us.

Between college and seminary, hands were laid on me to serve as summer pastor among farmer and rancher families in western Nebraska. The hospitable community of Brethren gathered in Enders, a town of a few dozen souls with its picturesque, little white meetinghouse. The Wine clan and their neighbors were fortunate to have been served over forty years by brother and elder D. G. Wine. Large in stature and graced by a gentle, warm heart, this free minister without formal education became my mentor, shaping my views of ministry and beliefs of the church. He was in his eighties; I was barely twenty. Yet we discussed a great variety of issues, ending in the wee morning hours only when my eyelids began to droop. When he shared from his library of a thousand books, this neophyte sensed Wine knew more history than many college professors.

I lived in a different home each week, and the stories *by* Brother Wine were augmented by stories *about* Brother Wine. My favorite one is about the church. A Baptist preacher appeared in Enders. He had been told that Enders needed a Bible-believing church and was led by God and other Baptists to accept this challenge. When he moved in with his family, the Brethren turned out to help with strong backs and favorite carry-in dishes. When the preacher posted a sign of welcome and announcements on the window of what had been an abandoned building, the Brethren showed up for the first meeting. They believed there were too few mortals in the vicinity of Enders for two congregations. They continued to appear for fellowship and worship at the preacher's Sunday and revival meetings. It seemed that every time he turned around, there were Dunkers to help him.

A few months passed. He planned and publicized a very special meeting. Neighbors arrived from surrounding towns and farms. He rose and confessed how he had been told that there was a real need for a Baptist-minded Bible congregation in Enders. But he had been misled. With emotion, he confessed: "Enders is very well churched. I need to move on to where I am needed." After several decades of being told, this story may be embellished. For me, however, it is a Brethren story that effuses the spirit and ecclesiology of our heritage. I share it as a way to express thanksgiving for an early gift of grace flowing through one of the most influential people and communities in my pilgrimage.

Church as Called-Out Community

The Greek word for church, ekkl*esia*, literally means "the called-out ones." The English derivative, ecclesiology, alludes to the study of the doctrine of the church. A favorite text of those who sense the chosen nature of the people of God is lifted from a sermon to the newly baptized: "You are a chosen race, a royal priesthood, a holy nation, God's own people" (1 Pet. 2:9). The community of faith is called out to be priests in the body of Christ. This favorite verse reveals why Brethren from their beginnings have embodied a high doctrine of the church.

Called Out to Be the Church. Here "high" does not refer to highly structured and liturgical embodiments of the church. Rather, a high view for the Brethren refers to the importance, even necessity, of the community of faith. A low view does not regard the community as essential to salvation. A high view holds that people, even two or three gathered in the name of Jesus, be the primary means whereby the Spirit calls individuals to accept Jesus and his way. Christians are called out to be God's people, not isolated disciples. New Testament faith teaches us to love one another, our neighbors, even our enemies. Our relationship with God cannot be separated from the nature of our relationships with one another.

The early Brethren leader Alexander Mack believed that one who accepts Christ will do what Jesus wants, namely be baptized and join a community that exists in Christ Jesus. The close-knit sense of fellowship that has characterized anabaptist-like communities finds expression in a highly valued, community-centered theology, which is neither Catholic nor Protestant.

Called Out to Be with and for Others. From a family that neglected the church, Bonhoeffer felt called out. He regarded the Christian community as a wonderful gift: "The physical presence of other Christians is a source of incomparable joy and strength to the believer" (*Life Together* 29). Bonhoeffer speaks of the dreams we have in ways that articulated my condition at first reading. In college and seminary, I often dreamed of an ideal congregation. Bonhoeffer reminded me that whoever loves one's own dreams of community more than the Christian community becomes a destroyer of the latter. I had envisioned people who would be members of my church. Bonhoeffer claims that God quickly frustrates such dreams. Communities have failed because people enter with their own demands and ideas of community. This clarified for me what had been difficult to understand: "Christian community is not an ideal, but a divine community."

Bonhoeffer adds that the "community is a spiritual, not a psychic reality" (35). For him psychic reality refers to entering community for self-centered reasons, such as seeking a position of power and influence. Even an emotional conversion experience can be used to overpower others to accept one's leadership and desires. Rather than psychic love, Bonhoeffer advocates a spiritual love. Here spiritual is used in the biblical sense of right relationships with God and others. Spiritual love will speak to Christ about a brother or sister more than dogmatically telling others the truth about Christ. Spiritual love strives to participate in ways that are helpful for the community. The basis of a psychic community is selfish desire; the basis of a spiritual community is light. For "God is light. . . . and if we walk in the light as [God] is in the light, we have fellowship with one another . . . " (1 John 1:5, 7).

Called Out from Domination Powers. The sense of being called out was basic to the radical Christians' general disillusionment with "Constantinianism," the dream of a Christian empire where all were baptized into the established church and uniformity needed to be enforced by the sword. The vision of the church existing as the empire in prayer was replaced in radical circles by the suspicion that the fall of the church occurred when it became aligned with the interests of the Roman Empire. As already noted, Brethren sensed fundamental differences between the way of Christ and the ways of the worldly reign of death that characterized the so-called religious wars of the sixteenth and seventeenth centuries. The concept of *corpus Christi,* the called out body of Christ, has continued to be important. This view is distinguished from the idea of *corpus Christianum,* the body of Christians in which membership in the state is coterminous with membership in the established church.

The Constitution of the United States provides religious freedom. Apart from some exceptions, Brethren have not experienced the most blatant fruits of state church mentality. Nevertheless, equating Christianity with American society has been pervasive enough to foster current concerns with the myth of a "Christian America." In an attempt to oppose the tendency to wrap our militaristic and violent culture in the Stars and Stripes and unfurl it before the world, many Brethren propose following the commandments of Jesus to love all people, even our enemies. Our security lies with Christ more than with weapons of our nation. The Brethren propensity is to choose faithfulness to the teachings of Jesus above all other allegiances.

Most Brethren approve of flags outside or inside schools and public buildings as symbols of love of our nation with its pledge of liberty and justice for all. At the same time, many members in peace church traditions do not accept displaying national flags at our places of worship. We are members of communities of faith that transcend national loyalties. In light of our heritage, it seems right to follow Paul's teachings that we not unnecessarily offend brothers and sisters of other nations and our own members who experience the flag as being connected with a battle hymn that glories war. In our worship we desire to focus on our loyalty to the Jesus way of love, service, and reconciliation.

Church as *Gemeinschaft*

Foremost for the Brethren, the church is *Gemeinschaft*, a German word that is difficult to translate with one English word. The word expresses the intimate sense of unity that exists when people share commitments to live the love of Jesus in community.

Theology of the Meetinghouse

For Anabaptists and Brethren, the church is essentially people. People do not go to church as much as people are the church. For more than a century, the church was a house church movement. Walls were attached to ceilings with hinges. This allowed members to lift the walls of one or two rooms in order to provide a meeting place. For larger gatherings of their love feasts, they met in barns. When they began to build special houses for love feasts and worship, they were still reluctant to call a building a church. Instead, the church—the people—gathered in a "meetinghouse" for the purpose of affirming the sanctuary of God in all of life. The same was true of other plain groups in early America, who in refusing to name any building a church referred to their neighbors' church edifices as "steeple-houses." Today, most Brethren call the primary place of worship their church, perhaps to accommodate sentiments of their neighbors. Some congregations and members hold to the historic name. Others, who use the word *church* more inclusively, continue to affirm the theology of the meetinghouse.

Marks of the Church

Oversimplification often helps a saying to stick. Such is true of the proverbial sayings of Bethany's church history professor, Floyd Mallott. In describing marks of the church, he asserted that Roman Catholics and Lutherans go to church to worship God. Calvinists in the Reformed tradition, who place the Bible on a centered pulpit, meet to be instructed from the Word of God. Brethren gather inside and outside the meetinghouse to see one another. True, but not the whole truth, as many Brethren believe they occasionally worship and absorb texts of edification and guidance from the Good Book. We might add that in seeing each other we relate in ways that hopefully enable us to better serve our Lord.

Emil Brunner, a Swiss theologian in the twentieth century, offered similar views of the church. In his *Systematic Theology,* he expresses his attraction to American Christianity, observing that the church is a fellowship more than an institution. Many theologians judged that he held an invisible view of the church, one lacking concrete visible marks and practices. He responded by maintaining that a caring, sharing community is very visible. Brunner adds that though the church is defined primarily as people, nevertheless, people do establish institutions.

For the most part, Brethren can accept the two marks of the church defined by Luther—wherever the Word of God is truthfully preached and the sacraments duly administered. The Reformed tradition adds a third mark, the necessity of order and discipline. Though not agreeing with Calvin's implementation of this mark at Geneva, the Brethren have struggled with what it means to be a disciplined community. One reason that Anabaptists and Brethren quote Bonhoeffer is that he adds to Luther's two marks the mark of fellowship *(koinonia)* in defining the nature of the church.

In order to be a genuine church, Anglican bishops have proposed four essentials, namely the authority of the Bible, at least two sacraments, the apostolic succession of bishops, and the apostolic faith of the ancient creeds. This Lambeth Quadrilateral has influenced the agenda of the ecumenical movement.

Brethren have concurred with the mark of biblical authority, and in subsequent chapters I will discuss other requirements that are necessary for being the church. Foremost, however, Brethren believe that churches could have all four essentials and lack the most essential mark of the church, namely, loving one another. Along with early Christians, Brethren believe others will know we are Christians by our love.

Sacramental Nature of the Church

There is something to be said for the Roman Catholic view, which in Vatican II named the church to be a sacrament. Sociologists need to regard the church the same as other institutions that can be studied, such as colleges, sports teams, corporations, and governmental agencies. Like them, congregations or denominations have a collective spirit, a spirit of enthusiasm, sadness, mission, or other characteristics that can be named and studied. But Christians claim the church to be both divine and human. The divinity of the church results from Christ's presence. The church is both a community of sinners and a community of saints. In a Christian community, the Holy Spirit permeates the objective spirit. A Christian community is understood through sociological analyses from the outside, but only from within do members experience the authenticating nature of revelation, the Divine Spirit coming to us through others, Christ existing as community. It is truly a mystery how sinners like us can be the body of Christ.

The word *sacrament* appeared as the Latin successor to the Greek word *mysterion* (mystery). For Brethren there is a sacramental quality in face-to-face relationships. Walking through a beautiful forest on a sunny day, I sense a divine presence. Alone, I meditate with the classics from saints of the past, and their spirituality flows through my being. Yet, I feel God's presence more deeply than in any other way when I am empathetically sharing with a brother or a sister. Bonhoeffer states that we are in communion when Christ is present between us. Communion is defined as believers relating to one another in the Spirit of Christ, of love. The smallest incarnation of Christian community exists when the Spirit of Jesus abides with two or three gathered in his name (Matt. 18:20).

This biblical truth points to the power of the church. Since the outpouring of the Spirit at Pentecost was integral to the birth of the Christian church, doctrinal books have connected the Third Person of the trinity with doctrines of the church. The Holy Spirit, especially present in the church, fosters assumptions of Anabaptists that no one can come to God except with a brother or sister. Thus, the neighbor constitutes an essential element in one's personal redemption. When a believer is baptized in the name of the Holy Spirit, prayers petition the Spirit of Christ to flow through the community and the believer who is empowered to walk in newness of life for others and the kingdom coming. The laying on of hands is a powerful and beautiful New Testament symbol embodying the truth that the Spirit calls, nurtures, and guides us through the living faith of brothers and sisters.

The Church as Covenantal Community

With tongues in cheek, Presbyterians often name 1 Corinthians 14:40 as their golden text. A professor from their tradition shared with our class: "When folks really get to know us, they will discover our golden text: '. . . all things should be done decently and in order' " (1 Cor. 14:40). Though ordered discipline has not been regarded as one of the essential marks of the Brethren, elders and mothers have embraced Paul's admonition. For we cannot separate our covenant with God from discerning proper relationships with one another.

The Meaning of Covenant

Many congregations greet each other as brother and sister. In this familial heritage, respected leaders were often addressed as aunt and uncle. An extended family requires a covenant community. Covenant implies agreements and responsibilities. Community members who live closely together and share a common purse have discovered the necessity to have common agreements. Egalitarian desires to have community without leaders have often led to abusive activity by capable people. Members have discerned that leaders are needed. But they have learned that leaders need to be chosen, supported, and made accountable.

Religious communities have generally survived longer than secular ones. This is likely because they acknowledge a transcendent authority. In the Hebrew Bible, covenant refers to the religious bond existing between God and Israel. The promises of God inspire visionary hope. The will and laws of God foster responsibility in the spirit of love. Because we embrace a familial style, we are aware of the strong ties that bind us together in Christ Jesus. We have inherited memories of the covenant of the first Brethren, who if required would lay down their lives for one another.

Pietist-inclined Michael Frantz, an early leader of the Conestoga congregation in Lancaster County, focused on the covenant in concrete ways. He described the visible manifestations of communion that exist in warm brotherly compassion, cooperation, and sharing what is needed. In response to God's love and love of neighbor, the disciple of Christ "must not call his property and whatever he has his own." Frantz added, "If I had three hundred acres of land and much other property and money besides, I would be able to be its steward . . . until need became evident in the community. Then if the need demanded it, no more of the above would be mine but what were my necessities of life" (Durnbaugh, *The Brethren in Colonial America* 458-59).

For Brethren, covenant occurs when vows are recited and affirmed in baptism. Covenant is present when promises of both church and members are made in calling pastors, deacons, and others for special ministries by laying on of hands. Covenant is involved when disputes are settled according to Matthew 18:15ff. Covenantal spirit is present in self-examination services conducted by a deacon or in quiet meditation before the love feast. Covenant is part of anointing services in which the anointed are asked to confess or profess whatever is close to their hearts. Covenant happens in a variety of ways in what has been called discipling.

Covenant of Annual Meeting or Conference

Count von Nikolaus Ludwig Zinzendorf traveled from Germany to visit Pennsylvania in 1741. The renowned Moravian leader believed his presence could bring about greater manifestations of unity among German sects and churches. The five Brethren representatives experienced the count to be overly dominant. More than that, they feared the re-institution of a state church with infant baptism. After three synods and discussions about possible union with the Mennonites, the Brethren left the gatherings sensing their own need to come together. A meeting in the spring of 1742 laid the groundwork for what came to be known as the Yearly Meeting. The name and democratic consensus style reveal Quaker influences. Later, perhaps to avoid confusion, Yearly Meeting was changed to Annual Meeting. Local members often referred to it as the "big assembly" or "big meeting." Growing attendance and structures may have fostered a desire to resemble mainline denominations; thus, this extended family reunion has come to be known as our Annual Conference.

An intangible unifying factor has been the familial reunion of our cultural clan, to which we attach the word *fellowship*. We play a favorite game: "Who do you know or who are you related to that I know?" There evolved a large love feast for elders and ministers. Now ministers have a connected conference. Fostering unity, the heritage of singing together continues. The community of faith, usually reluctant to feature sacred days of the church year, set Pentecost as the date for the big meeting. Now, instead of scheduling around the varying dates of Pentecost, the Conference has evolved to most often meeting near or on July 4.

The original purpose of preserving our unity through covenantal decision-making has survived. Queries come from congregations. These are processed by Standing Committee, made up of representatives from the districts. The business then comes before the entire body. In 1866, decisions by consensus of everyone present were replaced by voting delegates from congregations. A Quakerlike custom continues in that anyone is free to make a speech or offer a motion, an opportunity that is rarely possible in most denominational conferences. Ethical and polity issues are often difficult to distinguish from theological concerns. A spirit of openness to new light lingers in that decisions do not remain cast in stone. In the nineteenth century, efforts to maintain simplicity, such as opposing carpets (a sign of wealth at the time) and lightning rods (a symbol of distrust), appear again and again in the context of increased industrialization and higher standards of living. It is also difficult to regard decisions as normative that have been passed by a bare majority.

Historically, covenants to preserve unity led to the frequent advice to "forbear patiently" the behavior and beliefs of brothers and sisters. Theological issues, such as universal restoration of all souls, were not voted on to be accepted or rejected. Rather, in answering queries on such issues, admonitions advised that it was wrong for a brother to espouse one view privately and preach the opposite publicly. Yet, decisions were more legalistic in the nineteenth and early twentieth centuries than in subsequent more pluralistic decades that have followed.

The best theological analysis of covenant-making at the large gathering may be that which is found in the first printed collection of Annual Meeting minutes. In the introduction to the minutes, Henry Kurtz comments on differing opinions about decisions of Annual Meetings. There were those who "perhaps esteem them [decisions] somewhat too highly, taking them as rules and laws of equal authority as divine writ. . . . Others again put perhaps a too low estimate upon them, considering them as a bundle of human traditions of . . . elders, which we cannot too soon forget and lay aside." He expresses his own judgment that Annual Meeting minutes were neither laws nor vain traditions, but represented "a solemn act of renewing our covenant, into which each one of us had entered. . . ." He adds: "Let us look upon the counsels and conclusions as solemn agreements or covenants upon which our fathers brake annually the bread of communion, and considered them as bonds of love, to bind them together in union of the spirit" (*The Brethren's Encyclopedia* iii-vii).

In his day, Henry Kurtz had two factions in mind that years later either walked out or were ruled out of the church, leaving the Conservatives as the large group existing today as the Church of the Brethren. The Progressive or Ashland Brethren opted for a more congregational polity in which the Conference exists primarily for fellowship and mutual planning of cooperative endeavors. The Old German Baptist Brethren insisted on greater adherence to the decisions of the Big Meeting. Though Kurtz's middle-of-the-road position affirmed decisions to have more authority than what has developed in present ambivalent attitudes, it may be helpful to apply his theological analysis to our situation.

There are many today who advocate strict obedience for some, but not all, decisions of Conference. And there are many who are indifferent to Conference decisions. They judge business meetings at Conference to be a waste of time, too controversial, and not relevant to the life of most congregations. Perhaps the majority, at least the dedicated Brethren who spend large amounts of time and money to attend Conferences, have consciously or unconsciously adopted a middle view. Whereas Conference decisions cannot be absolutely binding, they should not be ignored. They deserve our consideration. We need to respect and have dialogue with the majority of brothers and sisters who initiate, process, and approve queries.

In a session of Standing Committee, when abortion was the major concern, I remember a sister sincerely wondering: "Why are we wasting our time? We will all leave believing the same as when we came." A medical doctor rose and replied: "I deal with this problem daily and I want to know what my church believes about this issue." Throughout the educational, inspirational, and business sessions of Annual Conference, Brethren are participating in covenantal activities that many believe have kept us together. Our differences are not to be glorified, but they do provide an opportunity to lead to greater faithfulness, truth, and unity in our bonding in the Spirit of Jesus.

On one occasion, following a controversial decision, I passed a huddle of college folk who were being told that they were not required to abide by what had just been adopted. After they had separated, I challenged the college president in the way that I often need to be challenged: "You are probably right. Your college legally need not adopt this policy. But I wish your board would have prayed about it longer before immediately rejecting the will of the delegates."

Church as a Disciplined Community

During a preaching mission many years ago, a ninety-year-old sister sent word that she wanted to see me. Though bedfast she obviously enjoyed relating her life story. From a wealthy Philadelphia family, she had savored all of the advantages. She enjoyed dancing, voice, piano, and violin lessons and had a wardrobe fit for her recitals. As she grew older, she would have become a debutante. But it was her fate to meet the Brethren. Curiosity led her to walk into a meeting one Sunday. She was intrigued with the simplicity, sincerity, and genuine love of the plain folk for one another. In spite of this admiration, she felt she could never join them. She would need to forsake her beautiful wardrobe. The community did not even approve of using a piano. And she would be wearing black dresses and stockings. Ultimately her growing interest and their nurturing love led her to seek baptism.

As a new member, she pledged silently to devote her life to keeping the best she was receiving from the Brethren. At the same time, she would strive to change their nonconformity to what had been beautiful and precious for her. The story ended with a twinkle in her eyes and a slight smile as she uttered her punch line. "Don't you think I have been too successful!"

In our demeanor, values, and lifestyles, we sometimes long for the best of what attracted our sister at the same time we would not sacrifice what our sister did in order to become a member of an extended family of nonconformist Christians. Discipline comes from the same word as disciple. The word can lead to encouraging and building up a person or the body. Or it can mean confronting and speaking the truth in love. *Disciplining* is a word used in Mennonite circles for both. *Eldering* is a traditional synonym used among the Quakers.

Examples of discipline from the earliest communities of faith no doubt influenced the Brethren. In one of Paul's epistles to the Corinthians, he advised them to deliver a member to Satan so that his spirit might be saved (1 Cor. 5:4-5). Here the purpose of discipline is reclamation of a member, restoring the person to fellowship. The highest concern is the true welfare of the member. The author of the epistle to Timothy advises the young church leader to rebuke those who persist in sin so that the community may learn what is right (1 Tim. 5:20). For the sake of the health of the body, there are times when it is important to engage in current practices of conflict transformation.

Alexander Mack believed that a greater sin than many sins was the refusal to be sorry for one's sin. He advocated the ban, which involved some kind of separation of a person from the community. In historic practices the greater ban removed a person from fellowship; the lesser ban barred the member from participation in the Lord's Supper. In the context of early Anabaptists and Brethren, in an environment much different than ours, the ban could be considered a soft liberal practice compared to the disciplines of established churches that imprisoned, made refugees, tortured, and executed those who deviated from orthodoxies of faith or practice. In contrast, the early Anabaptists simply required separation and this often for security reasons. They wanted to protect themselves from those who were seeking to capture and kill them.

The first controversial case of church discipline occurred in the congregation at Krefeld where the migrating Brethren had found refuge because of the political dominance of the Dutch who held to the more liberal policies of the Netherlands. The dispute is known as the Hacker affair. Johann Hacker was a young member married to Eva op deen Graef, the stepdaughter of a Mennonite merchant who was also a preacher. In spite of social and doctrinal congeniality with the Mennonites, the marriage evoked sharp criticism. Early teaching at Schwarzenau required that a couple be one in true faith in Jesus Christ. Christian Liebe, literally "Christian Love," led the opposition to the marriage, perhaps due to his brave faithfulness as a galley slave before being released as a celebrated leader. Liebe was successful in having the young groom placed in the ban.

Johann Naas, celebrated as the first conscientious objector in the tradition, favored a milder discipline. One of his sons married a sister of the same family. The withdrawal of Naas and others contributed to the first large migration of Brethren to America in 1719. It is speculated that the congregation may have lost some hundred prospects for membership as a result of the unpleasant infighting. Since the more liberal party emigrated to the new world, the first controversial case may have contributed to more tolerant attitudes of discipline among Brethren in America.

Misuses of Discipline

The motive for discipline too often results from efforts to protect the reputation and purity of the church than from loving concern for the person. The concern is more with the offense than the offender. At other times the concern can shift from reconciliation to a desire for vengeance. Often the sins of the weak are featured while the more destructive sins of pride, greed, or gossip are ignored. This fosters hypocrisy, the sin Jesus vigorously renounced.

In high school, an English teacher immediately showered me with disproportionate attention. Puzzled about my potential status as a teacher's pet, I shared this with my parents. I learned that they had a high regard for my teacher. She was the daughter of a founding elder of our congregation and had been disciplined by the church for wearing a hat when she returned with a degree from McPherson College. My parents' generation reacted to what they considered to be petty and harsh expressions of church discipline by the previous generation, while disregarding their own sins, as we too are inclined to do. In any generation when love and sharing disappear, discipline tends to become impersonal and lacks possibilities of redemption.

Positive Stories and Principles

We were privileged to host Harry Ziegler, an elder from eastern Pennsylvania, in our home. He was visiting his son Edward, pastor in residence at Bethany where his son Jesse had taught for many years. I asked Harry to tell me how it was when they engaged in church discipline. And he related this story, which was similar to those of other congregations.

It became known that a young unmarried woman, a member in good standing, was pregnant. This meant that she would appear before the congregation at the next council meeting. There she confessed her sin and expressed her sorrow if she had disgraced the community. The young man in question was absent because he was not a member. After some admonitions the church voted that she was no longer in fellowship with the church. However, at the same meeting, following subsequent affirmations of support and forgiveness, the meeting expressed forgiveness and voted to receive the young woman again into the fellowship of the church. That meant that every sister present would greet her with the holy kiss and every brother would receive her with the right hand of fellowship.

The presiding elder admonished the congregation that if they learned of anyone who continued to gossip and talk about their sister, that person would be called before the church council. The young woman was freed to come to meetings as a member in good standing. The congregation shared expectations and preparations for the arrival of a new life. And the birth was celebrated with joy and caring responses from members of the congregation.

The way this congregation dealt with the sister probably would not be viable for our communities. In our more independent impersonal culture, members are not as intimately acquainted as are congregations in a less pluralistic environment. The same issue surfaced when I was growing up. The community had abandoned the practice of discipline but, nevertheless, displayed attitudes that shunned a young woman in the same condition. The difference that permeates these similar stories is that brothers and sisters in the earlier story dealt with the sister and congregation in ways that brought them together, making it easier to abandon attitudes of condemnation and to restore warm relationships. Though not a detailed paradigm for us, the earlier story provides an example of church discipline at its best in displaying love and good intentions.

The story suggests that a disciplined community can be a community with genuine concern. In *Life Together* Bonhoeffer deals with the possibilities of the grace of God becoming apparent when we deal with sinners. Not despising sinners, but being privileged to bear with them, means we are not required to give them up for lost. Then we are able to accept them and preserve community with forgiveness. He adds that Christians can speak and help one another because we realize that we are sinners helping other sinners (102-105). But, he adds, when another falls into obvious sin, God's Word calls for admonition. "Nothing can be more cruel," Bonhoeffer writes, "than that leniency which abandons others to their sin. Nothing can be more compassionate than that severe reprimand which calls another brother or sister back from the path of sin" (105). He realizes that the problem is that we may not care enough to speak the truth in love to a brother or sister. The disciplined community is not to be identified with assumptions that we have a perfect community. Rather, discipline is needed because we all are sinners and need help beyond ourselves.

We should not forget that discipline is not limited to admonishing, correcting, or confronting a brother or a sister. Discipline involves encouragement, praise, and advice that nurture in ways that inspire others to be faithful servants in the kingdom. We need to consider Paul's advice to the Thessalonians as discipline at its best: "Therefore encourage one another and build up each other, as indeed you are doing" (1 Thess. 5:11). Defining discipline this way may convince many people today to accept the validity of discipline in the community of faith.

Proposals

To revive the right kind of discipline in building each other up, we need to seriously work on the meaning of church membership. In creating a new sense of identity and relationships, it will be necessary to envision that membership in the body of Christ involves commitment and discipleship.

Some congregations join in a periodic renewal of vows. Instead of deciding who is in and who is out, the task of pruning the church rolls offers opportunities to all the members to express their desire to remain active as much as they are able. Those who resist renewing their vows or who fail to respond in any way remove themselves. However, this does not mean that the community will not continue to be compassionately concerned about them.

Throughout the nineteenth century, those joining the church promised to settle differences according to Matthew 18:15ff. If one does as Jesus says and goes directly to a brother or sister to raise a concern, gossip is short-circuited. If there is reconciliation, great. If not, include several others and meet again. If there is still no progress, take it to the larger community. Because we tend to vacillate between restoration and the elimination of church discipline, we need more discussion about what it means to treat someone as a Gentile and tax collector, remembering that Jesus was criticized for eating and being with them. Likewise, we need more insights as to what it means to forgive seventy times seven.

Ideally, being a member of a loving community leads to a new freedom, the freedom to be open and honest. There is also the freedom to fail, be wrong, or defensive, because we know brothers and sisters will correct us. If we experience their love, we are motivated to be faithful because we know we are not alone in our struggle.

For some generations church discipline came to be regarded as a practice of rejection. We failed to model concrete examples of disciplining at its best. In recent years we have been experiencing a growing interest in new expressions of Matthew 18. We have a growing understanding of conflict resolution and conflict transformation. Women are calling for expressions of tough love as a result of a more widespread awareness and knowledge of the abuse of children and women. The demise of right discipline in our culture may have engendered a culture of vengeance and violence as the way to maintain law and order. The issue is theological; we are struggling to incarnate New Testament themes of redemption, forgiveness, and reconciliation in the context of our culture's belief that violence is the way to solve problems.

Church as Eschatological Community

Eschatological is a word that refers to end times. Since eschatological and apocalyptic prophecies spring up in every generation, this topic remains important for Brethren. It may be difficult to appreciate earlier views or to relate to contemporary expressions that are soon replaced by new predictions. Because views of our spiritual predecessors remain relevant for us, the focus here will draw from our biblical heritage. Future chapters that relate our faith to contemporary peace and mission concerns will relate to more recent millennial and apocalyptic beliefs.

In looking back at the early church to adopt models, we see that our forebears looked forward through the lens of biblical promises about the future. Though they may not have used the words, Anabaptists defined themselves as an eschatological community. Menno Simons wrote of two opposing aeons or kingdoms, the present age and the age to come. The present age or kingdom looks to the fallen creation. Our hope looks to a future age that will embody the fullness of the kingdom. This is not a dualism that regards material creation as evil in contrast to the nonmaterial world. Neither is it a dualism that places the kingdom entirely in the future.

Early and later Brethren have differed in the degree to which they have accepted premillennial interpretations of the biblical apocalyptic. For them the church is that part of the world that in small ways begins to make visible the future kingdom of peace and justice. Anabaptists have shared the biblical realism of the premillennialists, but have parted company from attempts to move the Christian way from the present into the future. Hochmann, who traveled with Mack on itinerant speaking tours, proclaimed the imminent coming of the millennial kingdom. Instead of the end, Christ's coming kingdom would saturate the present world with God's love and manifest actions of love between all peoples. The way to prepare for the second coming of Jesus is to follow him, to love our enemies, and so transform our lives into communities of love.

The first Anabaptists and brothers and sisters at Schwarzenau appropriated biblical metaphors such as *pilgrims, exiles, sojourners, aliens,* and *strangers* to define themselves as God's people. As pilgrims they sensed that their citizenship was not in this world but of the coming kingdom. Nevertheless, they were still in the world and compassionately concerned for it. Peter Nead, in the nineteenth century, offered the following admonition: "Brethren, recollect we are pilgrims, not children of this world; let us therefore live like pilgrims." To live like pilgrims was to live out the ethics of the future kingdom way in the present, to live as if the kingdom has already come.

In this the Brethren understood themselves as a messianic or kingdom community. Though the kingdom was not yet a reality, the community could experience a foretaste of the kingdom. This eschatological motif was articulated in the theology of the love feast. The meal together reminded believers of the coming marriage supper of the Lamb (Rev. 19). Though not experiencing perfect communion around the tables, the Brethren could nevertheless taste the first fruit of the nature of love and unity that God desires for all people.

In proclaiming the meaning of the messianic or kingdom banquet, Brethren sensed a theology of mission. Their views corresponded to Peter Riedemann's often quoted words concerning the mission of the church: "The church of Christ is . . . a lantern of righteousness, in which the light of grace is borne and held before the whole world, that its darkness, unbelief, and blindness be thereby seen and made light, and that men [and women] may also learn and know the way of life." For this Hutterian leader, the Sermon on the Mount imagery of the city set on a hill comes from the working of the Spirit of Christ within us for the sake of others and the whole world (*Confession of Faith* 77-78).

Free Church Communal Ecclesiology

The Hunger for Rootedness. With the scattering of extended families caught in the network of giant institutions, there is a hunger for warm intimate relationships. Because the nuclear family cannot bear all the needs provided by extended families of the past, there exists a contemporary yearning for familial-like communities.

Yearnings for God's Grace. Amid cultures of hate, ethnic wars, politicized attacks, believers in redemptive violence, and the belief that security exists in the escalation of armaments, the gospel of redemptive love inspires communities to follow the Jesus way of nonviolent peacemaking for their communities and the world.

The Appeal of a Church for Others. In a self-centered, competitive, greedy, materialistic culture, it is a liberating and wonderful feeling to belong to a sharing, caring, and serving community among members and for others. The church is a church for others.

The Presence of Hope. Multitudes patronize fortunetellers, depend on astrological charts for advice about their futures, and follow current fads of those who claim to know more than Jesus said he knew about the details and time of the end. It seems freeing and refreshing to encounter interpretations of hope that point to the ultimate nature of God's perfect kingdom. At the same time, it does not rule out the promise that the kingdom is among us now and that we can freely participate in God's coming kingdom of peace and justice which is not yet.

The Power of the Anabaptist Vision

In a world saturated with hatred, with weapons of mass destruction in the hands of one or more people or a nation that may trigger a holocaust, the option of prophetic, witnessing, suffering, supporting communities may become more necessary and viable. Consistent with its message that the church needs to be reborn in each generation, the anabaptist vision will continue to become flesh in places where it may be least expected (updated from "Communal Ecclesiology" by Dale Brown, *Theology Today*, April 1979).

Chapter 4

Original Blessedness or Original Sin?
Views of human nature

When I look at your heavens, the work of your fingers, the moon and the stars that you have established, what are human beings that you are mindful of them . . . ? Yet you have made them a little lower than God, and crowned them with glory and honor.
—Psalm 8:3-5

My God, my God, why have you forsaken me? . . . Yet you are holy. . . . But I am a worm, and not human.
—Psalm 22:1, 3, 7

As human beings, are we naturally good or bad? Opinions about human nature have not been extensively debated, divisive, or resolved among our people. In spite of assumptions of theologians that what we believe about this doctrine affects how we shape other convictions, Brethren have generally remained confused or silent about this one. The committee responsible for *The Brethren Hymnal* (1951) changed the first line of hymn number 433 to read: "Amazing Grace! how sweet the sound, That saveth men like me." At that time many ardently opposed calling themselves or others a "wretch," defined as a wicked or despicable person. Due to the growing concern for inclusive language, the next hymnal committee needed to change our identity again. So in number 143 of *Hymnal: A Worship Book*, published by the believers churches in 1992, we sing "Amazing grace! how sweet the sound, that saved a *wretch* like me."

A feminist member of our class had recently given birth to her first child. She glowingly testified to the wonderful birth experience and added that only male theologians could contrive a doctrine such as original sin. A Presbyterian classmate injected that she had four sons and loved them dearly, but still believed in the reality of original sin. In tears, another woman accused the others of assuming that if you have not borne a child, you are not capable of doing theology. It was a rare occasion when I was wise enough to keep the peace. The discussion that followed indicated that ambivalence may be a better word than confusion to describe the situation, for ambivalence refers to uncertainty that comes with mutually conflicting emotions or thought. Because of Brethren propensities for tolerating differences on this issue, this chapter will not presume to make definitive statements of our views of human nature, but will offer hints on how contributions of our heritage and life might enlighten our convictions about this ambiguous topic.

The Doctrine of Creation

The focus on the human species has often neglected the importance of ecological views of creation. Basic to Judeo-Christian convictions is the last verse of Genesis 1: "God saw everything that he had made, and indeed, it was very good." Such an affirmation of the goodness of creation is not universal. In some religious and philosophical views, the fall is equated with creation. In these views the material stuff of creation is less spiritual than what is invisible and nonmaterial.

This describes the stance of an old Brethren elder in Oklahoma related in a story by my grandfather. It was the first time either of them had tasted ice cream. His friend immediately responded, "Anything that tastes this good must be of the devil!" The elder articulated a brand of dualism that regards anything pleasurable, material, or fleshly as anti-spiritual or bad. This view is opposite the biblical Spirit-flesh dualism of being led by the Spirit or walking in the flesh (Gal. 5:16-24). For Paul, to embody the fruit of the Spirit is to live in proper relationship with our Creator and all of God's creation; but to pursue works of the flesh is to walk in ways that violate God and others and misuse God's good material creation. Some philosophers of science credit Judeo-Christian assumptions about the good creation to be one of the ingredients that propelled the scientific revolution of the last four centuries.

Hans Hut, an early anabaptist evangelist, traveled across southern Germany and Austria preaching "the gospel of all creatures." He cited examples of creatures close at hand, such as horses and cattle, sheep, pigs and fowl that lived and died in the service of humans. As they fulfilled their purpose, so did Christ and so should we live and suffer for others. Such an intimate relationship with other creatures had been exemplified by Francis of Assisi who articulated a basis for an environmental theology in his many references to brother sun, sister moon, brother fox, sister bird. What was basic to Francis was central to our early members. Brethren loved the good earth, often striving to leave the soil better than they found it. Our forebears named their meetinghouses White Rock, Shade Creek, Pleasant View, Maple Grove, Roaring Spring, Sugar Valley, Mountain Grove, Trout Run, and many other names that reveal relational attitudes to our surroundings. We are summoned today to revive our love and concern for what God has created. We need to seek justice for the rest of creation and join in God's redemption of the earth (see March 2001 issue of *Messenger*). The biblical basis of our Christian walk is related to contemporary concerns about our environment.

Because the doctrine of creation provides a fitting context for this chapter, some theologians claim that the creation story is the place to begin formulations of the doctrine of people. So many of the debates between creationists and theorists of evolution sidestep what is central to the biblical story. Both sides argue too often from an assumption that the Bible is a science book. Some, not all, creationists seem arrogant in knowing more about the history of the good earth than the best scientists. Defenders of evolution often reveal how little they know about biblical literature and faith. In not understanding the Bible as a book of faith, both groups fail to consider that it is by faith that the creation story leads us to affirm the goodness of creation and the sacred nature of humans who bear the image of God. In critiquing his tradition's doctrine of original sin, the formerly Roman Catholic theologian Matthew Fox has emphasized the doctrine of original blessedness. Having introduced biblical bases for original goodness, we need to first consider a variety of views of sin.

Biblical Realism and Original Sin

In the late 1960s, I remember driving to inner-city Chicago to an old house where the steps descended into a musty basement. My hunch is that I had been invited to offer a fatherlike or moral presence to weekly gatherings of draft resisters to the Vietnam War. They were passionately opposed to this war. Because they differed with Brethren, Mennonites, and Quakers who refused to fight in any war, they were denied conscientious objector status by the state. Their anger surfaced because they were dealing with three unfavorable choices: going to prison, leaving the country, or fighting half way around the world in a jungle war they believed to be grossly unjust. I was startled one night when they concluded the session by forming a circle with arms stretched around each other and singing "Amazing grace! that saveth a wretch like me." As tears ran down the faces of this foulmouthed group, I was perplexed as to why they were emotionally digesting a song made popular by the antiwar movement during these contentious years. Lingering, I discovered they had come to an awareness that they were part of the problem of the society they opposed. This was the story of many in the movement who were beginning to retreat from fervent activism in order to get their minds and lives straight. Many activists had come to realize that resistance against an evil does not mean that one is completely free from or innocent of that evil.

As with these draft resisters, many of us today cannot easily dismiss the same confession when we realize how we participate as citizens and consumers in the structural and corporate violence of a selfish, greedy, violence-prone society. Our sins are both personal and corporate. Biblical themes stress that "all have sinned and fall short of the glory of God" (Rom. 3:23). As Christians we discern the glory of God in the face and way of Jesus, which leads us to realize how far we are from living this way. Thus, people in the world who have suffered from our despicable air raids see the planes, paid for with our tax money, as "Christian" bombers. We are complicit corporately as Americans and personally as taxpayers.

"In Adam's Fall we sinned all." These words from a *New England Primer* express a familiar view of the solidarity of all people in the sin inherited from our first parents. Saint Augustine's life with a mistress before his conversion led him to associate sexuality with sinfulness. His views influenced many subsequent movements to believe that we inherit sin because each one of us is conceived by a sinful act. Augustinian presuppositions about original sin led the classical Protestant reformers to espouse themes such as the bondage of the will. The good news was that the sacrament of baptism eliminated the guilt of sin. This was accomplished through what has been named forensic justification, defined as a person's status before God being changed through forgiveness without the sinful nature being eliminated. For Luther and other reformers, Christians remain *simul justus et peccator* (always justified and always sinners). These views were asserted to emphasize that we are saved only by God's grace through faith, and that salvation is wholly of God.

Proof-texting selected Anabaptist texts can demonstrate their agreement with the classical reformers. Melchior Hoffmann, Dirk Philips, Hans Denck, and Menno Simons all held that the whole human race was corrupted, poisoned, and cursed through the transgressions of Adam, whose disobedience delivered all into the bondage of Satan (see *Spiritual and Anabaptist Writers, The Library of Christian Classics,* Vol. XXV, 352). However, in reading more of their anthropological texts (meaning views of human beings), one discerns many deviations from the doctrine of original sin.

Anabaptist Modifications

Though early anabaptist leaders did not reject the doctrine of original sin, some of their basic emphases were evident when they interpreted their rejection of infant baptism and the faith of believers. They denied deterministic notions of double predestination. A good God would not determine at birth a person's eternal destiny of going to hell or heaven. The will of the person is not in bondage, because mature people are free to choose whom they will serve. Balthasar Hubmaier came to believe that some vestige of the divine image escapes the damning consequences of original sin. In this the early Anabaptists were influenced by writings of the mystics who adopted notions of the inner word. This led them to believe that children inherited not only original sin but inner light as given in a golden text of the Quakers: "The true light, which enlightens everyone, was coming into the world" (John 1:9).

Baptism and the Second Adam. Anabaptist teaching came to incorporate the Pauline text: "as all die in Adam, so all will be made alive in Christ (1 Cor. 15:22). If Adam represents the fallen state of all humanity, so Christ, through his death, atoned for the sins of everyone and, thus, is the representative of the redeemed. Alexander Mack Jr., argued that we do not make the case against infant baptism by rejecting notions of original sin. Rather, we can proclaim like his father that "children are in a state of grace because of the merit of Jesus Christ" (Durnbaugh, *European Origins* 352). In this the Macks were part of a legacy that could accuse the major reformers of works righteousness by requiring an act of baptism to insure the salvation of infants. As Adam and Eve were in grace before their fall, so are children while in the age of innocence. Anabaptist leaders in southern Germany and the Netherlands preached that Christ would not have set little children before us as an example to follow if he had not seen something innately good in them (see Alvin Beachy's *The Concept of Grace in the Radical Reformation* 35-39).

Adam and Eve's Story Is Every Person's Story. This belief that children benefitted from Christ's grace before their fall led Anabaptists to espouse a salvation scheme that understands Adam and Eve's story to be every person's story. We are born in innocence; we fall short and rebel against what we were meant to be in creation; and God's redeeming activity through Christ then restores the divine image. To precepts of the first and second Adam, some leaders added motifs of first and second grace. Hubmaier defined first grace as the original created goodness and second grace as Christ's work in restoring the divine image following the fall. It is interesting that the emphasis on first grace closely resembles John Wesley's belief in prevenient grace. Instead of first grace, most Protestant salvation schemes begin with the notion of original sin that accentuates the need for God's forgiveness and redemption. Many Protestants add that this needs to happen through a definite conversion experience.

The propensity to view human nature not from fallen historical realities, but from the original created nature of humans, points to perceived inconsistencies in early anabaptist thought. These, however, can in part be attributed to the frequently unrecognized theological pluralism of the early leaders.

Pietist Pessimistic Optimism

While there are many Brethren who may heartily agree with anabaptist modifications, there continue to be many who identify with the views of Pietism. These two strands in our theology neither neatly coalesce nor greatly clash. Concerning human nature, Brethren may be more willing to think and let think than engage in legislative crusades at Annual Conference. My interpretations of pietist anthropology are expressed more thoroughly in a book by Gary Sattler entitled *Nobler Than the Angels, Lower Than a Worm: The Pietist View of the Individual in the Writings of Heinrich Muller and August Hermann Francke*.

Pietist Pessimism. Though the belief that the image of the goodness of God is never completely eliminated in pietist theology, most pietist language would lead one to think otherwise. Francke's reflections more frequently begin with sin than creation. This is clear from the following passage:

> *Corruption / which is* inward */ and thus all the more hidden; . . . the corruption / which is upon all people / which is in one word the poison of sin / which runs in the veins of the natural person / and which cannot be sufficiently explained. I know myself to be a poor, and wretched worm / who with its original and actual sin / has merited God's wrath and displeasure and eternal damnation.* (Sattler 31)

Though the worm is no doubt chosen from scriptural references, early Pietists echoed prevalent sentiments that humans sink even lower than animals. For example, a wild beast will not harm you unless it is forced to do so by necessity and/or hunger. In their inhumanity, humans are often worse in their desire to hurt others of their own species.

Original sin is assumed to be the cause of actual sin. The spiritually blind person who does not discern this needs conversion. Francke uses the language of Platonism in believing our immortal spirit to be trapped in the prison of the body. Our conscience convinces us to be ashamed of our sinfulness. Our self-will, which is struggling with God's will, must be broken, if not in childhood then in adulthood. Pietists adamantly stressed, however, that the will is free. The decision of faith, the decision to focus on the mind of Christ to change one's wicked heart, is freely chosen. For it is contrary to the manner of the kingdom of God that any would be coerced; for this is a kingdom of love. Jesus said, ". . . if any *want* to become my followers" (Matt. 16:24). Our Savior would not be served by outward coercion (Sattler 80-81).

Optimism About God's Grace. It has been asserted that the essence of Pietism has been to combine pessimism about human nature with optimism concerning God's grace. Gottfried Arnold, a Radical Pietist, portrayed early Christians by articulating this typically pietist view: "To this end the heavenly Father cleansed the hearts of his true children through the Holy Spirit, for lacking this, the human heart is full of malice, deception, and lies. This good Spirit now filled their souls with truth and taught them to behave towards their neighbor as if they were always walking under the eyes of God" (*Portrait of the Early Christians,* Book 5, 50). Spener, often called the father of Pietism, preached often about the necessity of a new birth. But he gave even more sermons about possibilities for new life. A slogan about Pietism says it well: "The God who is good enough to forgive us is powerful enough to change us."

Unlike Spener who seemed to have been pious since his childhood, Francke's disposition and actions required a powerful and freeing conversion experience, which came about from stress. His conscience was worrying him as he approached a deadline while preparing to preach a sermon he did not believe in his own heart and mind. Believing God did not exist, he knelt. Through prayers, confession, and tearful struggle, he rose with joy believing there was a God. In reflecting on this experience in his autobiography, Francke exclaims: "The streams of the living water were so lovely for me that I could easily forget the stinking swamps of this world" (*The Pietists: Selected Writings,* The Classics of Western Spirituality, Peter Erb, ed. 106).

The Image of God in Pietist Circles. In another essay in the same anthology, Francke proposes similar views of the image of God as found in the writings of earlier Anabaptists. He believed people experience a joyous relationship with our gracious Lord when "the image of God toward which a person was initially created is awakened in him once again." This happens when one is enlightened by the Holy Spirit and eyes are opened to how wretched life is apart from the true way that is possible in Christ Jesus (149).

In some conferences of the Christian feminist movement, the image/language of Sophia was appropriated in worship and discourse. Critics immediately accused the women of worshiping a pagan goddess. It may have stimulated the conversation, if Brethren representatives were aware of what their maternal forebears knew from the writings of Gottfried Arnold. These writings helped to shape the early movement. In *Das Geheimnis der gottlichen Sophia (The Mystery of the Divine Sophia),* Arnold uses this personification of wisdom to interpret the creation story in ways that speak to analyses of human nature. After interpreting Sophia or wisdom as the image of God in us, Arnold added views that bear on Brethren beliefs about baptism:

> *Although this wisdom was taken away through sin and no longer dwelt in corrupted man in a paradisiacal manner, nevertheless, she did not cease to speak to each child of Adam internally in their hearts and to bid them to reestablish the lost treasure. . . . Sophia's proposal is nothing other than a divine call to obedience. . . . If anyone wishes to know when and at what age this hidden inner speech and seeking is accustomed to occur, the answer is to be found in the Scriptures in which it states that it occurs from youth on and that it remains with a person so long as the person does not oppose it.* (219-20)

The Natural and Awakening. Though the word *natural* in pietist language usually refers to wicked and sinful human nature, Bonhoeffer has led me to consider another view of what is natural. In reflecting about an affirmation in patristic literature that God became human in order that humans might become divine, Bonhoeffer proposed another possible truth, namely, that God became flesh in order that people might be truly human. For Bonhoeffer, Christ was God's revelation of life at its best. What is really natural is anything that points to Christ. The unnatural is what does not fit the mind and spirit of Jesus. Instead of giving folks an out when they claim they were only doing what comes naturally, Bonhoeffer's way of discerning what is natural is Christ-centered.

The completely self-centered actions of infants have been cited to support views of original sin. However, if sin is relational, however, infants are relating to others in developmentally *appropriate* ways in order to further grow in favor with God and others. If they keep behaving the same way years later, they are no longer acting in developmentally appropriate ways and are out of proper relationship with God and others. The mystery that exists when we regard the child as sacred bears fruit as we strive for right relationships.

When pietist and Wesleyan revivals were called great awakenings, not revivals, they must have had this in mind. Awakenings suggest that people were being called to wake up and restore what they were meant to be in creation. In Bonhoeffer's words, this is what it means to be truly human. Our tradition believes we perceive this true humanness in the face and life of Jesus (2 Cor. 4:6).

Affirmations from My Pilgrimage

In returning from brief trips when our children were small, I would often tiptoe in quietly to look upon them as they slept. Behold, I envisioned haloes gracing their angelic faces. I was confident that the children were bundles of goodness. However, the haloes would slip and horns seemed to burst forth the next morning amid their screaming and cries as one of them pulled my hair.

Similarly, when I was younger, I was surrounded by a sense that the world was getting better and better, because of the goodness of people and the benefits of industry and scientific advances. But over the span of my life, the twentieth century turned out to be one of the worst if measured by our inhumanity to our own species. The Great Depression, two world wars, the growing gap between the haves and the have nots, eruptions of hatred, and the presence of ethnic cleansing have spawned a pessimistic philosophy of history. Dreams of past generations that the twentieth century was destined to be a Christian century were deflated.

I resonate with Martin Luther King, Jr.'s essay that sketches his "Pilgrimage to Nonviolence." He identifies with Reinhold Niebuhr who rejected the superficial optimism of human nature he had absorbed as a youth. At the same time, he was dissatisfied with a neo-orthodoxy that defines human nature in terms of its capacity for evil. King concludes, as have many Anabaptists, that the truth lies in some kind of synthesis of both. However you come out in weighing the influences of environment or inheritance, humans are born with inclinations for good and inclinations for evil.

From this background I have contemplated views that emphasize both original goodness and the universality of sin. This has led me to prefer inclusive *Creation-Fall-Restoration* categories over the two-fold *Fall and Redemption* schema of many Protestants. My study has revealed that Pietists may espouse varieties of original sin more than Anabaptists. Yet both historic streams offer affirmations of the sacred nature of each person created in the image of God. When we fall far short or turn away from this blessed state, both anabaptist and pietist sources would engender an optimism that original goodness can be restored and nurtured. For both conjoin degrees of pessimism about humans with enthusiastic optimism about what the Spirit can do through and among committed disciples.

Pitfalls of Anabaptist and Pietist Anthropology. We are called as Christians to confess weaknesses and to be in dialogue about problems that others and our own members discern in what we claim and how this is applied in our lives.

1. *Legalism.* From emphases on walking in newness of light of the restored image of God, it is easy to structure rules and lifestyles in ways that often obstruct the love of God from permeating our lives. Our heritage has been prone to making a god of goodness instead of living in response to the goodness of God.
2. *A mind-flesh dualism.* In posing distinctions between spirit and flesh derived from Greek more than Hebraic thought, there have been temptations to focus on sexual sins more than sins of disposition. Sexual aberrations, which are sinfully subversive to right relationships, have been punished more harshly than censorious spirits who manifest malice and gossip, for example.
3. *A church-world dualism.* Anabaptists generally reject possibilities of complete perfection on the part of believers. Still, tendencies to locate all purity with the redeemed in the church has often resulted in both overlooking sin within the church and not seeing activity of the Spirit beyond our communities of faith.

Strengths of Anabaptist and Pietist Anthropology. Though our strengths may be perceived as liabilities by others, it is good to testify about virtues that are not of our own doing, but given to us by the grace of God.

1. Political contributions have emerged from our anthropological assumptions. Separation of church and state and religious freedom have been nurtured in part by anabaptist and pietist views that stress freedom of the will and the loving, nonviolent nature of God's grace and activity.
2. The discernment of the human condition from its created nature highlights the doctrine of creation along with doctrines of redemption.
3. Contrary to a church-world dualism, an anthropology derived from the work of the second Adam extends the activity of God beyond the borders of the church. The rejection of predestination led to proclamations of universal atonement, namely, Christ died for everyone. This makes possible, at least, applications of forgiveness of the second Adam, for example, to the developmentally disabled or to those who have never "heard" the gospel of Christ.
4. There may be contributions from what others consider to be heretical synergistic tendencies, tendencies to stress human roles in salvation. Our ethical heritage joins James in combining works with faith. But this is relevant to active ecological and peace concerns regarding our greedy and self-centered culture that squanders billions of dollars and millions of lives in misusing God's good creation in making and selling weapons of death.
5. The conviction that both innate goodness and the restored image are gifts of the work of grace offers possibilities for transformations of naive humanism. We can relate to those whom we name as secular who have compassionate concerns for others. For example, most of us would accept the offer of an atheist to help rescue a drowning child. Yet the tradition from Jesus offers a more basic foundation for humanist concerns. If we love others because they are naturally lovely, we might join disillusioned liberals when we are disappointed by unlovely manifestations of sin. However, if we love others because God loves them, even as God loved us when we were sinners, then we can keep loving even when tempted to think others are unworthy of our love (Rom. 5:8).

Chapter 5

Jesus the Christ
Jesus of history and Christ of faith

Let the same mind be in you that was in Christ Jesus, who, though he was in the form of God, did not regard equality with God as something to be exploited, but emptied himself, taking the form of a slave, being born in human likeness. And being found in human form, he humbled himself and became obedient to the point of death. . . . Therefore God also highly exalted him and gave him the name that is above every name, so that at the name of Jesus every knee should bend, in heaven and on earth and under the earth, and every tongue should confess that Jesus Christ is Lord, to the glory of God the Father.
—Philippians 2:5-11

This early Christ hymn is filled with christological statements. Christology is a word that refers to thoughts, interpretations, or convictions about Jesus. Brethren have been interpreted to be a people who keep their eyes on Jesus and center their minds on the mind of Christ (Mallott, ch. 31). Since the hymn declares Jesus to be the form or likeness of God, it generates questions both about the nature of God and how God is known and experienced.

A small girl was absorbed in drawing a picture. Her curious mother asked her what she was doing. She replied, "I am drawing a picture of God!"

"But," her mother answered, "no one knows what God looks like."

Her child prodigy immediately responded, "They will when I get through!"

It seems that many popular efforts to know God through our minds, intuition, mystical experiences, or moral behavior resemble that of the little girl. I have appropriately been reminded that my joy in telling this story should not negate genuine expressions of simple faith often lost by adults—like theologians, for example.

The Nature of God's Revelation

Revelation means God's self-disclosure. How did and how does God get through to people? On the other hand, how do we know God's nature, ways, or will? Here are some answers.

A Book. Some religions regard a book to be the primary source of revelation of knowledge and relationships with God. For example, Muslims believe the Koran to have been delivered by God's messenger, the angel Gabriel, to Mohammed as he meditated in a cave. Venerated as absolute literal truth, the Quran was not to be translated and published in any language but Arabic. Unlike most of Christendom, in Islam the book is more esteemed than the prophet.

An Institution. In many religious movements, including portions of Christendom, revelations from God have been identified through infallible institutions and hierarchical structures. Though holding to a high view of the community of faith, Anabaptists have generally opted for the final authority to reside in the Lordship of Christ. The body of believers needs to be the body of Christ.

Rationalist Views of Truth. Believing the world to be orderly and rational, both secular and religious thinkers conclude that people know God or truth through reason. Such philosophical views grant that our minds will only discern shadows and inklings of truth with a capital *T*. And our rationality may be corrupted by desires of the flesh. Nevertheless, there exists an optimism that through reason people will grow in understanding of God's truth and laws. Though practical Brethren have honored common-sense reasoning, they have often observed how great minds can be appropriated for chauvinistic destruction of the things that make for peace. From pietist and anabaptist roots, Brethren believe that God's word, which became flesh among us, was full of grace as well as truth.

The Mystical Inner Word. Mystics have often testified to direct encounters with God. Through meditative ladders of ascent or more passive listening to the "still small voice within," hearts and minds are enlightened and redeemed. Our pietist and anabaptist forebears were attracted to medieval and current mystical emphases on the Spirit's presence. However, this led them to insist that in the community of faith, the mind of Christ is the measure whereby we know whether something is from God or from our own psyche.

One or Many Gods. Christianity emerged as a popular option in the ancient milieu of over thirty thousand known gods and idols. Large numbers of Gentile converts joined Christian house churches through the labors of Paul and other missionaries. Many were named God-fearers, which was the common name to refer to Gentiles who were attracted to the one God of Judaism. This popularity of monotheism no doubt influenced subsequent Christian theologians to formulate a doctrine of the trinity that emphasized three-in-one or one God with three manifestations.

Person. Though ways of encountering the divine in such as the Bible, the church, and prayer are basic, the faith of Christians centers on a person. In a sense this remains a mystery; we can never completely be in control when revelation is personal. God remains, in a sense, like the Bible says, hidden in Christ. We know in part, our knowledge is imperfect, and we see in a mirror dimly (1 Cor. 13:9-12). For we relate to a person who acted in many different ways and who has been interpreted by a myriad of believers.

Yet, in another sense, there is logic in the way Christians believe God revealed God-self to us. If God wanted to get through to people, what better way to do it than to become a person? When God placed a call to the human race, it was person to person. And since God's nature is unveiled and found to be a person, our heritage leads us to proclaim the dignity and worth of each and every person.

I-It and I-Thou. It was a Christian theologian, Emil Brunner, who applied the fascinating three-small-word philosophy of Martin Buber to the incarnation. Because this emphasis was highly relational, Buber's Jewish orientation was not violated by Brunner, but extended to another context. I-It relationships, according to Buber, refer to the relation of human subjects to inanimate objects. Scientists have learned much about our physical world through I-It relationships, including the fact that material objects may have more life than previously imagined. He does grant that if scientists or others are moved deeply by a sunset or majestic illuminations of trees in changing seasons, it is possible to have an I-Thou relationship with a beautiful sky or tree.

As an existentialist philosopher, Buber's main focus was that we live in a culture in which people more and more are defined impersonally as numbers, mere statistics. This can lead to naming civilian causalities of so-called clean bombs dropped from the sky as collateral damage. Our culture increasingly depersonalizes people. I-It relationships replace I-Thou ones.

I-Thou relationships are between people. In relating to a person, we relate to another subject. How do we know another person? If the person remains mute, we may guess that the person is intelligent, but we only know a person when the person chooses to reveal himself or herself by relating with us. It is true that health technicians can probe cells and genes and know the chemical make-up of a person through an I-It relationship. This may be necessary and helpful for proper diagnosis. Buber's contribution, however, was to highlight the difference and value of I-Thou relationships.

Out of his Jewish heritage, Buber applied his philosophy to our relationships with God. Through rational propositions and doctrines, we often strive to relate to a God viewed as an object. Buber opens possibilities of I-Thou relationships with God. God is no longer an object to be known, but a living subject. This insight led Brunner to apply Buber's philosophical scheme to the incarnation. As we cannot know another person apart from a person's willingness to be known, so it is with God. Our faith as Christians believes that God chose to be known. God spoke a word to us and the Word was Jesus Christ (John 1:1-4).

Brethren Focus on Jesus

An Episcopal student enrolled at McPherson College in Kansas, my alma mater, where I had returned as campus pastor and teacher. After several weeks he appeared in my office with a puzzled look on his face. He said that he had grown up hearing much about Christ and Jesus Christ. Never, however, had he been in a place where there was so much talk about Jesus.

In 1994 our denomination hired Communicorp, a communications group, to discern words to describe our denomination. Some chided the church for needing to hire others to define who we are, perhaps due to lacking convictions and creativity that would enable us to do this for ourselves. After visiting with and listening to a variety of Brethren in different congregations, Communicorp came up with the phrase "Continuing the work of Jesus."

Jesus, Christ, Jesus Christ, and Lord Jesus language permeate the early writings of our founders. Yet the focus on the humanity of our Lord expresses motifs that have survived throughout our history. Alexander Mack admonished members to "look alone to Jesus your Redeemer and Savior."

Mack frequently referred to the mind of Christ, the phrase lifted from Paul's introduction in Philippians to the Christ hymn. And he stressed the necessity to be obedient to the teachings and commandments of Jesus. Nineteenth-century brother Peter Nead emphasized that "Jesus Christ is our exampler, and it becometh us to pattern after him—to walk in his footsteps." *Nachfolge* (following after Jesus), discipleship, and imitation of Christ have consistently been prominent motifs among the Brethren. (See the excellent article on christology by Warren Groff in *The Brethren Encyclopedia*.)

As a youth, like it or not, I sat with my parents through informal services every Sunday night. We sang out of a paperback that was regarded more fitting for the service than the Brethren hymnal. As one who became a preacher, it is humbling to confess that I remember words of the songs more than any themes from the sermons. These words, sung with gusto, periodically invade my consciousness: "Be like Jesus all day long, in the home and in the throng."

The emphasis on the life and teachings of Jesus may be regarded as a corrective more than a substitute for dominant themes related to the divinity of Christ of mainline Christianity, for it is difficult to faithfully follow Jesus and his way unless we believe something about him. At a believers church conference on christology in 1980 at Bluffton College, John Howard Yoder challenged us with a presentation from which I have retained the following excerpts:

> *A high christology is a prerequisite for the renewal of the believers church. . . . Only if Christ is, both formally and materially, more and other than the distillate of the rest of our best wisdom, only if his call is imperative, his message irreducible to other equivalents we already knew about, only if his right to demand our allegiance comes from beyond the world in which we are at home, can there be that change. . . . Only if the call of Jesus is ontologically founded, connected to the arc from creation to apocalypse, can it give us the leverage to challenge our conformity to our own age.*

Brethren have generally avoided the abstract, metaphysical language of theologians and creeds. Such expressions should never take the place of the biblical writers' witness to Jesus as the way, the truth, and life. Nevertheless, it would be inaccurate to claim fundamental differences with the creed or wisdom of theologians. For the Brethren, Christ was the center of the apostolic witness. Their focus on the humanity of Jesus was joined with affirmations of a special transcendent presence in the crucifixion of Jesus and the risen Christ.

Expressions of the Human-Divine Paradox

There have been many ways to interpret complementary and contradictory aspects of the human-divine nature of Jesus. The reason for speaking of Jesus as the Christ is that Jesus was a common name given to many. Christ was the Greek word for Messiah, the title for a special person anticipated by Jews. And the title Jesus the Christ or Messiah was connected with Jesus, who Christians believed to be the Promised One.

Very Man of Very Man—Very God of Very God. A paradox has been defined as claiming two opposite statements to nevertheless be true. If we neglect the divinity of Christ, we may be in danger of weakening the power to be faithful to the Jesus way unto death, as Yoder suggests. On the other hand, if in defending Jesus' divinity his humanity is diminished, believers can unconsciously adopt the early gnostic heresy that denied that Jesus was entirely human. This heresy leads to the worship of one who is so heavenly as to be impossible to follow, a tendency that subverts the call to discipleship. Christian tradition has articulated that we affirm both truths of this ancient Christian paradox.

Jesus of History—Christ of Faith. Brethren have wondered whether to pursue the religion of Jesus more than the religion *about* Jesus. Similarly, Amish preachers are expected to preach more from the four Gospels than from the rest of the New Testament. In anabaptist circles the focus on Jesus has, covertly or openly, often led to a similar acceptance of a canon within the canon. Brethren have found many congenial additions to the four Gospels in texts like Romans 12, 1 Corinthians 13, and the love passages of the Johannine epistles. In addition, many members in our tradition have personally realized that our ethical tradition can seem like bad news if we neglect the good news about the Spirit's power in Acts and the grace and faith of the full theology of the New Testament epistles.

Lord and Master—Savior. A declaration that Jesus is Lord was courageous in a world in which citizens suffered severely by refusing to reverently burn incense in naming Caesar as Lord. Lord and Master suggests one we want to follow. Others prefer Savior as one who offers salvation through forgiveness and a new birth. Brethren often signify the merging of salvation and discipleship in naming Jesus as both Lord and Savior.

Humility—Exaltation. The Christ hymn at the beginning of this chapter is difficult from some perspectives; the text says that Jesus did not want to exploit any notion of his equality with God. Instead, he adopted the role of a slave, a servant, and humbled himself in being human. The old Brethren taught that we should have this same spirit of Christ and be meek and lowly of heart. When a man ran after Jesus and said, "Good Teacher,"

Jesus answered, "Why do you call me good? No one is good but God alone" (Mark 10:17-18). This confession of Jesus supports the surprising nature of the Christ hymn.

Many women today are uncomfortable with the term *Lord* as it mirrors the inequality of our structures in family, church, and society. In dealing with the dispute of his disciples about who is the greatest, Jesus answered that in the kingdom we do not lord it over others like the rulers of the Gentiles, but the one who is greatest is the servant of all (Luke 22:24-27). Is it possible to join such humility with the message that God in the Christ hymn exalted Jesus and gave him a name above every name? For many, adulation comes easily for those who are sincerely humble and genuinely live for others. Brethren historically have strived not to be proud. Others have often smiled in believing them to have pride in their humility. In the older Brethren's Card, Brethren seemed to be sincere in referring to themselves as little children. My wife was in agreement with Floyd Mallott who emphasized that the Jesus taught us how to be great in being the servant of all.

Jesus Mysticism—Christ Mysticism. Jesus mysticism is characterized by an affection and identity with the personality and will of the historical Jesus in our prayers and meditations. The sentiments of heartfelt love constitute ways of feeling, knowing, and living like Jesus. The succession of Jesus, or practical mysticism, passes from Bernard of Clairveaux, Francis of Assisi, and George Fox.

Christ mysticism has been named the mysticism of classical Protestantism, a devotion focused on the mystery of Christ dying for our sins.

Offensive—Attractive. Yet Jesus remains offensive to sensibilities of our popular culture. He associated, even ate, with despised tax collectors and sinners. He defied the mores of his day by openly conversing with a woman who had known many husbands. His woes and accusations of hypocrisy directed to the religious leaders of his day apply to many of us (see Matt. 23). In driving out merchants who were selling wares in the only place the Gentiles had to worship, he created disorder in the temple, possibly because of his passion for justice. The great majority of us are rich compared to the majority of people in our world. And Jesus informs us that it is easier for a camel to go through the eye of a needle than for those who are rich to enter the kingdom of heaven. He commands us to wash dirty feet, put away the sword, take up the cross and suffer and die for others.

Yet Jesus has remained tremendously attractive not only to Christians, but to multitudes of people in the world. In our worship we often sing "Jesus loves me" as a message to proclaim the love of Jesus for children. He began his life as a refugee. Throughout his pilgrimage he often had no place to lay his head. His courageous good deeds and message led him to be nailed on the cross as a terrible criminal. He has become the most famous, attractive, and loved person in history.

Like Us—Not Like Us. I processed a senior thesis with a student who was dealing with questions and doubts about Jesus. He personally wrestled with what he read, and he experienced both doubts and affirmations. During some visits he declared that Jesus could only be his Savior if Jesus were human like himself; it would be impossible to follow in the steps of some kind of heavenly, angelic person. In other sessions, he struggled to believe that Jesus would only be his Savior if Jesus were not like himself. He confessed: "If Jesus were only like me, I could not experience the redemption and transformation that comes from allegiance to one who exemplifies the wholeness of life far more than I will ever be able to attain." This is but another way to point to the paradoxical necessity of Immanuel, literally meaning God with us, like us and not like us.

Low Christology from Below—High Christology from Above. In college I struggled with some of the same issues as the young man above. I was influenced by friends who believed that Jesus was just a good man. Though I had already been baptized, a subsequent conversion experience occurred at a Student Christian Movement conference in beautiful Estes Park. The Bible study focused on John 7:14-18, a passage in which Jews were astounded by Jesus and what he was teaching in the temple. In a different way, the Jews asked my question: "How does this man have such learning, when he has never been taught?" Jesus answered: "My teaching is not mine but his who sent me. Anyone who resolves to do the will of God will know whether the teaching is from God or whether I am speaking on my own." This passage spoke to my being, "Try it, follow his teachings, take the leap of faith, then I will know whether the teacher and teachings are divine." My conversion was to a higher christology, and John 7:16, more than John 3:16, became a golden text for me. I learned later in a classroom at Bethany that this experience identified me with a large group of pragmatic Brethren.

My experience represents what is named "christology from below." Many are attracted to the life and teachings of Jesus and in belief and action are led to declare Jesus truly as the Son of God. An influential Quaker once testified to his community: "I did not join the Quakers to find Jesus; I was drawn by their deeds and quality of life. But, after I became a Quaker, Christ found me."

Others are raised in an atmosphere of affirmations of a high christology. They agree with all creedal statements and accept Jesus as a divine personal Savior. Then they discover that simply holding a high view about the nature of Jesus does not mean one will follow his teachings. They may read in his Sermon on the Mount that Jesus said, "Not everyone who says, Lord, Lord, will enter the kingdom, but only those who do the will of God" (Matt. 7:21). They depict what is called a "christology from above."

The pilgrimage of some begins with Jesus, leading to an acceptance of Jesus as the Christ. The pilgrimage of others begins with a high christology, leading to faithfulness to the way of Jesus. This reality raises problems with programmed conversion experiences that require everyone to accept and experience Jesus Christ in the same way.

Particularity—Universality. The scandal of particularity refers to a seeming lack of fairness of the biblical concept of the chosen people. Biblical texts make it clear that Abraham and his descendants were chosen not because they were more moral or as a special privilege; rather, they were chosen to be a blessing to all of the families on earth (Gen. 12:1-3). The same problem and answer can be applied to the choice of one person as Savior of the world.

Sensitive Christians often worry about what will happen to people who have never heard of Jesus or who adhere to other world faiths. Are they going to perish in hell? John Toews, a Mennonite biblical scholar, helped my understanding. He offers evidence that biblical texts that insist Jesus is the only way are intended for Christians. The texts emphasize that believers who live in a pluralistic society with many gods, not unlike ours, must give their wholehearted allegiance to Jesus Christ.

In Peter's first approach to the Gentile Cornelius, Peter began his evangelistic approach with a more universal note: "I truly understand that God shows no partiality, but in every nation anyone who fears him and does what is right is acceptable to him" (Acts 10:34-35; see John Toews, "Toward a Biblical Perspective on People of Other Faiths," *The Conrad Grebel Review,* Winter 1996; Dale Brown, "Can Christ Be Both Exclusive and Inclusive," *Messenger,* March 1996). The particular nature of the incarnation inspires a universal mission of loving service and understanding to all as a way to witness in deed and word to our Lord. In Christ, particularity and universality are joined together.

Another Way of Defining High Christology. A Mennonite brother rather shocked me when he claimed that Brethren have a higher christology than they. I protested his assessment in insisting that Mennonites more than most Brethren hold to confessions of faith that affirm the divine nature of Christ. "But you do not understand what I mean," he responded. "You Brethren are more ready to allow Jesus Christ and his teachings to apply to all aspects of life."

A short time later, my eyes scanned letters written to the editor of *The Christian Century.* The title given to one read: "The low Christology of Billy Graham." During the long period of the Vietnam War, this good man and famous evangelist refused to express any opinions about this war. The letter named his refusal to apply his Christian faith to a major divisive issue for millions of people as a low christology. The writer assumed that a high christology names the One who is Lord of the church to also be Lord of all of life and all of life's issues.

Quest for the Historical Jesus

During the last decades of the nineteenth century and early decades of the twentieth century, there was a flurry of popular and scholarly biographies of Jesus. Jesus was depicted as a successful sales or business man. He was also considered an ideal teacher, psychologist, social reformer, or nineteenth-century intellectual. Later analysts observed that Jesus often was described as the mirror image of the author. One of the most famous of these critics was the admired missionary Albert Schweitzer. In his book *The Quest for the Historical Jesus* (1906), Schweitzer discredited the biographies and at the same time substituted his understanding that the biblical accounts depict Jesus as the apocalyptic Messiah of the imminent coming of the kingdom.

Because of their focus on Jesus, many Brethren became involved in the dispute surrounding the biblical studies of Rudolph Bultmann, who maintained that the biblical authors did not intend to give detailed historical accounts of Jesus. Rather, they were scribes who shared proclamations of faith of the early Christians. Biographical data only appears in relation to the message of the apostolic community of believers. The only historical fact we need to know is that Jesus died on the cross. Bultmann's views came to be referred to as "the no quest."

Some of Bultmann's followers desired to offer a corrective. They agreed that it is not possible to reconstruct an accurate account of the life of Jesus from the Gospel writers. Instead, they focused their studies on authentic teachings and pericopes (selections or extracts from the larger life story). Conservatives who had opposed the first quest because of the liberal social views of these "questers" now joined what became known as "the new quest for the historical Jesus," for they wanted to defend the integrity of the biographical accounts about Jesus in the Bible.

During the latter decades of the twentieth century to the present, there have been many seminars in which biblical scholars have searched for the authentic texts about what Jesus said and did. They have engaged in redaction criticism, which involves the attempt to separate the authentic words of Jesus from those added later by believing communities. Some Brethren have been friendly to, others critical of, the efforts of these scholars. My long-time interest in this debate has led me to be somewhat critical, but not very disturbed. Whether the words are the exact words of Jesus or interpretations added later, all of the words have become part of the corpus inherited by the church through the centuries. How Christians have responded in word and deed to the teachings of Jesus in the New Testament can likewise be important. At the same time, we can learn from technical deciphering of the scholars. Brethren can thank the scholars for drawing attention to the life and teachings of our Lord. What they have chosen to be authentic are often verses dear to our tradition.

Believers Church Interpretations

Anabaptist leaders generally agreed with emphasizing both the humanity and divinity of Jesus. However, Menno Simons with a few others (Hoffman, Rothmann, and Dirk Philips) articulated a strong emphasis on Christ's divinity. They believed that Jesus did not receive his flesh from Mary. Instead, his heavenly flesh made him completely free from sin. This high christology fit their deep concern for the purity of the church. It provided the basis for the harsh discipline of early Dutch Anabaptism. Contemporary Mennonites recognize this as a docetic view, which literally means that Jesus only seemed to appear to have human flesh. Docetism denies that Jesus was really human. Critics have somewhat humorously referred to this early belief as the Teflon view of Christ's entry into the world. As interesting as this may be, it is important to emphasize that all major anabaptist confessions about Jesus Christ were combined with the necessity of obeying his words. Faith without obedience is, by definition, nothing.

To this strong focus on obedience, the pietist milieu of the early Brethren added an emphasis on a devotion to Jesus. A conversion experience in accepting Jesus means a new life in Christ. It involves openness to the Spirit's presence to lead us to become more like Jesus. In addition to obeying the words of Jesus, one will imitate the love of Jesus in embodying the fruit of the Spirit (Gal. 5:22). Colonial Brethren imbibed doses of Pietism and mysticism to inspire and appropriate anabaptist motifs. In the nineteenth century, the Brethren reflected to a greater degree anabaptist emphases on obedience and the purity of the church. A more ecumenical outlook in the twentieth century has revived the love ingredients of the christology from above of the early Brethren. At the same time our acculturation has often led to a lesser focus on our obedience to Jesus. Large numbers of Brethren have ignored or opposed some of the Jesus commandments so important to our anabaptist heritage. We have failed to honor traditional teachings related to oath-taking, going to law, washing feet, nonresistant and nonviolent peacemaking, and membership in secret organizations. Nevertheless, in many ways Brethren continue to embody a strong devotion to Jesus Christ and his way.

Because Jesus remains central to who we are as Brethren, I have written and several times revised the following sermon. Initially it came to mind when Kirby Page led the Bible study sessions at the first National Youth Conference in Anderson, Indiana, in 1954. The well-known tennis player concluded each Bible study with this admonition: "Never accept any idea of God that makes God less good than Jesus."

A Believers Church Sermon

What is God like? People brought little children—noisy, dirty, unruly little creatures—to Jesus. His disciples did not wish their Master to be bothered by such persons at the close of a busy day. But Jesus said, "Let the little children come to me, and do not stop them, for it is to such as these that the kingdom of heaven belongs" (Matt. 19:14). *Christians believe that God is like that.*

What is God like? The disciples were plucking grain and eating it as they walked through the fields on the sabbath. This was in direct violation of the customs of the day and the laws of strict religion. The religious leaders protested to Jesus. He replied, "The sabbath was made for humankind, and not humankind for the sabbath" (Mark 2:27). *Christians believe that God is like that.*

What is God like? It was a great religious feast day in Jerusalem. People traveled great distances to make their sacrifices at the temple. They desired to change money in order to purchase offerings of animals and goods. The merchants might have been cheating. Or possibly they were interfering with the worship of Gentiles who could enter no farther than the outer courts. Jesus entered the temple and began to drive out those who were selling and buying. He overturned the tables of the money changers and the seats of those who sold doves, and he would not allow anyone to carry anything through the temple. He said: "Is it not written, 'My house shall be called a house of prayer for all the nations'? But you have made it a den of robbers" (Mark 11:17). *Christians believe that God is like that.*

What is God like? The disciples were gathering for their last meal together. In a dramatic action, Jesus arose from the table and assumed the role of the lowliest of servants. He began to wash the disciples' feet. Over their protests, he lived out what he taught: The greatest must become the servant of all. *Christians believe that God is like that.*

What is God like? Jesus' last trip out of Jerusalem was to a hill, Calvary. He was dragged. They scourged him, mocked him, spit on him, nailed him to a cross, and pierced him in the side. In the midst of the most unjust trial and punishment of all time, Jesus prayed for those who were killing him: *"Father, forgive them; for they do not know what they are doing"* (Luke 23:34).

Christians believe that God is like that. What is God like? Christians believe that God is like Jesus, the Christ. "For it is the God who said, 'Let light shine out of darkness,' who has shone in our hearts to give the light of the knowledge of the glory of God in the face of Christ" (2 Cor. 4:6).

Chapter 6

Living in the Spirit
Biblical definitions of the Holy Spirit

Create in me a clean heart, O God, and put a new and right spirit within me. Do not cast me away from your presence, and do not take your holy spirit from me.
—Psalm 51:10-11

You yourselves are our letter, written on our hearts, to be known and read by all; and you show that you are a letter of Christ, prepared by us, written not with ink but with the Spirit of the living God, not on tablets of stone but on tablets of the human heart.
—2 Corinthians 3:2-3

Gottfried Arnold, a Radical Pietist whose writings influenced the new Baptist movement, portrayed apostolic Christians as people who loved to sing. They sang at mealtimes in their homes, extensively in their house meetings, and with enthusiastic and joyful hearts in love feasts. Rising from baptism, one early convert wrote: "I was deeply moved by voices of the sweetly singing congregation. The emotion of the worship kindled an inner passion. My tears burst forth so that I felt myself to be wholly united with them." These so-called primitive Christians taught their children, farmers, and wine growers songs they could sing from their hearts while playing and working. Arnold revealed a prejudice likely imparted to the first Brethren. He regretted that in subsequent generations singers or cantors were appointed to replace congregational voices. By the seventh century, bells, cymbals, and pipe organs made so much noise that common folks became more and more silent (*First Love . . .1696*, Book 2, Chapter 2, Sections 4-12). Arnold was not alone in his assessments. Church historians have often described the first Christians as an enthusiastic sect within first-century Judaism.

In studies of Brethren hymnody, Hedwig Durnbaugh reveals that the first Brethren, likewise, loved to sing. Their own members added many hymns to those of their German pietist associates. In the hymns they authored, Spirit language was not used profusely. Nevertheless, such language was implied in expressions such as "penetrating light." Hedda's research discerns that for the most part the mysticism of the Brethren expressed "a desire to seek spiritual union with Jesus rather than God" (*The German Hymnody of the Brethren* 30).

A visiting Lutheran minister, whom we had invited to our congregation, seemed surprised to find a larger number of Holy Spirit hymns in our hymnal than in other traditions, including his own. One of the most loved and popular hymns in our denomination was written by Kenneth Morse:

> *Move in our midst, thou Spirit of God.*
> *Go with us down from thy holy hill.*
> *Walk with us through the storm and the calm.*
> *Spirit of God, go thou with us still.* (See No. 418, *Hymnal: A Worship Book*.)

In 1962 I was asked to lead a Bible study focused on the Holy Spirit at the National Youth Conference in Estes Park. Some staff-planners were dismayed. They feared youth would be turned off by the topic. A degree of openness on the part of youth and my stubbornness to save the topic surprised the adults as the youth became involved in symbols and beliefs related to their biblical faith.

A more thorough Bible study came sixteen years later. Our denomination was struggling with differing opinions about popular charismatic manifestations. Perhaps my previous studies of our pietist heritage led our press to request a book about the Holy Spirit. Convinced that there were already commendable books available and wondering if it might be sinful to chop down more trees to add yet another, I hesitated. I was told that many of our members, who would not read other books, would read one written from a Brethren perspective. Ultimately, *Flamed by the Spirit* (1978) has been read by more Brethren than any other piece I have written. Since this book is no longer available, I will adapt and abbreviate here the same four biblical definitions of the Holy Spirit in the context of our theological heritage.

I. The Spirit Gives Life:

"For the letter kills, but the Spirit gives life" (2 Cor. 3:6).

When children sing about Jesus and his love, inevitably their faces light up with the joy of the Holy Spirit. Similarly, the presence of the Holy Spirit is reflected through us when we are connected to God and live out our faith.

Word Definitions of the Spirit

The Hebrew word for Spirit, *ruach*, literally means breath or wind. The word is found in the second verse of the Bible. The Spirit of God was blowing or perhaps flapping her wings over the waters. Through God's breathing, chaos becomes cosmos (an orderly universe). In Deuteronomy 32:11, *ruach* describes an eagle hovering over her little ones. Later rabbinic traditions name the bird of the Genesis story to be a dove, a sign of a new creation. These texts explain why the Hebrew word for Spirit is generally feminine, a fact that women cite for using Mother, she, or her to refer to the third person of the trinity. The creation story is our story. Life begins with each one of us as God gives the gift of life by breathing into our nostrils (Gen. 2:7).

As God's *ruach* can breathe new life into dry bones (Ezek. 37), biblical metaphors such as "mighty wind" and "tongues of fire" point to the presence of *pneuma*, the Greek word for breath or Spirit. *Pneuma* was powerfully present on Pentecost, fifty days after Easter. Then and now, the Spirit is the personal, moral, active power of God. For the most part, the Bible does not divide a person into parts as a body-soul division or a three-part nature of body, soul, and spirit. Rather, the Spirit is that which gives life and quality to our entire being. In the Pauline sense, to be fleshly is to center our lives in such ways that our emotions, minds, and desires are not in relation to God and others. To be spiritual is to be so filled by the Spirit that our total being is oriented toward right relationships with God, others, and God's good creation. To live and walk in the Spirit is to respond to God's gift of life by loving with all our heart, soul, and mind.

Zeal of the Early Brethren

Inasmuch as Brethren imbibed the flavor of German Pietism, they stressed the necessity of Christian experience. As a new fervent movement, they acquired Mennonite names through marriages to anabaptist descendants about whom Alexander Mack sincerely expressed a backhanded compliment in wishing the whole world were full of these "deteriorated Baptists." In contrast, the zeal and enthusiasm of the early Brethren were cited by others. One questionable caricature of the Brethren by Radical Pietist Johann Georg Gichtel claimed "they yell so loud that one's ears hurt."

Caricatures are usually exaggerations that contain grains of truth. This may be the case with descriptions by a radical pietist immigrant to the colonies in 1750. The author cleverly described four fictitious meetinghouses, which he placed on one intersection in beautiful Philadelphia. Here we omit the Quaker and Ephrata communities. The last line depicting the Mennonites extends Mack's inference: "Their meetings are often very sleepy affairs." In contrast to the shabby meetinghouse of the Mennonites, the author reported that the Brethren house struck the eye because of its beautiful color. But the Dunkers' meeting going on inside of that house does not escape the clever scrutiny of his pen.

> Over the door was a lamp that had been knocked over with this inscription above it: "We sing and preach with great outcry, if only the spirit could be thereby." . . . Their clothing is middle-class. Most of the men wear beards. They do not tolerate infant baptism. When they become adults and wish to be baptized, they go where water is and have themselves immersed three times. They hold communions or love feasts often. Their meetings are zealous and their preaching and praying often take place with great clamor, as if their God could not hear them well. One hymn chases another as if they lack [inner] silence. They teach their cherished truths after the letter. (Donald F. Durnbaugh, "Relationships of the Brethren with the Mennonites and Quakers, 1708-1865," *Church History*, Vol. 35, March 1966, 42)

Incarnations of Spirit Movements

James McClendon reminds us that the Spirit baptism in Acts 2 is not only remembered but replicated today. This has been especially true in the birth and enormous growth of the Pentecostal movement in the twentieth century. He refers to Bishop Newbigen's little book, *The Household of God* (1954), which regards Pentecostals, along with sixteenth-century Anabaptists, to be paradigms of a "third force" in Christianity that is neither Protestant nor Catholic. Sociologically, both movements have attracted people on society's fringes. McClendon names the Spirit's gift as ecstasy to those who are weary of injustice, alienation, and insignificance. The pentecostal message offers a voice for the voiceless, strength for those weak of soul, and guidance for mission to the world. Pentecostals have broken down racial barriers and placed women in the highest of leadership roles (*Doctrine* 434-451). Spirit movements of many kinds have contributed to freeing many of us to allow the Holy Spirit to be present in fresh ways and with new power.

I experienced this in the civil rights and peace movements. While attending black churches, what they identified as "soul" rubbed off on me. My memories took me back to my childhood. We drove through what we then called colored neighborhoods on our way to and from church. Since their services lasted longer, we would stop on a summer evening when their windows were open and roll down our car windows to listen. Enjoying what we heard, especially the singing, we were filled with a kind of patronizing spirit, but at the same time we felt a sense of authenticity. Our attitudes spoke: That's the way those folk are, emotional. If they could be more educated like we are, then they would worship in more dignified and rational ways like we do. In the civil rights movement, my attitude changed from one of superiority to envy. I began to wish that I belonged to a congregation and a church in which there were more spontaneous, warm, genuine, and communal manifestations of the Spirit.

Pitfalls of Spirit Movements

When Spirit movements overreact to valid concerns about the "deadness" of much Christian life, they are tempted to equate emotionalism with the Holy Spirit. Like Pietists who prefer heart religion over head religion, some charismatics minimize the part of the greatest commandment that requests us to love God with all our mind. They fail to grasp the biblical understandings that heart and soul are words that encompass the total person.

I was privileged to participate in a week-long sharing about our heritage as part of an educational program for Dominican Republic pastors and spouses. There were positive expressions of appreciation for Estella Horning who, in her week with them, taught them much they had never known about the Holy Spirit. Before joining together with the Brethren, they belonged to independent pentecostal congregations characterized by demonstrative expressions of the Spirit. Without forsaking this enthusiasm, the people reported that after the sessions with Estella, they appreciated sermons that combined content with emotional fervor. Estella led them to biblical understandings of the Holy Spirit they had never heard.

In focusing on powerful manifestations of the Spirit, there is also the temptation to capture and program the Spirit. At a charismatic conference for Brethren, a visiting leader recognized this danger by relating the story of a brother whose conversion experience resulted from falling into a well. In frantic desperation he made many promises to God about how he would change his life and accept Jesus if he were spared from drowning. He was found and a rope was thrown into the pit. Following his rescue, he kept his promises, for the most part. Since this event was the turning point in his life, he began to push anyone he could into wells. Tendencies to control the work of the Holy Spirit may apply to some in the holiness movement who insist that believers must have an experience of "praying through" or "entire sanctification." This concern applies to those Pentecostals who maintain that believers do not possess the baptism of the Holy Spirit unless they experience the gift of speaking in tongues.

Nevertheless, most of us need to be open to a greater sense of expectancy concerning the possibilities of the presence, outward manifestations, and gifts of the Spirit. We are admonished to "quench not the Spirit" (1 Thess. 5:19), for the Spirit brings life.

II. The Lord Is the Spirit

"Now the Lord is the Spirit, and where the Spirit of the Lord is, there is freedom" (2 Cor. 3:17).

At Pentecost, as in other settings, Christians experienced what they had been taught in the Scriptures about the powerful presence of the Spirit. For them the radical new thing was the Spirit of Jesus. They did not make fine distinctions between the Spirit, the Spirit of God, and the Spirit of Christ. It is true that the presence of the Spirit was named and defined by Old Testament allusions before the advent of Jesus. Early disciples came to believe that Jesus had become the bearer of the same Spirit. The activity of the Spirit was evident in the people and events surrounding Jesus' birth, at his baptism when the Spirit descended as a dove, through his dispensing the Spirit in acts of healing, and in bearing the fruit of the Spirit in proclaiming the dawning reign of God's kingdom.

Testing the Spirit and the Spirits

A sister, who suddenly had ample inheritance money to spend, began to testify that the Spirit instructed her to purchase lavishly priced dresses. Some friends hesitated to spoil her wishes, but they did question whether the voices within came from God or from her unfulfilled dreams. Perhaps you have known zealous brothers and sisters who have testified that God authored nearly everything they were led to do. Some sincerely believe they have a direct pipeline to God.

In 1 John 4:1-3, we are advised to "not believe every spirit, but test the spirits to see whether they are from God . . ." and that we do this by relating what we desire to our confessions about Jesus. The story of Stephen, one of the first deacons, offers a striking example. Stephen challenged the members of the council with their own biblical story, accusing them of opposing the Holy Spirit and persecuting the prophets. His prophecies about the temple resembled those of Jesus. The text describes Stephen as being "filled with the Holy Spirit." He looks upward and envisions the glory of God and Jesus standing at God's right hand. The rulers are enraged as they stone Stephen. In his martyrdom he takes his cue from Jesus who prayed for forgiveness to those who did not know what they were doing. Stephen cries out in a loud voice: "Lord, do not hold this sin against them" (Acts 7:60).

We have noted several times that our heritage as Brethren teaches us to test what we hear and experience with the mind of Christ. The freedom that comes with the Spirit of Christ is different from popular views. Our culture stresses that freedom is to be free from the control of others, to be free to do anything we wish. We can agree with interpretations that advocate civil rights for all, including ourselves. The Apostle Paul writes, however, that we are often in slavery to our self-centered lives. If we are freed from sin, we are free to be for others and the Jesus way of love and justice (Rom. 6). This is a Christian way to test the spirits.

The Trinity

It has been frequently assumed that the Bible offers little support for the doctrine of the trinity. Others maintain that the trinity is implied, if not explicitly stated, by New Testament writers. Many who adopt strong monotheistic teachings about one God in Judaism, Islam, or Christianity have difficulty accepting and understanding trinitarian beliefs. Most of Christendom, however, assumes the doctrine to be necessary in order to explain more fully the nature of God. For example, Zinzendorf, the pietist founder of the Moravians, formulated a doctrine of the trinity with three persons: Father, Mother, and Son. Early Pietists in their greater openness to the priesthood of all believers were thereby ahead of contemporary discussions about more inclusive ways to think of God.

In Eastern Orthodox traditions, it is important to believe the third person of the Trinity, the Holy Spirit, to be equal with the other two persons. Their mystical tradition cultivates direct relationships with God in prayers and liturgies. The schism between Eastern Orthodoxy and the Latin west in 1054 resulted from a variety of issues, a major one being the addition of one little Latin word *filique*, literally *and the Son*, to a creed. The Western Church added the phrase in agreeing with Augustine who emphasized that the Holy Spirit proceeds not only from God but also from the Son. The Eastern Church taught that the Holy Spirit proceeds from the Father alone. This indicates they want the Spirit to be on the same level as Jesus in the trinity. This early debate relates to our next chapter, which discusses the inner and outer word in Brethren life and thought.

The mystery of how one can be three and three be one has provided the impetus for much theological and philosophical speculation. Though Brethren have definitely been trinitarian and appreciated the explanations of others, it appears to me that one of the most helpful ways to talk about the trinity for pragmatic Brethren is to look at it as emerging from the biblical story. The doctrine was not dreamed up in a vacuum. Rather, it happened. Michael Green, in his book *I Believe in the Holy Spirit*, speaks of three happenings in the historical drama. Act I highlights the Jewish background of the first Christians. They were monotheists who believed in only one God, who was so holy the name could not be pronounced and whose nature was too inscrutable to be reproduced in any image. In Act II a man lived among them. After being with Jesus, his followers were convinced that he brought God into focus. God's nature was revealed through Jesus' life, teachings, character, and the manner of his death. In Act III we find Jesus' disciples discouraged and defeated following the crucifixion. Through the mysterious appearances and pentecostal presence, they were convinced that God's activity was still in their midst. They experienced the continuing work of Jesus. The early communities treasured words of Jesus such as reported in John 14. Jesus promised: "I will not leave you orphaned" (14:18). They were comforted in knowing that the Spirit of Jesus remained with them.

The trinity can be experienced in a multitude of ways by each of us. Gazing into the starry firmament, deeply aware of our finitude, we might ponder an awareness of One who is beyond our little systems, feeble efforts, and provincial lives. Or in moments of special encounters with the good, the beautiful, and the true, we may call those glimpses of the ultimate divine. When we engage people whose lives exemplify and identify with Jesus and his way, we are encouraged by glimpses of the abundant life that can be ours as well. And in those moments when we receive the fresh power of new perspectives, faith, and hope, we know the presence of the Holy Spirit, the continuation of the Spirit from the Abraham-Jesus tradition.

III. The Fellowship of the Spirit

"The grace of the Lord Jesus Christ, the love of God, and the communion of the Holy Spirit be with all of you (2 Cor. 13:13).

There have been so many awakenings led by Spirit movements that it is difficult to discern where the Brethren fit in. If we have a special contribution, it is likely that we highlight the communal definition of the Spirit. We have the experience of our anabaptist heritage that no one can come to God except together with a brother or sister. The neighbor constitutes an essential presence in one's personal redemption. How can anyone love God, whom we cannot see, apart from the love of brothers or sisters who can be seen (1 John 4:20). James McClendon, in a book designed for anabaptist theology, conjectures that "the Spirit in individuals may come to nothing apart from the Spirit in the community" (*Doctrine* 343).

Brethren, who rejected hypocritical expressions of many holidays for decades, chose Pentecost as the time for the big meeting. The special outpouring of the Spirit at Pentecost was a vital part of the story of the birthday of the Christian church. In this the elders agreed with theologians who, in statements of faith and books on dogma, have joined doctrinal statements about the church with those defining the Holy Spirit.

Spirit and Baptism

It is difficult for Brethren to separate baptism from membership in the body of Christ and ordination of the priesthood of all believers. Following the threefold immersion in water in the name of the persons of the Trinity, hands are laid on the newly baptized to acknowledge the presence of the Holy Spirit. In his diary Brethren martyr John Kline identified the third dip with possibilities of the loving Spirit flowing from the community of faith through the believer for ministries of love (Funk, selected passages). Whereas other traditions express a similar theology through baptism of infants and confirmation coming later, Brethren join baptism and confirmation in one service.

For this reason some biblical stories have been subject to Brethren interpretations. For example, many have wondered about the story of Samaritans who were baptized only in the name of the Lord. The text relates that they did not receive the Holy Spirit until Peter and John came from Jerusalem and laid hands on the Gentiles, who "received the Holy Spirit" (Acts 8:16-17). This was somewhat similar to Saul's world-shaking conversion experience on the Damascus road. The Spirit was certainly present in Saul's visionary encounter with Jesus. Nevertheless, the text relates that Saul, later known as the Apostle Paul, received the Holy Spirit when he arrived to meet

Ananias, a disciple who laid hands and baptized him so that "he might be filled with the Holy Spirit" (Acts 9:1-19). In these stories baptism occurs either directly before or after the laying on of hands. In both stories, however, receiving the Holy Spirit is related to substantial relationships with the community of faith.

The Wind or Spirit Blows Where It Chooses (John 3:8)

With the Gospel of John, we realize that the Spirit cannot be caught or possessed. Rather, one must be possessed and moved by the Spirit. She or it or he can be present before or after baptism. Such is illustrated in a narrative from the Book of Acts (19:1-7). Paul comes to Ephesus and meets new disciples. He asks whether they have ever received the Holy Spirit. They respond that they have never heard of the Spirit. Paul seems puzzled and asks into what then were they baptized. They respond that it was "into John's baptism." Many converts in the early community, who were attracted to Judaism, had received the baptism for repentance by John the Baptist. Then Paul baptized them in the name of Jesus, and the Holy Spirit was on them, and they spoke in tongues and prophesied. This is the text Pentecostals quote to make the case for a second baptism of the Holy Spirit as a new experience following the first baptism. Brethren have generally believed, however, that this may have been necessary only in this context. Though Brethren have generally accepted subsequent fillings of the Spirit, most would feel that it need not be tied to a "second work" experience.

Brethren discern workings of the Spirit within the community of faith. For us the laying on of hands is a beautiful New Testament symbol that points to the reality that God's Spirit comes to us through the lives of sisters and brothers. Moreover, the above text teaches us that the Holy Spirit can be discerned beyond the borders of the church. Both inside and beyond the walls of the church, we can discern, receive, and cooperate with manifestations that embody the Spirit of Jesus. Missionaries have often testified that the Spirit of Jesus had preceded their arrival.

Professor Floyd Mallott was sensitive to those who worried whether they had received the Spirit when they would hear of miraculous happenings of others who had experienced a dated second baptism of the Holy Spirit. He would attempt to comfort such feelings by asking whether anyone present had a loving mother whose love was nurtured by a devotion to Jesus. If so, he could pronounce: "Very early you received a baptism of the Holy Spirit." He would continue: "Has anyone placed hands on you to encourage, comfort, or admonish you in the Spirit of Jesus? If so, accept the reality that you have received the Holy Spirit. Have you ever awakened in the middle of the night and suddenly received a scriptural truth that came alive with new freshness and meaning? If so, the Spirit was bringing life." These insights are supported by the text that promises, "If you then . . . know how to give good gifts to your children, how much more will [God] give the Holy Spirit to those who ask" (Luke 11:13).

Gifts of the Spirit

Have you ever pondered how little you had to do with your birth? Through the eyes of faith, the creation story tells us that life is a gift of the Spirit. The variety of gifts listed in 1 Corinthians 12 and elsewhere are given by the same Spirit. A manifestation of the Spirit is given to each one not for self-actualization, but for the common good. The purpose of the gifts is to build up the body of Christ. Paul begins with the word *pneumatikon*, literally spiritual things or gifts. In most other places, he uses *charismata*, which means gifts graciously given. In popular usage, those who emit a mixture of charm and genius are judged to have charisma. Such gifts can be used for good or for taking unfair advantage of others.

There appears to be a standard of equality in New Testament communities. The gifts are not reserved for the spiritually elite. Each has received a gift (1 Pet. 4:10), and there is no pressure for any one to have all the gifts. Paul seems to prefer some gifts over others. Those who receive the gift of tongues should recognize that others may receive the gift of utterance of wisdom, and those who know the gift of prophetic utterances against social wrongs need to acknowledge those who know the gift of working miracles of personal wholeness. The presence of a variety of gifts reveals that grace may manifest itself in many different ways.

In thinking of gifts named in biblical epistles, there are specific categories and common gifts. One distinction is between the gift of people and gifts that are given to people. In Ephesians 4, apostles, prophets, pastors, and teachers are listed as gifts for the purpose of equipping the saints for the work of ministry. A lengthy list concludes 1 Corinthians 12: apostles, prophets, teachers, workers of miracles, healers, helpers, administrators, and speakers in various kinds of tongues. Contemporary pastors and leaders indeed might cherish being perceived as gifts rather than hired hands or employees. The laying on of hands has been used to signify the Spirit's enabling power as members call others for special responsibilities.

Classical Pentecostalism has focused on the cluster of nine gifts listed in 1 Corinthians 12:8-10. The nine may be grouped into three categories of three each. The first three are gifts to proclaim. In an earnest hope that the Corinthians would desire spiritual gifts, Paul seems to prefer the gift of prophecy. Prophecy may have included predictions and inspired teaching. Pauline scholars indicate that it is a gift to say the right word at the right time for guidance and edification of the community. The gift of tongues was associated with prayer, praise, and thanksgiving to reveal the presence of the Spirit. Christians have found a basis for defining this gift as speaking in other languages or in strange utterances that need to be interpreted. Because confusion occurred in some settings, Paul proposed the gift of interpretation. Two chapters later Paul expresses his preference for words of understanding. In relating to problems in worship, he declares that God is not a God of confusion, but of peace. And the fourteenth chapter concludes with an admonition that everything be "done decently and in order" (1 Cor. 14:40).

A second trilogy includes gifts of doing: healing, miracles, and faith. The first two will be discussed in the chapter on anointing. It is generally agreed that faith in this context is not faith by which one responds to the grace of God. Rather, here it is a special faith so as to be able to do wonderful things such as removing mountains (see 1 Cor. 13:2). Faith is the gift to keep on trusting and living against all odds, to have the courage to challenge and live in an atmosphere of apparent hopelessness.

The remaining three gifts are knowledge, wisdom, and discernment. The word *gnostic*, meaning knowledge, refers to elitists who claimed to have knowledge of salvation not available to others. In an atmosphere of unhealthy divisiveness, Paul wished to stress that the knowledge given by the Spirit is that of doing God's will and having charity toward others. In light of what Paul probably wrote to the same community, wisdom is not something we claim for ourselves. Rather, he is speaking of a Christlike wisdom that he acknowledges may appear to be foolish in most cultures. Nevertheless, the gift of wisdom is illuminated by the Spirit for understanding the purposes of God, the way of Christ, and the sacred writings.

Discernment, an Important Gift for Anabaptist Traditions

Discernment, the last of the nine gifts listed above, has taken on an important function in anabaptist circles—that of naming the gifts of brothers and sisters in the body. The community of faith discerns and calls out leaders while respecting the wishes of the one being called. Brethren have believed that guidance by the Spirit shapes local and Annual Conference decisions. A greater openness to this gift could lead to shaping the program of the church by discerning the gifts of members rather than always fitting individuals into offices and slots.

People of anabaptist traditions, such as the Mennonites, think highly of the text they name as the rule of Paul: "Let two or three prophets speak, and let the others weigh what is said" (1 Cor. 14:29). In testing the Spirit, this rule is to be added to previously mentioned tests of discerning the mind of Christ and what serves best the body of Christ and the common good.

Unity in Love, the More Excellent Way
". . . making every effort to maintain the unity of the Spirit in the bond of peace" (Eph. 4:3).

Paul concludes the chapter on gifts by pointing to a more excellent way. Then he interjects his beautiful love chapter (1 Cor. 13) between two chapters that deal with the gifts. He shows the primacy of love over the gifts: If I [have the gift] of tongues of men and of angels, but have not love, I am only a resounding gong" (NIV). He proposes that in loving we strive for greater unity in the Spirit. There has emerged perhaps an unnecessary debate as to whether love is the greatest gift or a virtue that needs to permeate all the gifts.

The text emphasizing the variety of gifts, but the same Spirit (1 Cor. 12:4) is one of the most abused passages of Paul. It has been interpreted to glorify a variety of differences. There are simply too many passages in the New Testament that call us to be of the same mind and the same Spirit to be satisfied with a glorification of differences. Pauline emphases do not support an "everybody believe and do your own thing" way of keeping unity in the church. Nor does he suggest that the activity of the Spirit implies an enforced uniformity, an approach characterized by "everybody believe or do my thing or else." Some err by attempting to maintain institutional unity through doctrinal indifference and individualism. The opposite temptation is to attempt to preserve unity through a rigid and legalistic style. This leads to clarity without charity, to laws divorced from the law of love. We must rise above our own views to seek together the mind of Christ. Rejecting either liberal glorification of differences or conservative legalism, we should rejoice in the varieties of gifts, service, and working that can be dedicated to the same Spirit, Lord, and God. In love, we need to strive for greater unity of the Spirit.

The Unpardonable Sin Against the Holy Spirit
"Therefore I tell you, people will be forgiven for every sin and blasphemy, but blasphemy against the Spirit will not be forgiven. Whoever speaks a word against the Son of Man will be forgiven, but whoever speaks against the Holy Spirit will not be forgiven, in this age or in the age of come" (Matt. 12:31-32).

In stressing the close kinship between the Spirit and the community of faith, we offer an interpretation of a passage and doctrine that has often been puzzling. Upon first consideration, it seems our Creator does not want to forgive. Yet biblical writers tell us that grace is basic to the nature of God. Even God's wrath is nothing other than a working out of an expression of God's love. For God is long-suffering and patient. Our Creator has given freedom to each one of us. Thus, as long as we remain within the community of the Spirit, there is a possibility for restored relationships with others and God. Every other sin can be forgiven (even the blasphemous way the so-called entertainment industry profanely and repeatedly utters the name of Jesus Christ). Whenever we remove ourselves from any possibilities of restored relationships, however, there is no opportunity for forgiveness. The sin against the Holy Spirit is the sin of removing ourselves completely from the divine activity and messages of those in fellowship with the Holy Spirit, the Spirit of Jesus.

IV. The First Fruits of the Spirit

"We know that the whole creation has been groaning in labor pains until now; and not only the Creation, but we ourselves, who have the first fruits of the Spirit, groan inwardly while we wait for adoption, the redemption of our bodies. For in hope we were saved" (Rom. 8:22-24).

Metaphors of the mighty wind and the tongues of fire have revealed the power of the Spirit to bring genuine change and dramatic experiences in our lives. From Pietists and Quakers, we have learned that the Spirit also speaks in a still, small voice. There is another metaphor of the prophets who have pictured the Spirit being poured out on us like a stream of water. The effect brings fruitfulness in the land. John in Revelation pictures the river of the water of life flowing from the throne of God through the middle of the street in the New Jerusalem. On either side is a tree of life producing twelve kinds of fruit; the leaves of the trees are for the healing of the nations (Rev. 22:1-5).

The Nurturing Fruit of the Spirit
The Spirit gives different gifts, but the same Spirit strives to produce the same fruit in all. The biblical images of the Spirit as life-giving waters depict the Spirit as the nurturer of Christian growth. Pentecostals name the Spirit as power to point to the availability of miraculous gifts. Holiness groups' emphases of sanctification stress Paul's affirmation that we presently have "the first fruits of the Spirit." The pietist insistence is that newness of life validates notions of a new birth and fosters a spirituality that digests this fruit.

In Galatians 5, the characteristics of the fruit of the Spirit are preceded by a list of the works of the flesh. These manifestations of sin are our works. In the Bible, when evil is attributed to the demonic, it is always in a way that includes human responsibility. On the other hand, virtues we may have are identified as the fruit of the Spirit of God, of Christ.

This Pauline teaching has been referred to as "the paradox of grace." It is named a paradox because it seems illogical and unfair. It did not make sense to the lad at school who complained that when he was bad he got blamed, but when he was good, this was attributed to having great teachers and good parents. Likewise, when the children of Israel suffered reverses, it was due to their sinfulness. However, when they experienced good times, this was attributed to God's redeeming activity. Though this paradox may defy the laws of logic, it still makes good human and divine sense. This is especially manifest when we observe the opposite—the person who blames others and unfortunate situations when he or she does something wrong, but brags and struts in taking all the credit when accomplishing anything worthy.

"The fruit of the Spirit is love, joy, peace, patience, kindness, goodness, faithfulness, gentleness, and self-control. There is no law against such things" (Gal. 5:22-23). When Christians meditate on this list, they may readily think of the character of Christ. The qualities that the Holy Spirit seeks to give to Christ's people are the characteristics of Jesus. The Gospels give us the picture and religion of Jesus. But no better description can be found of Christlikeness than Paul's word-picture of the fruit of the Spirit. If we are led by the Spirit, we will become more Christlike.

Christlike Virtues

A review of the nine fruits will likely tell more about what Brethren believe and who we are than a Brethren's Card or confession of beliefs. As Paul's list of nine gifts has been divided into three categories, the same seems to fit the fruit. The first three are so basic as to be the essence of a Christlike disposition. To have these three—love, joy, and peace—sheds light on the last phrase of our text: "There is no law against such things." That is, to have these qualities of character engenders a freedom from self-centeredness and a freedom to be for others in a way that is all the law requires and even more.

Agape Love. In response to God's grace, one does not ask, "What is there in it for me?" Instead, there is a quality of love that contributes to the perfection to which we are called. In defining perfection, Jesus asks that our love be inclusive, like the love of God who makes the sun shine on the good and on the evil. If we only love those who love us, how are we acting differently from tax collectors and others? (Matt. 5:43-48).

Joy. Paul implies that if we walk in the Spirit, our lives will radiate joy. This is not always external jollity; for walking in the Spirit often embodies a deep joy that nothing will be able to take away. I have been amazed at references to joy in the *Martyrs Mirror*. One typical account relates the execution of four early anabaptist brothers in AD 1546.

> *When they were being led out to slaughter, they boldly and joyfully sang. . . . They then blessed each other, and exhorted one another to steadfastness, to be strong and of good cheer. . . . Thus all four were beheaded with the same sword and undauntedly and boldly surrendered their necks for the name of Christ. (van Braght's edition 475).*

Peace. *Shalom* is the Hebrew word that provides the foundation for New Testament words for peace and salvation. It implies a strong sense of wholeness and well-being. Shalom leads to a desire to live as much as possible in harmony with all of God's creation and creatures.

In our popular religious culture, there is a tendency to domesticate the Spirit. Recently, a brother was sharing with me why he joined our tradition. Though still appreciating his holiness background, he related that among the Brethren he discovered an emphasis on the Spirit's priority to seek first the kingdom over worldly success motivated by individual concerns.

Christlike Relational Virtues

The next three virtues—patience, kindness, and goodness—focus on the way we should relate to one another.

Patience. Patience is a form of love. In the classic love chapter, we learn that "love suffers long and is kind." This disposition is slow to anger, ready to forgive, and willing to bear with those who annoy us. As God has accepted and forgiven us, we should patiently do the same to others. As a boy, I remember when Mr. Meeker scolded us for having our baseball diamond touching his property. My father had assured us that the spot under scrutiny was on our lot. We appealed to our father to intervene and tell Mr. Meeker off. Father responded in the spirit of the patient man he was: "Mr. Meeker has a hard time at his job. Everyone who is above him bosses him day after day. He may need some place where he is the boss. He might feel better if we move the diamond to avoid more arguments."

Kindness. Marked by gentleness in dealing with others, kindness goes much deeper than just a basic concern for the feelings of others. Kindness results in a positive benevolence that wishes the best for all people.

Goodness. This quality, like the others, is one of being as well as doing. Characteristic of virtue ethics that focus on the person more than on the laws by which a person lives, goodness is not concerned with individual happiness alone. A good person is sensitive to the needs of others and is compassionately involved in the agonizing problems of the world. Floyd Mallott, from whom I learned church history, named goodness as a basic fruit and identity of pietist movements.

The gifts of the fruit of the Spirit are corporate as well as individual. In such communities the infilling Spirit will overflow in "psalms, hymns and spiritual song among yourselves, singing and making melody to the Lord in your hearts . . ." (Eph. 5:19).

Wesley's Views: Witness and Fruit of the Spirit

"It is that very Spirit bearing witness with our spirit that we are children of God" (Rom. 8:16).

This verse became a golden text of Methodism. Converts quoted it frequently in testifying to the doctrine of assurance. The text became known as the direct witness of the Spirit. It answered questions as to whether we know we are in favor with God. Before his conversion experience, John Wesley later explained, he had the faith of a servant, doing the right things for Christ and the church. After his heart was strangely warmed at Aldersgate, he felt loved and accepted by God and testified that he now had the faith of a son.

But Wesley also continued to stress the indirect witness of the Spirit. Whereas the direct witness involved joining God's Spirit with our own spirit, the indirect witness nurtures the presence of the fruit of the Spirit in our lives. The direct witness makes us conscious of *justification*, God's forgiving acceptance. The indirect witness brings *sanctification*, the Spirit's empowerment of Christlike qualities in one's life. Wesley continued to preach the good news of the direct witness of acceptance but emphasized that the direct witness must be manifested in the indirect witness. And one of the ways to meet the test was to have others discern whether the daily walk revealed the fruits of the Spirit.

After struggling with self-righteousness and false testimonials by zealous converts, Wesley concluded that one could have the indirect witness without the direct witness. There can be beautiful Christians whose character shows forth the fruit of the Spirit, yet who do not testify to the assurance of a direct witness. Wesley was quick to add, however, that a person could not claim the direct witness of the Spirit without also disclosing the indirect witness. In this he strongly emphasized that if people testified to the direct witness of being assured of God's forgiveness, they must also give evidence of the Spirit's fruitfulness in their lives. Wesley's stance is congenial to Brethren propensities, possibly because his conversion experience was mentored by German Pietists. Brethren have continued to struggle with the call to witness while avoiding the arrogance of self-righteousness.

The Commissioning Spirit for Mission

"But you will receive power when the Holy Spirit has come upon you; and you will be my witnesses in Jerusalem, in all Judea and Samaria, and to the ends of the earth" (Acts 1:8).

We have seen how the Spirit builds up the body so that believers know a quality of fellowship that the world cannot give or take away. The goal of the Spirit is to send forth witnesses to share by word and deed the good news to all creation. With other Pietists, Brethren believed that the gifts and fruit of the Spirit were not only for the edification of the church, but also for the good of the world. In the tradition of the Radical Reformation, laying on hands is an anabaptist symbol to commission pastors, missionaries, peacemakers, service workers, and all believers who have been ordained for ministry by baptism for the work of the kingdom coming. Baptism involves both a call to nonconformity to a fallen society and a commission to serve for the reconciliation and liberation of this very world.

The word *witness*, which appears thirty times in the Book of Acts, became a favorite word among sixteenth-century Radicals. Witness describes both their martyr faith and missionary stance. They witnessed; the Spirit converted. This style was important in light of the prevailing compulsion in matters of faith and practice in the state churches. Anabaptists were among the first to propose the Great Commission (Matt. 28:19) to be the mission of all members. The root word for apostle is "sent one." Since they rejected infant baptism, Anabaptists needed to adopt a missionary posture in relation to their own children.

Those who are sent by the Spirit may participate in a bountiful harvest of the first fruits of the kingdom. Yet, the Anabaptists were sojourners in the land because the kingdom was not yet, but still in the future. But they could hold on to the promises by walking by faith and regarding the fruit of the Spirit as a down payment on the future kingdom. Such is a down payment and foretaste of the redemption of ourselves and all creation.

Pentecost revives memories of Jesus choosing a scroll from the prophet Isaiah in his home synagogue at Nazareth in order to define the Spirit's mission as good news (evangel) for the poor, release for those in prison, healing for the blind, freedom for the oppressed, and proclaiming the year of Jubilee in which property would be divided more equally. In defining the evangel, Isaiah and Jesus offer inclusive views of the work of the Holy Spirit. When we know a foretaste of the first fruits, we experience the kind of fellowship that God desires to give to all in the fullness of the kingdom. The down payment of the Spirit represents the power of the future kingdom breaking into the present.

In our tradition it has been difficult to maintain a neat separation between the gospel of salvation for the individual and the gospel of peacemaking for the sake of the kingdom. Evangelism and peacemaking belong together. The Holy Spirit leads us in redeeming activity more than it provides enlightenment to discern the evils and dates of the end time. As we encounter meaninglessness, broken relationships, hopelessness emitting from glorifications of violence, and despair of dominion of the powers and principalities, we can offer praise for the power and promise of the Spirit as first fruits of the kingdom of love.

Our Bible is replete with so many meanings, connotations, and workings of the Holy Spirit as to lead to both a degree of confusion and an awesome worship of God. Here, it is hoped that it has been helpful to relate biblical passages to the life-giving power of the Spirit, to the nature of the same Spirit embodied in Jesus, to the fellowship of the Spirit in bonds of peace in communities of faith, and to the commissioning Spirit leading and guiding us in ministries of salvation and loving justice. Brethren have both given and received many interpretations and manifestations of the presence and power of the Holy Spirit.

Chapter 7

Brethren and the Bible
Inspiration and authority

But as for you, continue in what you have learned and firmly believed, knowing from whom you learned it, and how from childhood you have known the sacred writings that are able to instruct you for salvation through faith in Christ Jesus. All scripture is inspired by God and is useful for teaching, for reproof, for correction, and for training in righteousness, so that everyone who belongs to God may be proficient, equipped for every good work.
—2 Timothy 3:14-17

Holy Scripture is a letter from God, which through the working of the eternal Spirit has been written to the human race. May we receive it so that the whole New Testament be written by the finger of God on the heart of the reader until his or her entire life becomes a living letter from God in which all can read the commands of Christ (paraphrase of 2 Corinthians 3:3).
—anonymous Brethren author, *Kierkegaard and Radical Discipleship*, tr. Vernard Eller, 419-20

The Wrapping and the Gift

"Jesus Christ is the supreme gift given to us in the wrapping of the Bible." This premise of one of my teachers resembles that of Luther: "The Bible is the manger in which Christ is laid." The metaphors intrigue me because the wrapping or composition of the Bible evokes a variety of responses.

Some contemporaries have not liked the bloodshed in the Bible, the cosmology (the three-story universe), and what appears to be an erroneous assumption that the world was created in seven days. Others object to what they regard as X-rated material, such as the sexual transgressions of David. Disbelievers of an inerrant Bible cite errors such as Matthew attributing the "thirty pieces of silver" to Jeremiah instead of Zechariah. Some college students in their first serious attempt to study the Bible become disillusioned about what they had been taught as children. In pastoral and evangelistic visits, I have encountered those who reject the Bible because of the hypocritical lives or loveless dogmatism of people who overwhelmed them with texts that named their sins. The sad misfortune is that in rejecting the wrapping, so many folks dismiss the book that contains the gift—stories of Jesus and his love.

Others appreciate and defend the wrapping so much that they fail to receive redemptive gifts of love in their hearts. They are tempted to worship the wrapping more than the gift. The Bible remains closed even for some who make infallible claims about it. Placed on a shelf as a sacred icon, carried by a bride down the aisle, opened only to record vital family statistics, the message and stories of faith, hope, and love are often ignored. We have known those who are so attached to a particular wrapping that they object to any new wrappings. This may explain actions of the few who have burned new editions of the Bible, opposing all changes in the wrapping as it came to them. Fundamentalist Christians generally are suspicious of biblical criticism. Other Christians regard theories of inerrancy as heretical. The resulting debates can seriously interfere with receiving the gift of good news.

Annual Conference Decision, 1979

As mentioned in the Introduction, one of the ways Brethren do theology is in considering decisions of the large delegate body at Annual Conference. This is a well-advised way to deal with the variety of views and debates about the Bible.

In 1977 a query was brought to Conference that raised concerns about views of the inspiration and authority of the Bible. Because the heritage has been known for its affirmation "We have no creed but the New Testament," the Standing Committee recommended that a committee of five be appointed to prepare a paper about our historic and contemporary understandings.

I was one chosen among others to represent a prevailing stream of Brethren views. There were areas of agreement as well as substantive differences among us. At first it seemed as if we would end up with both a majority and a minority report. If this had transpired, the delegate body would have voted to accept one or the other as the paper for discussion, amendment, and possible adoption.

In hindsight the committee avoided a rigid division by beginning our task with Bible studies. Each one of us was assigned to lead a study of an important or problematic text. This consumed major amounts of committee time, yet it was tremendously worthwhile. Through our presentations and dialogue, we came to respect the serious and high regard each one of us had for the Scriptures. Our experience has led me to speculate why liberals and conservatives often avoid earnest Bible study on basic issues that divide us. Conservatives often give the impression that they do not need the discipline, because they already know what the Bible says, whereas some liberals appear to not need to seriously study the Bible because their ultimate authority lies elsewhere.

Another way we came together was to agree on a document in which we could affirm what we all believed and then honestly state perspectives on which we were not yet agreed. This was especially true when we discussed the meaning of infallibility. Henry Kurtz, in his 1867 edition of *The Brethren's Encyclopedia*, stated that the fundamental position of the Brethren about the scriptures "was to take the pure word of God, and that alone, as the infallible rule of the faith and practice." Our committee learned that infallibility is sometimes used as a synonym for inerrancy in all facts and details. However, historically the word refers to a concern for the Bible's authority in matters of faith and practice. This implies the reliability and trustworthiness of the Bible for doctrinal and moral decisions.

This understanding provided the context for us to write a document that defines our basic consensus along with honest statements of disagreement. The following statement is probably most basic in answering the query. It serves as an example for other statements that follow this format.

> *We affirm that the Bible, rightly interpreted, is a fully trustworthy guide for our lives. In this sense we reaffirm our historic understanding of scripture as an infallible rule of faith and practice. With these and other expressions we honor and acknowledge the unique authority of the Bible for the church. We are not yet agreed on whether "trustworthy" means "inerrant." Some of of us believe that the Bible's witness to its own author-*

ity implies that the statements of scripture are without error of any kind, whether factual, historical, or doctrinal. Others of us believe that such a claim is both contrary to the intent of the biblical writers and a denial of the true humanity of scripture. ("Biblical Inspiration and Authority: a study guide to the Annual Conference paper" 27)

Since Brethren from the beginning have sought to imitate the early church, the document in the history section points out that "none of the creedal struggles of the great ecumenical councils involved a debate about the scriptures. The early creeds do not include the Bible as an article of faith" (12). Since our early forebears lived before the age of science and reason in Germany, they were not concerned about issues of biblical infallibility that have emerged in the late nineteenth and twentieth centuries.

In processing the work of our committee, I thought it would be interesting and would also facilitate a strong consensus to propose a one-sentence answer to the query, characteristic of many brief answers to queries in the nineteenth century. So I proposed that, like Henry Kurtz's concise statement, we recommend that "Brethren reaffirm their historic belief in the authority of the Scriptures in matters of faith and practice." Though somewhat intrigued, the committee rejected the suggestion, believing that a more lengthy decision included in a study guide would provide others with a meaningful experience similar to that of our committee.

A Baptist student read the entire study guide and was amazed that a church decision, which could be criticized for a flexibility that seemed to cater to modernistic pluralism, nevertheless, revealed a unity of the Spirit in holding one another in love and fellowship. He concluded that it "casts off any notions of scriptural indifference" (a student paper reference to pages 29-32 of the study guide).

Comparisons with Historical Understandings

The Annual Conference document agreed with historians who explained that the "Spirit-filled birth, dynamic growth, and struggles of the early church were soon accompanied by a movement toward more structure, order, and authority. The canon, which literally means a ruler by which to keep things straight, refers to the collection of books that were eventually approved by the church to be a part of the scriptures" (study guide 11ff.). By the year 200, the church had an authoritative collection of New Testament books, yet the canon was not officially closed for another two centuries. The following historical views of the Bible have provided the context of more official opinions to be considered in Brethren life and thought.

Eastern Orthodoxy. The Eastern Church holds a high view of the authority of the Bible. In standing for three hours of liturgies during a visit of a Brethren delegation to the Russian Orthodox Church, we observed the faithful, many who were illiterate, kissing and prostrating themselves before the Bible placed on a stand. It was explained that they do not worship, but venerate (regard with respect), the Bible, which for them is a verbal icon of Christ. Though the Bible is a form of the apostolic tradition, it is not to be placed over against the church. Every convert promises: "I will accept and understand Holy Scripture in accordance with the interpretation which was and is held by the Holy Orthodox Catholic Church of the East, our Mother."

Roman Catholicism. It is difficult to find stronger affirmations of scriptural infallibility than those of the Roman Church. Nevertheless, the tradition maintains that since the early councils and clergy created the Scriptures, the church remains the infallible guardian and interpreter of the Bible. Catholics give the writings of the Apocrypha equal status, which explains why Menno Simons, a former Catholic priest, established a legacy of using these writings in early anabaptist life. This may also explain Mack's few references to the Apocrypha. Following years of keeping Bibles from the laity, there has been a genuine biblical revival in scholarly circles and in popular usage of the Bible since the Vatican II Council (1962–65).

Luther. In the heat of battle, the father of the Protestant Reformation formulated the slogan *sola Scriptura*. Scripture alone, not popes and councils, was declared to be normative for life and doctrine. Nevertheless, Luther did not consistently identify scriptures with the "Word" of God. For Luther, the Word was Christ. The Word comes alive through the spoken word in preaching, the written word in the Bible, and the visible word in the sacraments. This distinction allowed Luther to make critical judgments. He wondered whether Moses had written all the first five books, he preferred the fourth Gospel to others, and he questioned the works theology of the Book of James and the value of the Books of Esther and Revelation.

Karl Barth, thoroughly immersed in biblical passages and themes, nevertheless, came to class one day and threw his Bible against the wall. The shocked students awaited his rationalization: "That book is not the Word of God, Christ is the Word of God!" For the most part, I could not afford to spoil treasured books or my reputation by desecrating the Good Book, but in writing curriculum for Anabaptist congregations, I did appropriate Luther's theme that Christ, not the Bible, was the Word of God. A designated reader from another denomination disagreed, accusing me of being too neo-orthodox, a theological movement beckoning back to the theology of Luther and Calvin. I satisfied him without compromising my emphasis by agreeing that the Bible becomes the Word of God when Christ comes alive for us in the Scriptures.

Calvin. Calvin and Calvinists gave the Bible a clearer and more authoritative status than Luther. The Scriptures should have the same authority with believers as if they could directly hear God's voice. Statues, the organ, and other trappings of worship were removed from the cathedral in Geneva, leaving only a central podium on which a Bible rested. Parishioners were instructed in biblical faith and sang only songs from the Psalter. This setting, along with Calvin's stress on the moral law of the Old Testament and its continuity with the New Testament, placed the Bible at the center of Protestant life.

With Luther, Calvin's doctrine of the internal testimony of the Holy Spirit defined the role of the Spirit almost exclusively as an aid in confirming Scriptures in the heart and mind of the believer. Though many have found in Calvin the origin of fundamentalist stances in reference to the Bible, others look to passages in which Calvin accented human authorship and defined revelation as something not to be identified completely with the Bible. In suggesting that biblical authors give a testimony to revelation other than the Bible itself, Calvin approached Luther's position in maintaining that the authority of Scriptures lie elsewhere—in Christ.

The above analyses have been selected from the committee's contributions to the Conference document. These historical stances are important, for they have frequently affected Brethren life and thought.

Brethren Hermeneutics

Hermeneutics can be translated as the attitudes and principles we assume and apply in interpreting scriptures. Though Brethren have often borrowed heavily from one or more of the inherited historical views, the following additional influences and emphases may converge to reveal another way of interpreting the Scriptures and doing exegesis.

The Context of Pietism

Pietism definitely represented a back-to-the-Bible movement. From 1712 to 1812, the Halle-based Canstein Bible Institute, the first Bible society, published more than two million Bibles and one million New Testaments. The movement placed the Bible at the center of Christian life. It spawned a revival of reading and studying the Bible for all and a new impetus for biblical theology among the more scholarly. Paul Tillich observed that "wherever biblical theology prevails over systematic theology, that is almost always due to the influence of Pietism" (*A Complete History of Christian Thought* 285).

Because the Scriptures were translated in many languages, Spener and Francke encouraged learning the biblical languages, Hebrew and Greek, in order to best understand the Scriptures. Students were to carry Greek pocket editions with them. Once students had progressed with the biblical languages, it was recommended that they commence with biblical Aramaic. Francke published monthly his *Observationes Biblicae*, one of the first theological periodicals. He was in real trouble when he often singled out badly translated passages in Luther's Bible.

Pietist views of inspiration held that the writers, not the words, were inspired by the Holy Spirit. Angelic beings did not dictate words directly to the authors. Instead, the Spirit gave divine truth through an enlightenment of the heart. Pietist views that recognized both human and divine elements opened the door to higher criticism. According to Francke, the sacred authors "wrote as they felt" at the same time they were "moved by the Holy Spirit" (*A Guide to the Reading and Study of the Holy Scriptures* 123).

Though their theories of inspiration did not basically deviate from their contemporaries, Pietists differed in their purpose and goals for reading the Bible. Scriptures must be a guide for life, not just a source of belief. The authority of the Scriptures is that we are led along the way as if Christ is walking with us. Groups and individuals study together or alone for personal edification, devotional life, and the reformation of the church and the world. Derived from the Scriptures, persuasive love, rather than dogmatic intolerance, should stimulate dialogue with those who differ. In summary, the pietist hermeneutic produced both biblical centrism on the one hand and higher criticism on the other. (For a more complete legacy of pietist hermeneutics, see my *Understanding Pietism,* ch. 3.)

Anabaptist Communal Hermeneutic

In defining their hermeneutic, anabaptist scholars have proposed that the locus of authority shifts from the text itself or the hierarchy of the church or technically qualified biblical and theological scholars to committed believers gathered around the Word. The Word is interpreted and studied with the mind of Christ. We have mentioned that Mennonites and others name 1 Corinthians 14:29 as the Rule of Paul, which advises the body to "let two or three prophets speak, and let the others weigh what is said." This involves a shift from "I" to "We" language, which is consistent with the overwhelming majority of New Testament passages.

It has been amazing to observe how this works out in congregational life. Several people are asked to teach a class that highlights biblical texts for children, youth, or adults. No one accepts the call. Finally someone reluctantly or perhaps enthusiastically agrees to do it. The congregation is relieved, whether or not the person knows very much about the Good Book or has engaged in any serious Bible studies. With the Bible and possibly some helps in hand, a novice is commissioned to interpret the Word of God. A great deal is left to the work of the Holy Spirit. It is incredible how the Holy Spirit often serves us well. At the same time, we experience that the fruit of the Spirit can unfortunately wither in the same process.

As I write I am reading articles and books that interpret contemporary moods in theology labeled postmodern or postliberal. These labels have emerged since I taught classes that discussed contemporary theological trends. Though I remain puzzled, I will attempt to relate these trends to the anabaptist hermeneutic.

Since my chapters intend to offer another way, I am interested in a stance that aims to be neither conservative nor liberal. James McClendon's theology offers an anabaptist version of post-liberal approaches to the Bible. Redaction criticism that attempts to tell us what Jesus said and did not say can be stimulating to those who help us better understand the Scriptures. But the best technical criticism will not keep the Bible from being a dead icon for many. McClendon adds, however, that in making a graven idol that receives greater homage the more it is misread, the Bible becomes a "paper pope." Borrowing from Reinhold Niebuhr, fundamentalists are mistaken in taking all biblical stories literally and liberals are wrong in not taking them seriously.

McClendon, with other so-called postliberal theologians, gives priority to biblical narratives. This is helpful for communities that identify with the anabaptist hermeneutic. The stories themselves, without conservative or liberal exegesis, have an impact on the listening congregation. Throughout history converts did not absorb Christian teaching intellectually and then decide to become Christians. They were attracted to what they saw and heard in the stories and in the faith and practices of the communities. The same is true with the best of Brethren evangelistic efforts. People have responded to stories that reveal why and how we strive to embody loving and caring communities.

Brethren congregations need not feel guilty in granting more credence to the Holy Spirit and to a teacher sincerely attempting to impart and exemplify the mind of Christ. Reading commentaries can help. Such suggests a Brethren amendment to the anabaptist hermeneutic. As we discern our biblical faith when we gather around the Word, we need to add that we often are influenced by scholarly authors. This is a shift of authority from a hierarchy to a community of faith that often appropriates wisdom from commentaries of favorite scholars.

Nevertheless, one does not need to be a biblical scholar to teach the Christian way. This supports a Pietist-Brethren hermeneutic that the authority of the Scriptures becomes a genuine living authority when stories and messages of texts make a difference in the lives of believers, even through vessels of clay.

Inner and Outer Word

There was a streak of mysticism in early anabaptist and pietist movements, felt especially in expressions naming the unwritten Word, the inner light, the inner illumination, or voice of God. Centered in the heart, it was the essence of the person's entire being. When we speak of "the heart of a matter," we retain something of the power of the metaphor that refers to our most vital organ.

Some southern German anabaptist leaders rejected the identification of the word of God with Scriptures. Hans Denck wrote: "I value the Holy Scripture above all human treasures but not as high as the word of God, which is living, powerful and eternal" (Klaassen, *Anabaptism in Outline* 140ff. See sections on the Holy Spirit and the Bible for views and sources of the early leaders.). These leaders did not reject the Scriptures, but they emphasized that they are not the wine, but the sign outside the inn that advertises the wine. Most Anabaptists, however, agreed that the outer Word, the Bible, can lead to the inner word. But if the outer Word was necessary for salvation, they were concerned about those who could not read. One can't help but wonder whether some of the early martyred leaders would be accepted in many contemporary anabaptist congregations. Generally, with Menno Simons, anabaptist movements have given a devotion of greater authority to the outer Word, especially as models for Christian teaching and church organization. Simons is quoted:

> *We certainly hope no one of a rational mind will be so foolish . . . as to deny that the whole Scriptures, both the Old and New Testaments, were written for our instruction, admonition, and correction, and that they were the true scepter and rule by which the Lord's kingdom, house, church, and congregation must be ruled and governed.* (Klaassen 151)

Pietists who were separated or expelled from Protestant congregations embodied a greater dose of mysticism. Jacob Boehme, often regarded as the primary source of Radical Pietism, is known for his extreme, subjective statement: "The entire Bible lies in me." Spener insisted that it was not enough that we hear the written word with outward ear, but we must let it penetrate to our hearts (*Pia Desideris* 117). He would agree with Gottfried Arnold who held that the inner word needed to be checked by the outer Word.

These radical pietist refugees who settled in Schwarzenau were integral to the formation of the new church. A few years later the Huguenot refugees, more formally named the Community of True Inspiration, settled in Schwarzenau. Prophets emerged in their midst whose inner voices were esteemed more highly than the Scriptures. The new anabaptized Brethren needed to relate to these Inspirationalists. Mack accepted the presence of the inner word through visions and leadings of the Spirit. Still, he insisted that "this law which is inwardly written by the Spirit of God is completely identical with that which is outwardly written in the New Testament" (Durnbaugh, *European Origins* 386). In this Mack agreed with mainline Pietism and his radical mentor Gottfried Arnold. Ultimately, for Anabaptists and the Brethren, the inner word and the outer Word become one. Through the Spirit's presence, the one Word becomes the living Word.

No Creed But the New Testament

In testifying against creedalism, the affirmation that we have no creed but the New Testament often becomes a surrogate creed. Brethren have admonished each other to remain a New Testament church. Both pietist and anabaptist traditions assumed a priority of the new over the old. In this they may have been influenced by Luther who considered both testaments to have law and gospel. He believed the old gave major status to law, whereas the new featured the gospel.

Spener, who attributed divine inspiration to all Scripture, nevertheless, differentiated between the two covenants. From the theory of progressive revelation that emerged in Pietism, Spener judged the New Testament to possess an unequaled brilliance and clarity. He believed that in it we have a higher revelation because it fulfills the Old Testament. A 1531 quote from anabaptist sources claims that "the New Testament fulfills the Old."

Even when Brethren have been tempted to regard as creedal the stance of noncreedalism, they have not rejected the Old Testament. Rather, they agree with the Anabaptists that the New does not replace the Old. Floyd Mallott has been reputed to have said: "The new is in the old concealed. The old is in the new revealed." The ability to distinguish between the two covenants supports two ethical emphases of the tradition, namely, nonswearing and the refusal to participate in warfare, though both had been permitted in the Old Testament.

A Christlike Hermeneutic

Alexander Mack's admonition to "look alone to Jesus your Redeemer and Savior" was central to interpreting the Scriptures. The old covenant needed to be interpreted in light of the message of the new, and both the old and the new by the mind of Christ. It is in Christ that the Scriptures are fulfilled and explained. The inner word is often defined as the presence of the Spirit of Christ.

Bernhard Rothmann, an early Anabaptist, said quite simply that an interpretation of the Scriptures is reliable if it leads to behavior that conforms to Christ. If such behavior is not there, scripture has not been understood (Klaassen, *Anabaptism in Outline* 141). Early anabaptist hermeneutics accepted teachings and laws of the Old Testament whenever they pointed to Christ. Any problems that emerge are not unique to our tradition. Others need to explain why they substitute Sunday for Saturday, the Jewish sabbath, or monogamy instead of polygamy, which was approved in the old covenant. Even Calvin, who stressed continuity between the two covenants, rejected the ceremonial law in favor of keeping moral laws such as the Ten Commandments.

More simply, we turn to a devout grandmother in our tradition. In raising questions about the command in Leviticus that all who curse father or mother shall be put to death (Lev. 20:9), she responded, "But Jesus wouldn't want us to do that!"

Comparing Texts with Other Texts and with Other Cultures

When we interpret passages with the mind of Christ, it often means that we need to compare texts with other texts. If we are indeed a New Testament church seeking the mind of Christ, it may be necessary to consider more than one proof text or even more than several proof texts on some issues. According to an old saying, "We need to search the scriptures in order to rightly divide the word of truth."

For example, consider an issue found in a letter to Timothy from an author identified as Paul. He instructs the young Timothy to "permit no woman to teach or have authority over a man; she is to keep silent" (1 Tim. 2:12). Some interpretations claim that if we had a better understanding of the culture and the problems of the early communities, this admonition would make common sense. Texts have many times been interpreted in different ways in different eras of Christianity.

We understand now that in his time Paul surprised his early readers in 1 Corinthians 11:4,5,10 that women were permitted to pray in church if they had a "symbol of authority, a covering, on their head." Anna Mow pointed out that this was to avoid scandal, because only prostitutes circulated with uncovered heads. We live in a culture that discerns the mind of Christ telling us to live out the nonconformist affirmation of the Apostle Paul that there is neither male nor female in Christ "for all are one in Christ Jesus" (Gal. 3:28). There are an increasing number of textual interpretations of the relationships of Jesus with women, whom he treated as equals and as leader disciples in his community.

Popular Affirmations About the Bible in Brethren Life

- You yourselves are our letter, written on our hearts, to be known and read by all; and you show that you are a letter of Christ, prepared by us, written not with ink but with the Spirit of the living God, not on tablets of stone but on tablets of human hearts (a biblical pietist expression from 2 Corinthians 3:2-3; a Brethren version appears at the beginning of this chapter).

- The Bible is best understood as the community of faith gathers around the Word (a common anabaptist expression).

- The Old Testament must be interpreted by the New and both New and Old by the mind of Christ (often attributed to Rufus Bowman).

- Adopting the New Testament as creed is not a rejection of the Old, but rather a fulfillment of it, foundation building on foundation (by many of us exposed to Hebrew Bible courses).

- The Bible is our infallible authority in matters of faith and practice (derived from statements by Alexander Mack, Henry Kurtz, and many Protestant traditions).

- We are to be open to new light as it breaks forth from the Word (an expression from the Reformed tradition that Alexander Mack, Jr., appropriated in the reasons he gave for changing the order of washing feet in the love feast).

- In the relational theology of Christianity, the Person is more sacred than the Bible. In the more rational, legalistic religion of Islam, the Quran is more sacred than the prophet (observations from students of world religions).

- We Christians have spent more time worshiping the signpost than following the road. For me, the New Testament is a gambler's handbook giving rules for betting our lives that Jesus is the way, the truth, and the life (from Moderator Dan West's address).

- Straightforward preaching of scriptural truth, reinforced by a lot of Christian living, is the best defense of the Bible that has ever been devised. . . . Practice will do more than proof to protect it from discredit (a *Gospel Messenger* editorial, 1919).

- The Bible's authority rests in the claim that it is a word from God to us. . . . Its images, its proclamation, its teaching have laid a claim on our lives. The authority of the Bible does not lie in what we can say about it but in what we discover in it. . . . Authority holds the power to explain life and make it meaningful. We cannot think of authority apart from its ultimate claim on us (Robert Neff, excerpts from "Taking Biblical Authority Seriously," *Brethren Life and Thought,* Winter 1983).

- Jesus loves me this I know, because the Bible tells me so.

We have no creed but the New Testament, but this creed is so long that we are often confused by our different interpretations. Readers are invited to offer other variations of our affirmations.

Chapter 8

Sacraments or Ordinances
Magic or mystery

I became its servant according to God's commission that was given to me for you, to make the word of God fully known, the mystery that has been hidden throughout the ages and generations but has now been revealed to his saints. To them God chose to make known how great among the Gentiles are the riches of the glory of this mystery, which is Christ in you, the hope of glory.
—Colossians 1:25-27

We have observed that Brethren theology can be defined by how we relate to others and God more than by propositional dogma. Likewise, Brethren heritage can be revealed through the stories we relish, our service ministries, and corporate devotional acts and celebrations. We have also noted the sacramental or spiritual nature of face-to-face relationships. However, sacred observances that others call sacraments, were called ordinances by our forebears. It may be helpful to examine these words in understanding our theology or lack of theology of sacred observances.

Sacramentalism

Sacramentalists hold high views of what they name sacraments. The sacred acts are regarded as outward signs of inward grace, the presence of God, the means of grace. The word *sacrament* means mystery, which believers experience to be strange, awesome, ineffable, and unfathomable. Extremely high-church dogma regards observance of sacraments to be necessary for salvation. Luther's influence led most Protestants to reduce the number of sacraments to two, baptism and the Lord's Supper (eucharist). The Roman Catholic and Orthodox Churches maintain an additional five: confirmation, matrimony, penance (confession), ordination (holy orders), and extreme unction (anointing). The mass embodies holy ritual for the eucharist.

I discovered the enduring power of sacraments when visiting an incarcerated Catholic sister who was doing time for radically demonstrating against weapons of mass destruction. Though very critical of hierarchical clergy and the political stances of her Catholic tradition, she confessed that when she wanted to partake of the holy elements, she would only accept a priest, one with the mark of ordination that placed him in the apostolic succession beginning with Peter. Many Catholics who boycott confession and ignore teachings against birth control seldom miss mass. Members of our tradition and other Protestants who have converted to Catholicism testify how they were attracted by the mystery and divine presence they sensed in the mass. Today many Catholics priests and theologians strive to transcend traditional beliefs that the sole locus of the body and blood of Christ is to be found in consecrated bread and wine. At the same time, members of many so-called free church traditions are considering anew historical expressions that relate our heritage to understandings of sacraments and ordinances.

Sacramentarianism

This long word would puzzle most quiz contestants in that it rejects usual understandings of sacraments. Marcus Barth, son of Karl Barth, was one of the first to moderate customary views of sacraments for me. In a series of lectures on sacraments at Bethany Theological Seminary, he specified that the word *sacrament*, meaning mystery, usually refers to what has been hidden throughout the ages but now has been revealed to the saints in Christ (e.g., Col. 1:26). He points out that in Greek biblical texts, mystery never refers to baptism, communion, or any ritual. Someone responded: "If we do not name the rituals sacraments, what do we name them?" Barth advised that we just name them what they are: baptism, christening, the Lord's Supper, eucharist, or communion.

Vernard Eller, one of our most popular Brethren writers in the twentieth century, introduced and translated our heritage in ways that were interesting to other Christians and secular readers. He named one of his books *In Place of Sacraments: A Study of Baptism and the Lord's Supper.* In the text he confesses that he probably should have chosen a more positive title. He definitely identifies himself as a sacramentarian. He opposes sacramental beliefs that proclaim we literally eat the body and drink the blood of Jesus when we come together. Eller believed the early Christians certainly did not mean to participate in such an abnormal incarnation.

In a lecture to the Midwest Theological Society, patristic scholar Samuel Laeuchli presented a belittling analysis of sacraments in a lecture entitled "Christianity and Magical World Views." He explained that the magical world view replaced animism in early medieval life. He defined magical views to be the art that produces effects by the cultic assistance of a supernatural magical power in mastery over secret forces of nature. The changing of bread and wine into the actual body and blood of Christ in a sacred ceremony administered by a sacred priest fits this definition. Laeuchli related how through the ages Christian thought often was joined in a synthesis with popular streams of the culture. He gave historical examples, such as the blending of philosophies of Aristotle and Thomas Aquinas in Thomism; Kierkegaard's synthesis of existentialism with Christian faith; and social and political movements that appropriate biblical concerns for justice. Such blending is inevitable and often helpful. But Laeuchli believed it to be unfortunate that a magical world view of sacraments remained in the church centuries after such views were outmoded in the culture. It is needless to say that his thesis elicited passionate and critical dialogue among the gathered theologians.

Heretics in late medieval centuries were persecuted, even killed, for refusing to "doff their hats" as was the custom in greeting a parade carrying the host, bread transformed to be the physical body of Christ. Heretics were sometimes buried with their hats on to indicate they had never been guilty of worshiping a morsel of bread. An early Waldensian leader spoke disdainfully against kneeling before bread. Hussites believed "that the substance of the bread and wine continue materially the same after consecration" (Leonard Verduin, *The Reformers and their Stepchildren* 146-47, 150).

Schwarzenau Brethren inherited views of these late medieval advocates of reform and anabaptist models of the church. Those who rejected sacramental views were generally against expressions of sacralism, which regarded the union of the church and state as the manifestation of God's kingdom. In recovering the priesthood of all believers, they were aware that the early Christians started out as a rare phenomenon with no concept of the sacrosanct (more holy by rite) priesthood. From their beginnings Brethren have believed the sacramental life to include the daily walk. The true mystery is the presence of the Spirit of Christ that exists in the total life of his people. Symbols, ordinances, and practices are celebrated both inside and outside meeting places of the people. Likely aware that the New Testament did not use the words *sacrament* or *mystery* to refer to covenantal acts, they spoke, instead, of ordinances. They especially desired to obey acts instituted by Christ.

Considering Sacramental Views

As Anabaptists we may need to confess vestiges of paranoia from our historical consciousness. We are reluctant to strive for normative understandings of the sacraments because Christians have too often left a trail of blood by conforming others to their confessions. It was out of the sacramentarian heritage that I began to consider documents and literature on baptism, eucharist, and ministry promoted by the World Council of Churches in the last decades of the twentieth century. It was amazing how denominations, both members and nonmembers of the council, were interested in sharing and listening to a variety of sacramental views. As already noted sacramentalism, in my mind, had been associated with Bonhoeffer's negative attitudes of religion often being a *deus ex machine*, in which God's grace, favor, will, and power to some degree come under the control of humans and their institutions. Marcus Barth and Samuel Laeuchli had convinced me that the sacramental system evolved from the magical world view of the mystery cults more than from biblical theology. Though the word *sacramental* embodies a biblical concept, we have noted how Barth revealed that the word is not linked to what Christendom has named sacraments.

In joining the discussions, I found myself considering broader expressions of sacramental presence. Deeply invested in the discussions, I came to feel that instead of naming myself and my tradition as anti- or a-sacramental, it would be more accurate to recognize that in many ways our tradition is very sacramental. Those who know me will agree that I am too stubborn to change quickly. I became aware that I had been encountering more positive ways to think of the word that was being discussed by so many. I need to acknowledge that the seedbed of this openness had occurred in earlier experiences with Quakers, Orthodox emphases, remarkable Vatican II documents of Roman Catholics, and Spirit emphases of my pietist-anabaptist church tradition. Most Christians are not aware of the strange quirk of language that named those critical of sacramentalists as sacramentarians. The two labels have mistakenly been regarded as synonyms. Now I have been led to believe that this mistaken identity may not be all that wrong.

Jesus Christ as Sacrament. It was from descendants of seventeenth-century Radicalism of Quakers on British soil that I first sensed that Jesus Christ is the sacrament. Jesus is the sacrament who steps into history. A favorite painting of the Quakers is "The Presence." A silhouette of Jesus appears in the midst of a Quaker meeting. For the Friends, gathering in the meeting is the most important visible sign of Christ's real presence. This may not be far from reformation thought. Karl Barth asserted that though sacraments do not redeem, faith in Christ has a sacramental dimension and form" (*The Teaching of the Church Regarding Baptism* 28). We have noted that the Greek word *mysterion* means mystery. For Christendom it has been a scandalous and awesome mystery how one man is regarded to be both very God of very God and very man of very man. Another mystery expressed in biblical studies is that God is both hidden and revealed in Christ.

The Church as Sacrament. The documents from Vatican II begin with accents on the people of God and confessions of the mystery of the church in terms of the paradoxical union between the human and the divine. Vatican II documents increased an awareness of what Roman Catholics have always felt, namely the sacramental nature of the church. In low church circles, it takes a miraculous leap of faith to believe that people like ourselves can be what Paul named us to be—the body of Christ. Anabaptists have strongly identified with affirmations of the presence of Christ in the church. We have noted how Brethren very early acquired an ecclesiology that viewed the church as a quasi-physical extension of the body of her Lord. Presently, in our life together it remains a mystery how people like you and me can truly be the body of Christ.

Sacramental Nature of All of Life. A similar sacramental ingredient influenced me to anticipate the mystery of divine presence in the total life of his people. The sacramental life is the daily walk, a journey that takes us to an infinite variety of meetings for worship, instruction, fellowship, and service. It is a promised mystery that when two or three are gathered in his name Jesus will be with us (Matt.18:20). When our bodies are dipped in baptism, anointed with laying on of hands, giving and receiving vows in marriage ceremonies, these and others acts can be regarded as sacramental times.

Conversion to a More Sacramental Perspective

So it was in October 1983 that I represented the Brethren at a BEM (Baptism, Eucharist, Ministry) conference in Hyde Park. In one of the sessions, we were divided into small groups. My group included an Anglican (Episcopal) theologian, a Presbyterian minister, an Orthodox priest, and perhaps one other representative. I had prepared to seriously question sacraments in articulating Brethren views expressed so well by Vernard Eller. I listened intently, contemplating how I might reply.

It suddenly occurred to me that instead of rejecting sacraments, I might interpret my tradition to be even more sacramental. I reasoned that for them a certain number, two or more sacraments, were believed to be qualitatively a means of redemptive grace due to the unique presence of Christ. In order to have and name a sacrament, Luther maintained that there were certain requirements such as the presence of a sign, faith, promise instituted by Christ. I suggested that it would be more sacramental to believe that sacraments pointed beyond themselves. This would mean that the presence of Christ is accessible in many other situations and places. Jesus did say that wherever two or three are gathered in his name, he would be with them.

The Orthodox priest responded with enthusiasm to what I was proposing. He invited me to come to his church and share with his people what I had said. The Anglican priest, whose facial demeanor expressed charity, looked at both of us and said, "You two are not as close together in your views as you think." I did remember our discussions of sacraments. I had been a member of a Brethren delegation to Russia during the Cold War, and it was surprising how attracted we were to the Orthodox style of spirituality. Perhaps here were mystical notes that were in tune with the mysticism of our radical pietist legacy. We discovered that for the Orthodox "Presence" is presence and does not need to be further qualified as real. When one of our Brethren asked them how many sacraments they have, the priest shared an oral tradition: "When we first encountered the West after the Protestant Reformation, we were frequently asked whether we had seven or two sacraments. We were puzzled, not having felt the necessity of such precise theological definitions. So we responded: 'If we must choose sides, we will have to go with seven.'" This then elicited a favorite story. When they shared with a wise theologian that the West was always asking about the number of sacraments, he said: "Just choose some number like 290 or 432 or any number." This answer appears to be derived from Orthodox emphases on the mystical presence of God in all of life.

Concrete Applications

The Body Language of Communion. Brethren tradition has been eclectic in formulations of the significance of communion or the Lord's Supper. The early leaders imbibed the sacrificial and memorial themes of the Mennonites, as well as their particular version of Christ's real presence. Anabaptists took seriously Paul's admonition that in eating or drinking, we should discern the body (1 Cor. 11:29). And the body, which they discerned was not just Christ's presence in or around or with the bread, but also his presence in his body—the church, as members broke bread together. Free church students of Greek find an openness for this interpretation in the four "this is my body" communion texts. Though the neuter pronoun for this is the same gender as *soma* (body), the fact that *artas* (bread) is masculine does not prove but allows the possibility that the pronoun may refer to the preceding act and not just the bread. This translation might help interpret Jesus' words to his disciples: "You are my body." In turn this might signify that Christ's body is the people breaking bread together, which is consistent with Paul's "body" language in his epistles.

In dialogue with Jesuit students in a joint seminar, one of our students discovered an article by a Dutch Catholic explicating something of the same, which he named *transignification*. The elderly Jesuit father, who had spent a great portion of his life in a mission to convert Protestants, immediately countered, "You have not discovered a Catholic teaching, but a Roman Catholic who is talking like a Protestant." On the other end of the spectrum, Quakers pose an interpretation that shifts the fundamental location of the presence of Christ as in the people. Another Friend logically asked: "Why not eliminate the bread altogether due to tendencies of participants to worship the consecrated bread?" To this most Anabaptists could reply: "Because of the goodness of God's creation, it is right to appropriate gifts of bread, water, and juice or wine in our spiritual or sacramental life together."

Expansion of Sacramental Happenings. If it is more sacramental to assume that sacraments point beyond their act to envision other experiences to be sacramental occasions, then the number of sacraments may increase. It becomes difficult to limit the number to two or seven. M. R. Zigler, longtime peace leader and Brethren representative to the World Council of Churches, sensed the failure of particularity in requirements for a sacrament. He sat through lengthy discussions that struggled with the inability of the different traditions to gather in communion around the same table. He is remembered as one who rose to propose that an even more powerful expression of the Johannine prayer for oneness might be for Lutherans to pledge never to kill Lutherans, Calvinists to promise to never kill Calvinists.

Though he evoked an embarrassing silence, he failed to gain support for his motion. The body correctly appraised his pacifist ploy. Anabaptist perspectives represent a small minority. Yet these perspectives constitute a modest hope that some new accents of a theology of sacraments might create a vision of the covenant by which becoming the body of Christ also helps us to participate in achieving the new humanity for which we have been created.

In understanding how sacramental observances also participate in the sacramental presence that they invoke, Paul Tillich helpfully defined differences between signs and symbols. He reasoned that a road sign points beyond itself to tell you what is ahead. If it informs you to turn, you wait until you get there to turn your wheels. But a symbol not only points to something beyond. It participates in what you have envisioned. A kiss is more than a sign that you love your spouse. It becomes a symbol when deeply felt love accompanies the kiss. As defined by Tillich, genuine sacramental acts embody the faith being espoused. I kiss my child not just as a symbol of my love; I kiss to love the child. Here is participation in what one wants to symbolize.

In naming as sacred every act in which we discern the presence of the Spirit of Christ, we may diminish the importance of special days and occasions. Early Puritans rejected holy days by insisting that every day is holy. They critiqued debauchery celebrations, such as Mardi Gras as a prelude for Lent. They reasoned that every day should be the time for piety and penitence. I was raised in a family that did not celebrate birthdays. Perhaps it was assumed that there were many other days in the year to demonstrate the joy of being with growing and beautiful children. The early Puritans shunned holidays only to end up creating another one—Thanksgiving—in appreciation for a successful harvest. For the most part, the early Brethren ignored special days in the church year. However, for years they held their big Annual Meeting on Pentecost, the birthday of the church. In thinking about this, a case can be made for special sacraments and days when they are symbolic of the value and joy of every sacred day. For example, birthdays are special events that let a child know she or he is special every day of the year.

Where Are the Brethren on Sacraments?

Many Brethren would minimize the importance of theological beliefs in the above analyses. Instead of applying our beliefs about sacraments, they believe it is more important to derive our beliefs from participation in the practices of our heritage, our love feast, baptism, and various contexts of anointing. For most of us, the love feast identifies much of who we are as

Brethren and what is most basic to our tradition. It may be another way of thinking, however, to reconsider our prejudices and discern where and how we know degrees of unity of the Spirit in the bond of peace.

How Many? This may be the easiest question to answer. We are definitely more aligned with the Roman Catholics than with Protestants who name only two. And though we do not know them very well, we are probably even more like the Orthodox who maintain an open Spirit in not officially choosing a number.

What Do We Name Them? Do we call them sacraments, ordinances, covenantal acts, community symbols, presentiments of our humanity, or name them one by one? Affable Brethren would be satisfied with almost any name. Some congregations that name sacred practices as ordinances are quite sacramental. I was invited to a love feast by a large Brethren congregation in which more people were present than at any other congregational event in the year. During the afternoon before we gathered around the tables, I was asked to join ministers and deacons in a separate room to consecrate the communion bread. Other congregations who might speak of sacraments, the name used by their neighbors, nevertheless retain attitudes that define ordinances.

Eller grants that all of us rejoice in the mystery of the incarnation that reveals a life for which we were made. Similarly, Dietrich Bonhoeffer emphasized that God became human not so humans can become divine, but that we can know what is truly human. This was why Vernard Eller chose *The Presentiments of Our Humanity* (13-15) as the best name for his book, although he recognized that it would not win the day in Christendom or with book editors. Eller also liked the name "celebration" for these special practices, but he believed it was too secularized to be appropriate. Eller finally joined most Brethren by choosing the name he favored most, namely, "ordinances." Though this name may connote practices that were legalistically required, this is the name used through most of our history.

Eller summarizes that the goal of our life together in the body "is not to lend variety to normal life by introducing occasional experiences of divine abnormality," but to participate in signs and symbols of "what life could be, should be, was created to be, and in God's grace is destined to become" (*In Place of Sacraments* 14). The pietist-anabaptist tradition does not deny that Christ's presence may be experienced more intensely in rites such as baptism and communion. It does affirm, however, that the presence of Christ in our everyday life, as promised through the resurrection of Jesus, is not qualitatively different from what most of Christendom experiences in special sacramental practices.

Chapter 9

Baptism, Love Feast, Anointing
Favorite manna

For just as the body is one and has many members, and all the members of the body, though many, are one body, so it is with Christ. For in the one Spirit we were all baptized into one body—Jews or Greeks, slaves or free—and we were all made to drink of one Spirit.
—1 Corinthians 12:12-13

Memories of eating quail, manna from a sweet substance of the tamarisk tree, and a honeylike sap sucked out by insects led the children of Israel to be thankful that they had been fed by God. For Brethren water in baptism, bread and juices in communion, and the oil in anointing one another are marks of God's presence that feed us both in the blessed times and in the wilderness periods of our pilgrimage. Like the Israelites of old, our three ordinances foster consciousness of the care of God. Both Jewish and Brethren communities savor memories of times when the presence of God's Spirit encourages and inspires us to keep the commandments of our God.

Baptism

As with Anabaptists of the sixteenth-century Radical Reformation, baptism has remained an important symbol since our beginnings at the crossroads of Pietism and Anabaptism in eighteenth-century Germany. This practice prompted others to bequeath nicknames such as "Dunkers," "Dompelaars," and "Neu-Taufer" (new Baptists) to the "peculiar" people. Yet fond memories remain of members walking through the woods to gather at waterside. First, a plainly dressed elder wades into the river or creek to determine the proper depth. Then one by one the applicants kneel in the water. Having publicly confessed their faith and vowing to be faithful to Jesus, his teachings, and the church, they are dipped three times forward in the name of God, Christ, and the Holy Spirit. Remaining in a kneeling position, the newly baptized receive the laying on of hands. A prayer is offered that bids the forgiving and enabling presence of the Holy Spirit.

The latter action can be thought of as Brethren confirmation, for it embodies the intimate connection between baptism and membership in the community of faith. In both past and present, tears of joy are often shed as the holy kiss, hug, or right hand of fellowship warmly welcomes new sisters and brothers into the body of Christ. The difference today is that in most congregations baptistries and other necessary facilities have been moved indoors.

To baptize or be baptized was originally an act of civil disobedience, a stance that espoused religious freedom, separation of church and state, and voluntary acceptance of the faith. Unlike most of our history, early converts needed to count the cost of possible imprisonment, banishment as refugees, and suffering even to death. In a safer nineteenth century, baptism at an earlier age seemed more feasible. A frequent historical caricature of Brethren preaching claims that whatever the text, the minister always managed to get around to the topic of baptism.

Baptism and Soteriology

Soteriology refers to views of salvation. Alexander Mack believed that a child who dies without water baptism does not suffer the loss of salvation. He judged children to be in a state of grace due to the merit of Jesus Christ. He insisted that believers do not look to the power of water in baptism, but to the Word, Christ, who commands baptism. Mack rejected accusations that Brethren participated in works righteousness in believing that the act of baptism saves a person. However, he did assume that if believers are saved from self-centeredness and if they desire to obey the love commandments of Jesus, they will do what Jesus wants them to do, namely, submit willingly to water baptism in joining the community of Christians (see Mack's "Rites and Ordinances" in Durnbaugh's *European Origins* 348-355).

For Mack, salvation was more than being saved to heaven when we die. Salvation is related to each meaning of baptism listed below. A story that frequently circulates in Lancaster County, Pennsylvania, tells the same. A brother was saved in a revival that swept through the country over by the big river. The congregation he was joining gathered around the horse tank on one of the farms. After the third dip, he leaped out of the water waving his hands in the air and shouting, "It is finished! It is finished!" The elder grabbed the back of his shirt and looked straight into his eyes. "No, brother," he said, "it's just beginning!"

Yet Brethren have not escaped beliefs that regard baptism to be necessary for salvation. A sister took me aside at a church retreat to confess that she had recently taken her infant son to be baptized in the Lutheran church where she was raised. She related why she had not shared this with her pastor or any members. We discussed her decision never to tell her son he was baptized as an infant. Her wish for him was that he would choose to be baptized later and become as enthusiastic in being Brethren as she was. And she confessed that she did what she did just to be safe, in case there was any truth in what she had perceived.

Biblical Meanings of Baptism

Conversion and Discipleship. After being inspired at Pentecost by Peter's sermon, the people asked, "What should we do?" Peter answered: "Repent, and be baptized every one of you in the name of Jesus Christ so that your sins may be forgiven; and you will receive the gift of the Holy Spirit" (Acts 2:37-38).

"Therefore we have been buried with him by baptism into death, so that, just as Christ was raised from the dead by the glory of the Father, so we too might walk in newness of life" (Rom. 6:4).

To repent is to turn around, to confess one's sins. One is justified, which means getting right with God in receiving and being empowered by the loving forgiveness of God and others. It can be a time of experiencing both the fruit of the Spirit (Gal. 5:22-26) and the gifts of the Spirit (1 Cor. 12). Some find it meaningful to think of baptism as a symbol of being buried and raised again in baptism so as to walk in newness of life. This walk is often explained by calling it *justification* (joy of acceptance as above), *regeneration* (being born again, the new birth), *sanctification* (growing in faith and holiness)—symbols that are more meaningful for some than for others.

Covenant. "For just as the body is one and has many members, and all the members of the body, though many, are one body, so it is with Christ. For in the one Spirit we were all baptized into one body—Jews or Greeks, slaves or free—and we were all made to drink of one Spirit" (1 Cor. 12:12-13).

Consistent with the Anabaptist heritage, it was natural that baptism meant joining the church, the body of Christ. In the story in Acts 8, it appears that the baptism of Samaritans was not complete until Peter and John were sent by the church at Jerusalem to lay hands on the newly baptized (Acts 8:14-25). For "Dunkers" past and present, baptism means joining a community of faith.

Ordination for Ministry. There has been a growing recovery of the emphasis that baptism means ordination to the priesthood of all believers. It has often been asked: "Why did Jesus need to be baptized?" It may be that for him baptism coincided with the beginning of his public ministry. Alexander Mack, Jr., in his *Apologia* (Durnbaugh, *The Brethren in Colonial America* 469ff.), faults an opponent "churchman" for pretending the baptism of Jesus and that of his disciples are not the same. Mack, Jr., adds: "Just as the Chief High Priest pledged himself . . . through his baptism to make the entire rebelling creation subject to Him, so all of His followers with their baptism have pledged themselves . . . to assist Him in this important task" (510). Mack refers to the classic statement in Peter's epistle to the newly baptized to support his emphasis on baptism as ordination:

> *But you are a chosen race, a royal priesthood, a holy nation, God's own people, in order that you may proclaim the mighty acts of him who called you out of darkness into his marvelous light. Once you were not a people, but now you are God's people; once you had not received mercy, but now you have received mercy.* (1 Pet. 2:9-10)

The following baptism formula has often been circulated as the charter for movements seeking social justice and equality:

> *As many of you were baptized into Christ have clothed yourselves with Christ. There is no longer Jew or Greek, there is no longer slave or free, there is no longer male and female; for all of you are one in Christ Jesus.* (Gal. 3:27-28)

Scholars interpret the baptism imagery of this text to point to transformation of ethnic, class, and sexual divisiveness of the Galatians to a sense of oneness in Christ. The notion of putting on the clothes of Christ influenced Brethren to add that baptisms signified equality between laity and leaders. Since new converts in apostolic times removed garments and were baptized naked, being clothed with Christ likely refers to putting on new white garments for the new life. Psalm 132 refers to priests clothed with righteousness and salvation. Thus, some interpreters would agree with Brethren views that baptized believers clothed with Christ in baptism are consecrated to be priests who participate in their Lord's ministries.

Form

On the American frontier, many schoolhouse debates between Brethren and advocates of other traditions focused on these practices. Brethren and Baptist apologists vigorously defended believers baptism against the pedobaptists (advocates of infant baptism). They quoted the church fathers and Luther in support of immersion instead of sprinkling and pouring used by other denominations. Many arguments were marshaled to buttress the threefold forward action against Baptist groups who dipped backward one time. Baptists argued that Christ was buried with his face looking upward. Brethren responded that the kneeling position fits better the death of Jesus on the cross with head bowed forward. One theory is that the unitarian Polish Brethren who immersed one time influenced the Brethren who adopted the threefold action to affirm their trinitarian beliefs and formulations. In this they were with the ancient Orthodox tradition that to this day immerses forward three times for adults. Very early in the Orthodox tradition babies were baptized with a threefold immersion when the babies were old enough to be dunked three times. In recent decades Brethren have not been as legalistic about the mode of baptism. Yet they have altered the mode only slightly and found few reasons to depart from forms adopted by the first eight in the Eder River in 1708.

Annual Conference Responses to Questions, 1980

At the time of this writing, the last statement on baptism was made by the 1980 Annual Conference in Pittsburgh. A query that came a year earlier was answered in a paper called "Baptism and Church Membership." The query asked how we should respond to . . .

> a. persons who wish to be baptized without becoming members of the congregation. *Answer:* "We find no justification in the scriptures or in

our theology for administering baptism to those who are unwilling to make a covenant with the body of Christ."

b. children who have experienced spiritual awakening and are desiring baptism, but who seem not yet mature enough to take on the responsibilities and privileges of membership in the church (such as voting on key issues or serving on boards). *Answer:* "We do not see baptism as necessary for the salvation of children within the congregation (1 Cor. 7:14). Nor do we believe baptism to be the most appropriate symbol of the religious and spiritual awakening, which many children feel in their pre-teen years. On the other hand, we are not willing to specify an age at which maturity and readiness for baptism and the ability to relate responsibly to the community of faith occurs. An understanding of baptism as ordination to ministry (1 Pet. 2; Gal. 3:27; and especially the stories of the baptism of Jesus, Matt. 3:13-17, etc.) would urge us to expect that baptism would not be appropriate before a higher degree of responsibility and maturity has been reached than is sometimes the case among Brethren."

c. persons who question Brethren teachings on adult baptism by immersion, citing our reliance on adult confession of faith in receiving into membership Christians who have been baptized as infants. *Answer:* "Because of the way in which we see baptism linked with repentance, with ordination to ministry, and with a conscious covenant with God and our brothers and sisters in the community of faith, we practice believer's baptism in what we believe is the biblical form of trine immersion. However, we affirm the working of the Holy Spirit in the lives of many who belong to those parts of the body of Christ where infant baptism is practiced. When it is the discernment of the body, and the faith of the person that infant baptism and confirmation have been, for them, acceptance of Christ as Lord and membership in His body, we shall accept their baptism, and congregations who so desire may receive them by transfer of letter as full members in full fellowship in Christ."

d. persons baptized at rallies or camp or other such temporary fellowships beyond the congregation. *Answer:* "We would encourage the celebration of baptism to be shared as an event in the life of the community of faith as well as in the life of the candidate. Where special requests are made for baptism at camps or conferences, application should be made to the congregation which will serve as the faith community of the candidate and, when granted, the celebration should include representatives of that fellowship."

e. persons who use baptism as a celebrative, often spontaneous, repeatable symbol of purification and consecration, not intending for that baptism to carry the weight of church membership. *Answer:* Instead, the church prefers several rites and ordinances as suitable for celebrating experiences of renewal and purification. Among these are laying on of hands; of particular significance is our use of feetwashing [and anointing].

Special Rites for Special Ages

The following section on puberty contains the recommendation of the Annual Conference paper. I have also included the sections on birth and baptism for the purpose of visualizing all three special rites if the Conference decision is to be taken seriously.

Birth-Consecration of Children and Parents. We begin with a practice that has been celebrated in various ways since our beginnings. Often referred to as dedication, babies and parents are presented before the Lord in the presence of the community. Both the gathered community and parents celebrate the miracle of birth in welcoming a precious new life, sometimes in a circle surrounding the parents, children, and set-apart ministers. It is genuinely Brethren to rationalize that what we are about is to be derived from the story of Jesus. We know that the infant Jesus was presented to the Lord in the temple (Luke 2:22). In recent years church parents have been chosen to stand with the parents in the rite of dedication of both parents and infants. Church parents, like godparents in other traditions, may carry out more concretely the promises of support pledged by the entire congregation.

Puberty. This is the time of bar mitzvah, confirmation, or baptism for many Jewish and Christian communities. In discussing ceremonies for the age of puberty, we might think of some ways to relate to the temple experience of Jesus at age twelve. In our history the average age for such ceremony for those who have grown up in the church has moved from the early twenties, a time closer to marriage and serious beginnings in farming or other vocations, to the age of puberty. The 1980 Annual Conference, however, asked the church to consider the following:

> *Recognizing that entry into puberty is a very important time for young people, and that a spiritual awakening and a response to gospel preaching often occurs at this time, we are still left without a ceremony to mark the occasion. Perhaps an investigation into the recovery of the ancient practice*

of the catechumen (those preparing for baptism) would be helpful to us. In this practice, the congregation recognizes with public ceremony those who make a decision for Christ at this age. They would be in a somewhat ambiguous position, neither outside the church nor completely within the church, but certainly within the care of the church and enjoying the benefits of its fellowship, nurture, and, perhaps, the Lord's Supper. They would be entered into a program of preparation and study in anticipation of a later time of baptism.

Baptism. Only a few congregations have adopted modifications of the above recommendation. If the suggestions were tried, the age of baptism would vary. Baptism would come at a time when those baptized would be more responsible and gifted to carry out portions of ministries in the body of Christ. Perhaps cultural influences are not compatible with this proposal. Both our educational systems and cultural expectations are aware that maturity comes earlier than in previous generations. Those who agree with the Annual Conference paper would ask whether any would advise a daughter at such an early age to take on responsibilities that come with marriage. But, again, there are differences between baptism and marriage. I first became concerned about this issue when I surveyed Brethren students at McPherson College. I discovered that some sixty percent resented their early baptisms in which they passively supported the wishes of peers and parents. However, forty percent were quite satisfied with both the reason and the results of their baptisms.

In reviewing historical perspectives, Brethren have shifted back and forth in their views and practices of baptism. They have shifted from a counter-culture stance to a more comfortable relationship with the world; from a discipleship to a soteriological [like getting to heaven] focus; from disciplined *gemeinschaft* (community) to more inclusive views of membership; from feelings of pride or resentment to feelings of good-humored embarrassment in being named Dunkers.

The Love Feast

The love feast has been a high point of our worship and identity and what we believe. Apart from it, Brethren are open to many styles of worship. Without it, however, Brethren may be a people in search of a liturgy.

For more than a century, the Brethren were a house church movement. Due to the need for more space, it was necessary to hold some love feasts in barns. Most of the first meetinghouses were called love feast houses. They were designed with a huge fireplace for preparing the meals for the weekend love feasts. Attics were divided into two dorms, one side for women and the other for men. Often a farm family would invite the young people to stay together with them. Hospitable hosts diligently provided food and lodging for members from distant congregations. The setting and meetings provided a large social gathering for all. At times it attracted rowdy young men who disrupted the meetings, shooting firearms to the skies. But if the sheriff was called, it was by others. The Brethren refused to throw out the rascals. From their experience, they knew that some who heckled and disrupted the meeting would be sitting around the communion tables in the future as the result of the patience and loving acceptance of the Brethren.

In preparing for the love feast, deacons conducted an annual church visit to each home. They asked whether members were still in the faith, still in peace with the church, and willing to labor with the Brethren for an increase of faithfulness. The family was given the opportunity to make suggestions to the church for the common good. If the members were in sufficient harmony, the date for the love feast was announced. All were invited to preaching services on Saturday in preparation for the three- to five-hour love feast beginning on Saturday evening. The weekend concluded with worship on Sunday morning followed by dinner for all.

Martin G. Brumbaugh, Brethren historian and governor of Pennsylvania in the early years of the twentieth century, described the first love feast at Germantown.

> *It is evening now. The old-time tallow-dips are lighted. They gather around a long table, a hymn is sung, and in the silent evening hour, with no witness but God, and curious children, these people begin the observation of the ordinances of God's house on Christmas evening, 1723. The sisters on one side, the brethren on the other, arise and wash one another's feet. Then they eat the Lord's Supper, pass the kiss of charity with the right hand of fellowship, partake of the holy communion, sing a hymn, and go out.* (156)

Today the weekend love feast has been shortened in most congregations. Frequently it is observed on World Communion Sunday and/or Maundy Thursday of Holy Week. In addition to two feasts each year, many congregations have additional bread and cup communion services, similar to those of other Protestants. There were other changes such as the long-time struggle to allow women to break bread with one another instead of receiving it from male elders; allowing grape juice in 1875, which gradually replaced home-brewed wine; changing from double to single mode of washing feet, which may have occurred early at Germantown but was only accepted gradually in adopting practices of far western Brethren in Illinois in the first half of the nineteenth century. Changes in the love feast often dealt with theological issues such as the role of women in worship. (More complete information can be found in Durnbaugh's *Fruit of the Vine*; index item, Love Feast, 667).

Biblical and Theological Foundations

The love feast has been an attempt to dramatize meaningfully the central events of the upper room experience of Jesus with his disciples. It appears to be an attempt to appropriate biblical narratives of the Last Supper. On the American frontier, where neighbors and strangers came to observe, it has been surmised that Brethren provided the passion play for pioneer communities. Previously, when there were more visitors, and even today when there are Christians who are participating for the first time, there has been an effort to explain and interpret basic parts of the love feast.

Theologically speaking, in the love feast, the Brethren have the visible drama of fundamental doctrinal emphases. It has been said that the love feast portrays the inseparable relationship of the two greatest commandments. The feast combines commands to experience a loving response to God's love and to love one another. Johannine epistles are basic: "No one has ever seen God; if we love one another, God lives in us, and his love is perfected in us" (1 John 4:12). "Those who say, 'I love God,' and hate their brothers and sisters, are liars; for those who do not love a brother or sister whom they have seen, cannot love God whom they have not seen" (4:20).

Feetwashing. After the deacon visit, which today is usually a brief period of self-examination, we have the first major part of the love feast named "The Sacrament of Serving Love" in one worship book and "The Symbol of Service" in another. The motif of service is prevalent in the lives and thoughts of Brethren. It is derived from Jesus who strongly stressed to his disciples, who were arguing who might be the greatest, that he was among them as one who serves (Luke 22:24-30). From this text some of us as children were taught that the way to be great is to serve. And Brethren Service initiated many of our church programs such as the one that birthed Heifer Project.

John 13 tells how Jesus washed the feet of his disciples. The chapter is read to prepare for the ritual. When a professor gave Luther's requirements for a sacrament, I raised my hands to say that feetwashing seemed to fit all of them. He immediately replied: "No, it lacks a promise."

My knowledge of the biblical account allowed me to demurely reply, "But Jesus says, 'If you know these things, happy are ye if ye do them' " (John 13:17 KJV). Perhaps more convincingly I mentioned that Saint Bernard, a dominant monk of the thirteenth century, advocated that feetwashing be accepted as one of the holy sacraments.

The text depicts Jesus engaging in a common act of hospitality usually assigned to servants or slaves. It is puzzling that our tradition has not related this rite more often to Paul's command to "contribute to the needs of the saints; extend hospitality to strangers" (Rom. 12:13). In building their houses, many Brethren families in previous generations reserved one bedroom for transients, who were aware that many Brethren homes were places to stop for bed and breakfast.

Another theological emphasis for feetwashing has been derived from Jesus and Peter's conversation about their relationship (see John 13:6-11). The response that not all of the body needs to be washed might have been used by some of us whose mothers insisted that we take a bath before going to love feast. But Jesus pointed out that not all are clean, obviously referring to Judas, whose feet were likewise washed. Thinking of the rite as cleansing has been meaningful for many members. As baptism refers to justification and regeneration, the washing of feet becomes a continuation of cleansing without which believers, like Peter and Judas, would have no part of Jesus. A new forgiveness, a new purification, a new sanctification is always needed. Perhaps the act of cleansing shares similarities with Catholic confession.

The act that symbolizes service also expresses humility. Some can readily wash the feet of others, but are reluctant to have their own feet washed. In doing both, however, one can be opened to the Spirit's way of diminishing the significance of pride. Participation in the rite acknowledges the egalitarian nature of the body of Christ as well as a willingness to respond to the call to adopt the servant role in relation to our friends, our enemies, and our mission to the world.

The act seems to contradict worship in that at times it may appear crude, awkward, and lacking in aesthetic finesse. Yet the washing of feet symbolically represents real-life servant ministries such as changing of bedpans, feeding the hungry, clothing the naked, or binding raw wounds. Some Brethren have been embarrassed to participate in the service in our contemporary culture; others fear that the act fosters pride. Nevertheless, the rite has survived, even revived, in spite of voices judging it to be dying from lack of participants. As I write, feetwashing remains an integral, meaningful part of the total love feast attractive to old and new generations.

The Agape or Fellowship Meal. Often referred to as the Lord's Supper in our tradition, this can be confusing to segments of Christendom for whom the Lord's Supper is the observance of eucharist or communion. Some Brethren would agree that the Lord's Supper includes both the fellowship meal and the bread and cup communion. Others identify the supper to be the entire love feast. Whatever we call it, this fellowship meal remains an important rite, one that portrays our communal theology, and is hopefully a time when our focus is on the last meal Jesus shared with his disciples. Though Brethren often attempt to have a meal similar to that of the disciples, they gave up mutton for beef, which was generally more available in our rural surroundings. However, the modest meal represents more than a legalistic attempt to duplicate literally the biblical accounts. This becomes clear in a statement by Alexander Mack, Jr.: "For Christ did not say that one should recognize His disciples by the feetwashing or the breaking of bread, but He said that by this shall every man [and every woman] know that you are my disciples, that you have love for one another" (Durnbaugh, *Brethren in Colonial America* 6).

For this reason the meal has often been referred to as the symbol of community. The meal represents more than mere togetherness. It is togetherness as a divine gift. W. A. Visser D'Hooft, World Council of Churches general secretary, who gathered with Brethren in Schwarzenau to celebrate the 250th anniversary of the tradition, once told our representative, M. R. Zigler, that Dietrich Bonhoeffer was the theologian for our people. In the following passage from *Life Together*, the famous martyr articulates a theology of community that we strive to celebrate in our love feast.

> *Like the Christian's sanctification, Christian community is a gift of God to which we have no claim. Only God knows the real condition of either our community or our sanctification. What may appear weak and insignificant to us may be great and glorious to God. Just as Christians should not be constantly feeling the pulse of their spiritual life, so too the Christian community has not been given to us to be continually taking its temperature. The more thankfully we daily receive what is given to us, the more assuredly and consistently will community increase and grow from day to day as God pleases. Christian community is not an ideal we have to realize, but rather a reality created by God in Christ in which we may participate. The more clearly we learn to recognize that the ground and strength and promise of all our community is in Jesus Christ alone, the more calmly we learn to think about our community and pray and hope for it.* (38)

I first heard old Brethren speaking of the meal as a messianic banquet before I understood any meaning in what they were saying. Simply, I have learned that a messianic banquet is a kingdom banquet. By grace, the love we experience in community becomes a foretaste of the bond of peace and wish for justice that God wants for all peoples. We are summoned to participate now in coming visions of the kingdom of love, peace, and justice.

Passing the Greeting to Bind the Community. Brethren in most of our history participated in a practice between the meal and communion that is worth considering in defining our beliefs. Only the Old German Baptist Brethren continue to include this as an essential part of their love feasts. One of the elders speaks of *passing the salutation* as he begins a rite of passing the holy kiss, which winds its way around tables until all participants have been so greeted and passed it on to the next brother or sister. The last table of men connects with sisters with a right hand of fellowship. This has been described as *binding the community*. This is the last act to prepare the church for bread and cup communion.

Bread and Cup Communion or Eucharist. Throughout the love feast in the Church of the Brethren, hymns are sung, prayers are offered, silence is observed, scriptural passages are read and interpreted, and confessions and exhortations are offered by the minister and various members of the community. In most love feasts, instead of sitting behind each other in pews, we sit so as to see the faces of our brothers and sisters. In such face-to-face settings, it seems important for Brethren to break bread for one another. And this, no doubt, motivated women to want to participate in the breaking of bread as well, instead of that action being reserved for elders and ministers. The priesthood of all believers and the equality of believers are incarnate in such widespread participation.

This helps us to understand the rationale and ways that Brethren participate in bread and cup communion. In the previous chapter on sacraments, it was stated that the real presence of our Lord is not located exclusively in the bread or wine. A broader discernment of the sacramental presence of Christ's body is in the people whom Paul names the body of Christ. It is this body who breaks bread together. For Brethren, unleavened strips of bread are broken, with a piece broken for another and the person who receives breaking it for the next person. Or smaller strips are placed on a table, which allows two people to hold one end of a piece of bread during a communion prayer. Then they break bread while repeating together versions of textual affirmations of the presence of Christ. This is followed by passing a common cup of wine or juice. More recently, small glasses are distributed and used while repeating meanings of the cup that incarnates the living presence. The participating body meditates on the life, crucifixion, and resurrection of our Lord. Bonhoeffer has written often about the Christ who is between us. Or another way of saying this is to recognize the Spirit of Jesus who blesses and guides our relationships with one another. To quote Bonhoeffer again: "In the sacrament the believer receives the Lord Christ in the body. . . . They [we] receive and meet each other as one meets the Lord, in reverence, humility and joy. They [we] receive each other's blessings as the blessing of the Lord Jesus Christ" (*Life Together* 29).

A Possible Time of Reconciliation. One of the purposes of the deacon's visit was to get right with others before coming to the love feast. This time of reconciliation is certainly supported by Jesus' teachings. He taught us that if in offering a gift at the altar we remember a brother or sister who has something against us, we should leave the altar and first be reconciled—then return and offer our gift.

I'm reminded of a similar story about a student prank in college. Late at night some of my dorm friends and I packed wet snow into waste cans and put them in front of the exit doors of the women's dorm, making it difficult for them to get out in the morning. When the head resident and his wife heard us, he climbed out the window, and scuffling and hostile words ensued. Someone, perhaps his wife, even called the police. What began as a "clever" prank ended in a bad scene.

We had nearly forgotten the event when several weeks later the head resident visited each one of us. He mentioned the forthcoming spring love feast and confessed his regret for his rude actions. Most of us, could think of nothing except to respond somewhat in kind, confessing our responsibility for doing something we later regretted. For most of us, the love feast was not on our calendars. However, he influenced most of us to show up. We found ourselves seated around tables in what became a memorable love feast. It was a model example of reconciliation for us.

Perhaps in our emphasis on getting everything right, some stay away from the feast because they do not believe they are reconciled with one or several members. This is regrettable because there are many stories that reveal how people have gotten right with each other during love feast. So, another story. This one is about Mary Geiger, a wealthy and influential widow who was a moving spirit in the Geiger Memorial Church in Philadelphia. The setting for the story was the first love feast for a black sister who recently had joined the meetinghouse close to her neighborhood. Mary observed that the women were attempting to position themselves so as to not sit by the new convert. She quickly walked over to the new member, put an arm around her, and they walked together to sit at one of the tables. Women looked sideways to glimpse the wealthy saint wash the feet, embrace, and give the holy kiss to the first black sister. This memory is but one love feast story among many in which attitudes were changed and reconciliation pervaded over personal grudges and cultural prejudices.

Anointing

"Are any among you suffering? They should pray. Are any cheerful? They should sing songs of praise. Are any among you sick? They should call for the elders of the church and have them pray over them, anointing them with oil in the name of the Lord. The prayer of faith will save the sick, and the Lord will raise them up; and anyone who has committed sins will be forgiven" (James 5:13-15).

In the biography about her husband, *A Man Called Peter*, Catherine Marshall recounts in a vivid way her reaction to his heart attack. At his bedside she remembers the words from the fifth chapter of James. She sends for oil and, with the Bible before her, administers in her own way this service of love to her husband. The difference between her and most Brethren is that through our heritage we can call for pastors and pillars of the church who will come and administer this simple service.

Perhaps we have cultivated a literal application of the text by stressing that "they should call for the elders" and have too completely left the initiative in the hands of the suffering. For in some communities it is the judgment of those learning about it for the first time that the anointing service is one of the "best kept secrets" of Brethren. As pastor, I remember when a retired couple in our congregation journeyed nearly a thousand miles to stand in line to receive laying on hands of a well-known faith healer. In dealing with cancer, they suffered needlessly from both a long trip and then waiting in line for several hours. When it was nearly their turn, they were stopped and instructed to come back the next afternoon. Disappointed and discouraged they drove back. When I heard about it, I was saddened that anointing was as close for them as their telephone, and we had failed to communicate adequately through our teaching, sermons, and newsletters. All repented and we experienced a meaningful anointing service. This story teaches us that a community of faith should rally in support of the sick and show itself to be in solidarity with them.

Usually the church learns about one who is suffering from illness or hurting in other ways. Oftentimes the condition is more than a minor illness, but the person need not be critically ill to request anointing. Sometimes anointing is requested before surgery. Increasingly it is called for in times of emotional or relational difficulties. Traditionally, two elders administered the anointing; today a pastor and a deacon or another member comes to the patient. The service is simple and can be conducted in a home or hospital, often in the presence of a few intimates or family members. The above passage from James 5 is read. There is an opportunity for confession of sins and of faith, vocally or silently. Sometimes the person will seek reconciliation or express regrets. Another may recall good memories. Some dream about how they will act, perhaps differently, should they recover.

A brief hymn, prayer, or scriptural passage may precede and follow. The time then comes when, with oil on the fingertips, the pastor anoints the person on the forehead three times—for forgiveness of sins, strengthening of faith, and restoration of health to body and mind. Ministers, deacons, and others lay hands on the head of the anointed and offer a prayer. Usually, brief parting words of love and encouragement conclude the service. Along with other attentive acts, this service helps to overcome the alienation that a person who is ill may feel.

Oil has a long history of being used for medicinal purposes in the Greco-Roman world. When Jesus sent out the twelve, Mark reports that "they cast out many demons, and anointed with oil many who were sick and cured them" (6:13). The practice was rooted in both the traditions of Israel and the ministry of Jesus. Early Christians were aware that oil had been used by the Israelites for the consecration of kings (1 Sam. 10:1-9; 16:1-13) and objects used for worship (Exod. 30:25-30). The Eastern Orthodox tradition anoints with oil all five senses, each one seven times, and another seven times in places that need healing. Roman Catholics anoint at the time of baptism. For them one of the seven sacraments has been named extreme unction or anointing, which for centuries has been administered when a person is near death or dying. In the last century, they have recovered the original name—anointing for healing. This has resulted in using it for both healing the sick and in last rites for the dying.

I was surprised to discover that at the Roman Catholic Council of Trent in 1545 they not only suggested healing along with the emphasis on extreme unction, but they also gave the threefold formula adopted by the Brethren more than two centuries later. These formulae provide theological and practical understandings for anointing today.

Forgiveness of Sins. Once the individual has had the opportunity for confession, the first oil is lightly rubbed on the forehead to anoint for the forgiveness of sins. In this the service acknowledges that psychosomatic factors are present. The release of getting things off of one's mind, of genuinely feeling forgiveness from one's sins or deliverance from cruel deeds of others, can abet and aid physical healing. Two examples of anointing as it relates to forgiveness come to mind.

In a visit to a congregation, I was asked by the pastor to join a family in anointing a woman who was physically healthy but suffering from what she believed to be sinful. Her friends, family, and doctor convinced her that she had to have an abortion because of the imminent danger to her life. In thinking of her husband and children, she agreed. But she had developed strong convictions against abortion. The time of confession, the love of those present, the anointing, and asking for forgiveness all helped her to overcome her guilt and to restore the self-esteem of the wonderful person she had been and promised to be.

The second example describes a rare use of anointing. A wonderful grandmother, a widow getting and feeling older, called me when her congregation was temporarily without a pastor. She had become a matriarch to her several children and many grandchildren. Partly her fault, perhaps, but they depended on her to mend their clothes, provide special dishes at their bidding, and take the children for her joy whenever they wished. She was feeling that the time had come when she could no longer do this. She hinted and even honestly shared her concerns, but to no avail. Members of her family responded by saying, "O, Granny, you do not mean this. You are so wonderful and healthy." She was led to do something more dramatic. She decided to call her family together and have an anointing service. In this service, she confessed to all that she was resigning from her office as matriarch of the family. She said that she still loved them but that their patterns must change. There were tears. We sang and family members said prayers of confession. The anointing worked. Her soul and the differences with her family were healed. The last I heard is that the family had, in fact, listened.

Strengthening of Faith. The anointing text in my NRSV Bible is entitled "The Prayer of Faith." The promise is given that "the prayer of faith will save the sick, and the Lord will raise them up" (James 5:15). William Beahm, seminary dean and mentor during my graduate program, suffered from cancer during the last days I knew him. Some friends and Brethren who meant well unfortunately wrote letters and cards with this advice: "Brother William, if you would have enough faith, you will get well." In addition to suffering terrible pain, he shared that he suffered from insinuations that he lacked faith. Faith healing movements have often given the same impression; by mistakenly offering health panaceas to all, they make a lord of health. The mystery of how God's mercy will be revealed to us in sickness or in health is in God's hands. Christ exemplified this in his suffering when he prayed that the cup of suffering might be removed. But he added to the prayer: "Yet, not my will but yours be done" (Luke 22:42).

Thus, we offer the second anointing of oil for strengthening the faith. This anointing may help to increase a person's strength for what lies ahead if healing does not take place. Most physicians appreciate that the anointing service often relaxes a person for a serious operation and/or prepares one to live through final days with love ones. This provides an atmosphere for tasting resurrection faith.

It is remarkable that I have experienced only one physician who seriously questioned our anointing service. He observed that his clients seemed to rest so peacefully after an anointing that they were not prepared for the necessity to fight zealously to stay alive. This second anointing for strengthening of faith can perhaps alleviate this concern.

Restoration of Health. The third anointing on the forehead followed by prayers of faith for the restoration of health imparts a sense of peace, mystery, and hopeful expectancy. The cherished rite is derived from Genesis and Christian emphases that life is sacred and good. It is wonderful when people who are ill in body and spirit are restored to doing the things they love to do for others and themselves. A popular booklet, *Anointing for Healing* by Warren D. Bowman, circulated widely in the last half of the twentieth century. More than thirteen thousand copies were printed. The pamphlet reveals widespread use of and appreciation for anointing among Brethren. His writing is full of testimonies of successful healings related to the rite. But he also affirms the role of the medical profession. The booklet lists positive statements by doctors about the contributions to health offered by communities of faith. A quote from Rufus Bowman, former president of Bethany Seminary, gives what might be a typical Brethren rationale for the service: "If anointing gets the patient in a better mental attitude and helps to get the patient right with others, self, and God, it is bound to have a healing effect upon one's body" (20).

Another story may help us gain some understanding of several issues often present in the practice of anointing. The fetus of a young couple was well developed and examinations indicated the infant would be born with major deformities. The doctor definitely recommended abortion. The couple refused and instead called for an anointing service in the presence of loved ones. On the birth day, behold, the infant boy appeared and was judged to be perfectly and beautifully normal. The story for our purposes does not end here. A few weeks later, I received a church newsletter that contained a note of thankfulness from the parents. I recall that the couple was indeed bubbling with praise and thanksgiving. Yet, they wanted others to know that they were not saintly people and could not guarantee that their actions and prayers would achieve the same results for others. They had known others who faced decisions similar to theirs and had responded prayerfully as well, but the outcome was different. They emphasized that they did not want to give the impression that they were better Christians.

What About Miracles?

A positive outcome in a very difficult situation can seem unbelievable, even miraculous, although the doctor is able to explain everything. As a pastor I ministered to a sister suffering from cancer with symptoms confirmed by X-rays. Following an anointing service, the physician was perplexed when he could not find any evidence of cancer. Several times I have been close enough to such situations that we might call miracles as to doubt my skepticism. Some solve the issue by believing in miracles.

There are some folks who refuse to accept anything as a miracle if it can be explained. For example, the "miracle" story of Jesus feeding the five thousand has been explained that Jesus in his sharing inspired others to share of what they had. Then there is the interesting story about two frogs at the bottom of a creek struggling without success to remove a large rock. Along comes a fisherman who kicks it with his boots. We can easily understand that to the two frogs this was a miracle.

In a class with theologian William Hordern, I copied from the chalk board his definition of a miracle: "A miracle is a particular intensification of the divine action of such degree and in such fashion that those in whose presence it occurs are obliged to cry God." If a cancer disappears in an unusual way without any explanation, it is a miracle. Hordern would agree. He also would regard it to be a miracle if a skillful surgeon removed a cancer so as to completely eliminate it. The miraculous is what leads us to discern the presence of the Spirit, even if it's considered to be a natural phenomenon. For example, a beautiful sunset is truly a miracle even though scientists can explain every aspect of the changing panoramic skyscape. And we know that quantum physicists have discovered the reality of the unpredictable.

How Do We Tell?

Brethren have so many wonderful stories to tell about the anointing service, yet others have observed that we do not talk about it. We do not advertise it. Members of the larger community often are not informed of the nature and availability of the anointing service. Perhaps we want to mimic Jesus who, after he healed, commanded the blessed to say nothing to anyone (Matt. 8:4). Though Jesus often said not to tell others, his disciples related the good news of the healings of Jesus. Historians have judged that this stance of Christians in the first centuries attributed to the spectacular growth of Christianity.

Brethren, however, have often been reluctant to tell their stories because they do not want others to think that they are better than others, or favorites of God. As Sermon on the Mount people, we believe that God sends blessings, like the rain, on the just and unjust. The testimony of the couple above about the miraculous birth of their son perhaps explains why Brethren who are disappointed in the crude commercialism and promotion of television healers are often reluctant to share their stories.

Private or Public Uses?

In recent decades, private and public uses of anointing have increased. In addition to historic uses, pastors have been encouraged to inform parishioners about a variety of contemporary uses. For example, anointing can express communal concern and ministry when someone has been injured, is experiencing emotional illness, coping with depression or disillusionment, preparing to make a weighty decision, weathering a marital separation or divorce, is worried after the loss of a job, and or where there are fractures in family, church, or work situations.

Public use of anointing is found increasingly in corporate worship in many congregations, at conferences, retreats, and camps. People are invited to a time of prayer and anointing. In large gatherings there are often various "stations" to which people can go to be anointed. Sometimes people are asked to anoint one another. Public anointing has been introduced for a variety of purposes. A traditional anointing for healing might take place with the entire congregation. For example, people might be invited to be anointed for the strength of faith to respond in Christlike ways, as one congregation did following the outbreak of war. After a sermon, people might be anointed for personal transformation. In reading the Old Testament, some Brethren have discovered uses of anointing for consecration of members for specific tasks and mission. Whenever there is any kind of brokenness at retreats, camps, conferences, or special times in the local congregation, anointing can be used to call everyone together to new life in Christ.

Hopefully, increasing public use will not lead to ignoring the intimate times of confessions, reconciliation, commitment, prayers, and faith that have been fruitful in small gatherings with loved ones and beloved representatives of a community of faith.

Chapter 10

New Testament Symbols
Keeping the love commandments

If you love me, you will keep my commandments.
—John 14:15

There is a cluster of practices, often symbolic for Brethren, that generally have not been learned from sermons or in Sunday school. For example, whether to swear an oath or join a lodge was more likely discussed as Brethren sat around tables or learned from experiences of family members and friends. I have referred to these practices as *adiaphora*, a word borrowed from the Protestant Reformation that referred to practices not considered to be as important as others. In addition to major doctrinal themes, Luther and other reformers had to deal with issues such as how much of the liturgy of the mass do you keep and how much of it do you change or throw out. For a peasant people simply desiring to be a New Testament church, the question became what commandments do we keep, and what do they mean?

We have noted that a nineteenth-century Brethren's Card modestly boasted to be little children who ". . . teach all of the doctrines of Christ, peace, love, unity, faith and works." Obviously, the fourth one comes from James: "So faith by itself, if it has no works, is dead" (2:17). Biblical commentators note that James is somewhat at odds with other epistle writers who maintain we are saved by grace through faith, not by our deeds. Most Brethren would agree with our forebears and those who cite James in advocating desirable moral imperatives of Christian identity for communities of faith. Although Luther had problems with James, calling the book "an epistle of straw," he did not reject the book in his exegetical works. He agreed that James did say some good things. Pietist leaders, who led what has been called a second reformation, loved to quote Luther's affirmation that true faith becomes very busy and active in love. Brethren have believed this.

Yet, our tradition has often seemed to many to be guilty of a moralism that makes a god of goodness instead of living the love of God. The tendencies of a legalism that requires strict rules of conformity to all of the commandments have been mellowed by our inheritance of a love theology of Radical Pietism. Jesus' love for us and our love for Jesus engender our desire to keep his commandments. Our forebears expanded this to address commandments other than those spoken by Jesus. Most of the following commandments reflect the Spirit of Jesus in pointing to lifestyles of faith and love. Perhaps, like Tillich, we can call them symbols, if indeed they point beyond themselves to expressions of basic teachings and beliefs of Jesus and his way. We consider them in a book on theology because they probably represent better what Brethren believe and who we are in our daily walk than detailed doctrinal statements.

Perhaps readers have wondered about the soft crosses that decorate this chapter. Their meaning may embody mysteries and memories of Bethany Theological Seminary. A few students circulated an overground paper representing the soft cross. They likely feared that our participation in commandments considered in this chapter are pale and squashy compared with the cross at Calvary. Our proud keeping of commandments may resemble soothing effects of a beautiful golden cross. For Anabaptists the cross is a manifestation of God's way of meeting evil in the world. Thus, the cross is not every backache we have, but the price we may pay for our nonconformity to this violent world.

Oaths or Yes and No

"Above all, my beloved, do not swear, either by heaven or by earth or by any other oath, but let your "Yes" be yes and your "No" be no, so that you may not fall under condemnation (James 5:12).

"James forbids oaths, because he desires a community of solidarity based on mutual trust. Such trust is possible only where speech is simple and unadorned with false religiosity" (*New Interpreter's Bible*, Vol. XII, 222).

"Again, you have heard that it was said to those of ancient times, "You shall not swear falsely, but carry out the vows you have made to the Lord." But I say to you, Do not swear at all, either by heaven, for it is the throne of God, or by the earth, for it is his footstool, or by Jerusalem, for it is the city of the great King. And do not swear by your head, for you cannot make one hair white or black. Let your word be "Yes, Yes" or "No, No"; anything more than this comes from the evil one (Matt. 5:33-37).

An interesting essay by Gordon Hoffert reflects on his experience as a seventeen-year-old preparing to depart for Germany as an exchange student. Applying for a passport, he found himself alone face to face with an official whose first words rang in his ear: "Do you swear . . . ?"

"Being alone it would have been easy not to force the issue. But I had just learned about my religious heritage. After the oath was read, I expressed my loyalty to my country. But did I make a big deal about saying 'affirm' instead of 'swear'!"

In reflecting on this experience, Gordon concludes: "I unknowingly revealed the first glimmer of my own sectarianism."

Gordon's story could be duplicated in testimonies of a myriad Brethren. One of my own stories fails to equal the good example of my student. I also was standing in a crowded line processing passports. Finally, when it was my turn, I failed to respond quickly like everyone else. In holding up the line, I perceived the official was disgusted with me. So I quickly explained: "I am sorry but I belong to a stupid church that teaches us not to hold up our arm to swear an oath or place our hands to swear on the book that teaches us not to swear." The only redemptive ingredient in this story is that when I looked at her face, she was smiling.

Most Brethren realize with Jesus that oaths are integral to public life. In both Gentile and Jewish worlds, an oath invoked one of many gods or Yahweh to guarantee the truth of what was said or to punish the one taking the oath if what they said was not true. For the tradition of the peace churches, nonswearing of oaths calls attention to emphases of our Lord.

Subverting Truth by Protecting Lies

In his work on discipleship, Dietrich Bonhoeffer maintains that Jesus rejects oaths because of his concern for complete truthfulness: The oath is proof of the existence of lies in the world.

> *If human beings could not lie, oaths would not be necessary. Thus an oath is meant to be a barrier against lying. But in providing this, it also encourages lying, for whenever an oath claims final truthfulness for itself, then at the same time room is also given for lying to take place. . . . Old Testament law uses oaths to reject lying. But Jesus rejects lying by prohibiting oaths.* (Discipleship 129)

In interpreting the Sermon on the Mount, Bonhoeffer concludes that when oaths are prohibited, it is clear that the goal is to be truthful. "The command of complete truthfulness is only another way of expressing the total claim of discipleship" (131). In the world of politics and secret activities of governments, it is obvious that lying is common and accepted as necessary. In public life lying is generally only a crime when one has sworn an oath in an American court.

Bonhoeffer does grant that in civil and personal affairs, there may be exceptions to his strong position. In a later book, *Ethics,* which he wrote when engaged in conspiracy activities against Hitler, he argues how a lie might retain truthful relationships with a neighbor. Such would be the case if a Nazi tracker knocked on the door and asked for the location of one hidden in your house, who, if found would be murdered.

Loyalty Oaths

Early Christians, who proclaimed Jesus, not Caesar, to be Lord, were willing to die rather than burn incense to Caesar. Similarly, some members of peace churches have refused to take an oath of allegiance to totalitarian-like military forces that give orders from the top down. Bonhoeffer believed loyalty oaths to be dangerous. Such oaths mean that Christians would not be able to control their future or the future of those to whom they are bound after loyalty is sworn (130). Generally, the peace church tradition advocates loyalty to a civil religion that speaks of the nation under God. But they reject a civil religion that regards the nation to be God. Whenever there is a conflict between the love commandments of Jesus and commands of the state, the ultimate allegiance belongs to Jesus and his way.

Simple Integrity

The simple, positive command "Let your 'Yes' be yes" signals that integrity is basic in our tradition. Glen Stassen's book, *Just Peacemaking: Transforming Initiatives for Justice and Peace,* develops fascinating triadic teachings of Jesus' commandments in the Sermon on the Mount. Such fits the discourse about oath-taking. First, Jesus refers to the traditional uses of oath-taking in ancient times. Second, he indicates how complicated it has become to distinguish between swearing by heaven, by earth, by the holy city, or one's head. Third, after referring to the variations and problems of swearing, Jesus gives an alternative that is simple, practical, and a witness to truthfulness and integrity (44-45).

From their lifestyle of simplicity, early Quaker merchants in Great Britain were weary of the bickering and bartering that had existed for centuries in the exchange of goods. So they revolutionized ways of doing business that were widely accepted by others. Instead of lying about the price in order to engage in bartering, they fixed a price they judged to be fair. In this way the purchase was simplified as all quickly knew the price that Quakers considered to be right.

Many stories from Brethren life have evolved from common assumptions about the integrity of the members. As a pastor in Iowa, I often heard the favorite line "a Dunker's word is as good as his bond." Stories abounded about a brother or sister who received credit on purchases without needing to write it down. It was said: "If a Dunker promised something, you could be certain that it would be done. If they borrowed or owed money, you would be confident it would be paid." In our family my brother was saved from doing time in jail due to the reputable integrity of our father. He made the mistake of pressing his foot to the floorboard of his souped-up little Ford, when he noticed a police car in his rearview mirror. The attempt to avoid being caught led to a dangerous chase around curves and through alleys, but he was eventually pulled over by an extremely angry policeman. My brother was fated to get the book. After questioning and discovering who he was, however, the officer mellowed and concluded that any one who was a son of Brother Harlow could not be as bad as he thought. So he let him go.

A popular Brethren folk song, words and music by Andy Murray, focuses on the integrity and truthfulness of a previous generation of Brethren characters. It is a treasure worth passing on, and I share portions here:

Grandaddy was a farmer
I guess he looked funny to some
With his big black hat and his plain cut coat
But he didn't look funny to his grandson.

He was stern and kind and strong and gentle
About the wisest man alive
At least that's the way he looked to a little boy
Who'd just turned five.

Grandaddy used to take me
When he'd haul his grain to town.
Something that always happened there
Made me think that he was quite renowned.
When we'd pull up close to the millhouse,
The miller would look out
As soon as he would see that it was Grandaddy Cyrus, you could
Always hear him shout

Chorus
He's a full measure man
He won't tell you a lie
When Cyrus rolls his wagon to the scales
Just wave him right on by
Level on the level, signed with a shake of a hand.
Unaffected, well connected
Simple, honest man.

I've often wondered if Grandaddy
Stood at the pearly gates
And Gabriel turned and said to St. Peter
We don't have to make this Dunkard wait
We can let old Cyrus walk on in
We don't have to check him out
If he says his name is down in the book
It's there without a doubt.

—Used by permission of Andy Murray

Secret Societies

In seven annual meetings beginning in 1804 and ending in 1862, Brethren revealed their prejudices about Freemasonry, Odd Fellows, Sons of Temperance, and other secret orders by ruling against joining such lodges. No doubt this came about because increasing numbers of members were joining lodges. Anti-lodge sentiments were also part of other nineteenth-century Protestant communions. Serving as a visiting theologian at Berea College in Kentucky, I noticed that this church college was established with strong convictions against slavery, lodges, and denominations. Neighboring churches and lodges in Kentucky had opposed abolitionist and social concerns that Berea College had imbibed from the New Measure Revivalism led by Charles Finney. Anti-lodge sentiments are also shared by Missouri Synod Lutherans.

> *The following anti-lodge decision was made in 1804, nearly a century after our birth: "Though we are not sufficiently acquainted with this (secret) association to judge in the case, still there are revealed many trifling things, frivolities and unfruitful works, so that it is considered to be highly improper for brethren to be members in their association, or to have fellowship with their works."* (Henry Kurtz, *The Brethren's Encyclopedia* 115)

Because Brethren lacked knowledge of lodges and there was a lack of similar organizations in the scriptures, our forebears searched the scriptures to find proof texts to support their decision.

Secrecy

"Then the high priest questioned Jesus about his disciples and his teaching. Jesus answered, 'I have said nothing in secret' " (John 18:19-20). Since oaths have been used to secure promises of secrecy, it may explain why Brethren were attracted to Jesus' claim that he said nothing in secret. The refusal to hide what we do and believe often signifies our integrity. I have brothers who are members of lodges, and I have attempted to chide them somewhat seriously about their membership. I have inquired why they have taken vows to something they cannot share with a blood brother like me. With tongue in cheek, I have boasted that there was nothing I needed to hide from them in my active membership in the church, yet I have confessed that what I hinted about the church is not entirely true. My most informed brother countered that if I would read and do a bit of research, it would be easy for me to find out anything I wanted to know. In today's environment, it is likely that secrecy in congregations and lodges are a trifle compared to the pervasive lying and secret activity claimed necessary by the Federal Bureau of Investigation and Central Intelligence Agency.

A Separate People

"Do not be mismatched with unbelievers. For what partnership is there between righteousness and lawlessness" (2 Cor. 6:14). Christians who were named to be temples of the living God are to be separate from those in temples of idols (2 Cor. 6:16-17). Brethren also quoted Ephesians 5:6-11, a passage that calls us to be children of light in all that is good and right and true. We are to have no part in the unfruitful works of darkness. In other passages, however, Paul approves marriage to unbelievers (1 Cor. 7:12-16). He also allows Christians to accept an invitation to dinner from an unbeliever (1 Cor. 10:27). It appears that in considering verses quoted by both sides, we might understand better the saying of a second-century apologist to the ruler Diognetus. The unknown Christian has frequently been quoted by Brethren in discerning that "Christians are in the world but not of it."

Sociological Factors

At Ocean Grove, New Jersey, in 1954, Annual Conference passed a paper entitled "Membership in Secret Societies." The committee discovered that "only a small percentage of our members are involved in secret societies." This means that lodge membership is probably a problem for only a few congregations. Where lodge membership affects a member's loyalty to the church, it was recommended that the church again state its convictions about oaths. The committee added that supreme claims of fraternities, social, and professional organizations should likewise be brought to the attention of members. If membership in a lodge involves compromise with standards, ideals, and mission of the church, it is recommended that the church seek counsel from leaders in the district. Otherwise, when members participate in secret societies, the committee "recommends churches hold them in loving fellowship." At the same time, church members are advised to seek to make the church so vital and its fellowship so genuine for all members that none will feel the need for associations such as those offered by the fraternal orders.

When we listen to brothers and sisters who are members of lodges, we learn that qualifications for membership often resemble Brethren qualities of outstanding character, good morals, good ethics, and belief in a supreme being. Likewise, lodges have service ministries, such as paying medical expenses and providing beautiful hospitals for families of victims who have been seriously burned. Lodge organizations give millions of dollars to charities that often resemble those we support.

I have reached this understanding through a small group Bible study in one of our congregations. In our discussion I mentioned that perhaps Brethren have cherished the ties that bind us together so much that we want the church to be the most important association of our lives. I added that Brethren may have been too fearful of jealousies resulting from divided loyalties. After an extensive discussion, one of the members shared that he belonged to the Masonic order. As the result of our discussion, he asked the group to observe his participation in the life of the church and his allegiance to Jesus Christ. He requested that they report to him if it ever appeared that his devotion to Jesus and the church was no longer the primary allegiance of his life.

That session validated my sociological hunch. As a young pastor shepherding a sizable youth group, I influenced two members who were considering membership in the youth section of a lodge. My motives were likely selfish, however, when I reasoned that one more allegiance added to many other activities in their lives would further complicate their lives and perhaps lessen their vital relationships with Christ and the church.

These experiences have led me to devise a theological statement that fits the decision of Annual Conference. It may also be considered a sociological statement. Although Brethren have never articulated their belief this concisely, my statement is based on my feeling about and understanding of the familial fellowship, the caring and sharing marks of our "fraternity," as it used to be called. I realize that my statement could be used to figuratively build walls that hinder mission and wonderful relationships with others, isolating ourselves from the good, beautiful, and true beyond our circles. But this is my statement: *The community that comes from Jesus is the primary paradigmatic community to embody God's intention for humanity.*

Historically, Brethren jealousy and sincere concerns have caused reluctance in allowing a brother or sister to have another primary social allegiance.

Non-Litigation

The church regards the methodology in Matthew 18:15-22 as the way to settle disputes. One should first confront the brother, then others, and if necessary the entire church. In this context Brethren stress the principle of non-litigation expressed by Paul in 1 Corinthians 6:1-7.

In this passage Paul is responding to lawsuits he observed at Corinth. He offers better and more practical advice to believers who were going to court against other believers before unbelieving judges. In the Greco-Roman world, only the wealthy initiated civil suits in courts. The body of Christ at Corinth had few such members. Writing to believers, Paul stresses that despised, worldly judges are not aware of how Christians should relate to one another. It is preferable to have out-of-court judgment of Christians who live and conduct themselves differently from the world. He envisions that believers will form part of the heavenly court in the final judgment.

From their views of the church, Brethren were predisposed to follow Paul's advice. Respected and reconciling members were chosen to be deacons. In their rural settings, deacons helped resolve disputed property lines between two members. Elders were chosen to settle disputes in neighboring congregations. Also, for long periods of our history, the church maintained prejudices against members becoming lawyers. In recent years a few Brethren lawyers have become mediators. Instead of having two lawyers, one representing each side, mediation involves one lawyer, or mediator, who serves both sides. He or she strives to achieve an agreement in which there is a win-win conclusion, which replaces the usual win-lose decision required in civil courts.

In discussing patience as a fruit of the Spirit, I mentioned the way my father dealt with Mr. Meeker, a neighbor who was chastising and chasing kids from our ball diamond. Against our wishes and complaints, my deacon father refused to keep the diamond adjacent to Mr. Meeker's property. After explaining our neighbor's propensity to boss other people around, he made us accompany him to move the diamond in order to retain relationships with Mr. Meeker and his family. I later learned that my father was well aware of Sermon on the Mount admonitions to turn the other cheek and go the second mile. Brethren sought to find nonviolent ways to solve disputes in their communities and in the church.

Mennonites seem to study biblically derived practices of our heritage more than Brethren. I recall a few of their conclusions from a weekend conference on litigation. They recommended that as individuals and congregations we remain faithful to Paul's advice to avoid lawsuits. They also encourage and provide leadership for the practice of mediation. In this gathering, however, they did discuss the current massive use of lawsuits and granted that there might be occasion when it would be necessary to sue an insurance company for funds paid for and promised in a policy. Or it might be acceptable to join a lawsuit to help the poor defend themselves from unjust practices, such as dumping poisonous chemical waste close to their neighborhoods. But in addition, in a society of many conflicts, multitudes of lawsuits, and financial incentives to sue "at the drop of the hat," it is good to have traditions that emphasize suffering servanthood and compassionate and forgiving responses, along with biblical emphases on the sin of greed.

The Holy Kiss

Caricatures of literalistic, simple folk may describe Brethren who, when they find anything commanded in the New Testament, are quick to demand, "Do it!" This could apply to the command "Greet one another with a holy kiss" (1 Cor. 16:20; 2 Cor. 13:12; 1 Thess. 5:26). In 1 Peter 5:14, "the kiss of love" is substituted for the "holy kiss." In the confines of early rural life, the holy kiss was natural whenever members met. When a brother met a sister, a warm handshake was extended. The practice was a natural greeting in a church that regarded *koinonia* (fellowship) to be an essential mark of the church. Their egalitarian views emphasized that the greeting was to be extended to all members, not just those whom one knew and liked.

It is interesting how many of our symbolic practices were present in the apostolic church. Stephen Benko, in his book *Pagan Rome and the Early Christians,* devotes a major chapter to the holy kiss. He points out cultural differences of the kiss. In some cultures it could be to rub noses or breathe into nostrils. He reminds us that God kisses humankind in the creation story. In European, especially Russian, culture there are three alternating kisses on the cheek. Benko reminds us that the noun kiss is derived from Greek *philema,* a verb "to love." Brethren practices have inherited rules from the early church. For example, in apostolic times there were widespread rumors of Christians being marked by lust and inappropriate sexual behavior. For this reason both the apostolic church and the early Brethren ruled that men kiss men and women kiss women. And kissing a second time was forbidden.

The author refers to Justin Martyr who, in the middle of the second century, recommended the kiss before the eucharistic service. In addition, the kiss was important in liturgies for ordination and before or after a baptism. If one can accept formal liturgical expressions of the kiss for Brethren, such was beautifully described in an older periodical.

> *We meet [kissing] in baptism our brother [or sister] for the first time upon the heavenly road, as a member of the body of Christ . . . in feet washing we show by the kiss, that love prompts us to perform this lowly service; . . . in establishing a deacon, a teacher, etc., we salute a brother or sister for the first time in that capacity, and show our willingness, in laying on a burden, also to help in bearing it.* (Monthly Gospel Visitor, 1852)

The practice of exchanging a kiss survives as a part of the feetwashing service. To a great degree the kiss has been replaced by a friendly handclasp or a holy hug. The warm greetings of members to new members remain a legacy to the spirit of the practice of the holy kiss.

Covered and Uncovered Heads

Because there are biblical references to the posture of kneeling in prayer, Brethren often assumed this position. In recent decades kneeling has been used on special occasions and observed more regularly in plain congregations. Likewise, it is logical that the Brethren followed the instructions of Paul that in prophesying or praying a man disgraces his head with something on it and a woman disgraces her head if unveiled (1 Cor. 11:3-5). For more than a century, sisters in our tradition wore special caps in simple styles. When many women began wearing them only at church, they were named prayer coverings and were related to corporate worship. Our tradition is not alone. There are many cathedrals, basilica, and other church buildings where women are required to have their heads covered. In some cultures, especially Christian ones, men don their hats from customs and feelings of reverence.

In 1 Corinthians 11, Paul is dealing with one of the many divisive issues at Corinth. There were women who were not covering their heads. Paul introduces his advice with the headship passages that tell the Corinthians that Christ is head of the man, the husband head of his wife, and God the head of Christ. In another chapter (1 Cor. 14), Paul advises the same members that God is not a god of confusion, but of peace. This could mean that here Paul is more interested in order than in authority. The best interpretation I have read of the prayer veil is by Graydon Snyder and Kenneth Shaffer in *Texts in Transit II*. Their thorough exegesis concludes that "it is an error to suppose that submission destroys equality." Our tradition has believed that we should compare a passage with other passages as much as possible with the mind of Christ. When James and John wanted to sit side by side in the kingdom, Jesus taught them how to be great—be a servant and a slave to all (Mark 10:35-45). Likewise, the household commandments written to the Ephesians begin by telling all to "be subject to one another out of reverence for Christ" (5:21). And in the same 1 Corinthians 11, after Paul has given instructions about the prayer veil, he uses the expression "in the Lord" to declare that "woman is not independent of man or man independent of woman. For just as woman came from man, so man comes through woman; but all things come from God" (11:11-12). This approaches the equality expressed by Paul's declaration that ". . . there is no longer male and female, for all of you are one in Christ Jesus" (Gal. 3:28).

In responding to the texts, it has been interesting to listen to opinions of our sisters and brothers. If Brethren were to canonize saints of the twentieth century, one of the first would likely be Anna Mow. Sister Anna attended our class at Bethany when we were discussing the prayer covering. She still wore one when she was with other sisters who did. However, she chuckled when stating that it doesn't cover much. "In fact," she said, "the Apostle Paul would probably not recognize it if he came back." More seriously, she explained how in Paul's time it was prostitutes who remained unveiled. Paul was attempting to foster unity in the church and respect by those outside the church.

In Bible study sessions with sisters who wore the covering, I would often ask them why. Most responded by talking about reverence. When they put on the prayer veil, they said they had a feeling of reverence, of getting ready to worship.

Henry Kurtz, who compiled the first extensive list of Annual Meeting minutes, often added personal opinions and recommendations in small print. After writing the response to the query that advised that both "married or unmarried women. . . . should have a covering on their heads (besides their own hair)," he wrote "In cases like the present, which concern the female portion of the church, would it be out of the way or contrary to the gospel to appoint a committee of elderly sisters (perhaps with an aged brother elder) to consider such questions and report thereon? It would seem to be consistent with the principles of equality, see Gal. 3:28, and their verdict would perhaps have more weight with their younger sisters" (*Brethren's Encyclopedia* 60).

Larry Dentler wrote an excellent research paper on the prayer covering entitled: "What the Brothers Told the Sisters About the Prayer Covering." He read many articles written primarily by men, and he interviewed nine sisters at North Liberty Church (Indiana). In addition to rationales from reverence and loyalty to biblical and heritage practices, which he named "the neutral track," he cites prominent leaders in our history who advocate "the authority track" and others who represent "the submission track." He reports that their essays were almost equally divided before 1926 when the Conference decision mollified strict dress requirements.

The authority track was advocated by S. Z. Sharp, an early educator, influential in founding some of our academies and colleges. In his *Gospel Messenger* article (1896), Sharp relates the experience of meeting with nearly a hundred people who studied Greek, along with other proponents who held the authority view. Sharp supported this view by referring to 1 Corinthians 11:10, which reads, ". . . a woman ought to have a symbol of authority on her head, because of the angels." The study group agreed that the Greek word in the text, *exousian,* often translated as "veil," would better be translated as a "sign of authority." The authority track, according to Dentler, believes the prayer covering symbolizes woman's authority to pray directly to God through Christ. This sign of the work of Christ restores woman to the position she occupied before the fall and leaves her in the original equality to man. Dentler discovered that many others, such as A. C. Wieand and Graydon Snyder, had similar views. In an article in *The Christian Century,* March 15, 1972, Robin Scroggs, a United Church of Christ biblical scholar, writes:

Verse 10 claims that the head covering is symbolic of the women's authority to lead the worship, and this right is then grounded in the following verses which affirm the equality of women in the eschatological community in the Lord and from God.

Dentler traced *the submission track* to Peter Nead's *Theological Writings* (1866), which remain a favorite source for beliefs of the Old German Baptist Brethren. His work sets the tone for interpreters of this track. Nead's position, probably more accepted in the nineteenth century, interprets the prayer covering as symbolizing the woman's submission to man. In the views of Nead and others, women must accept the headship order as given by Paul. She may pray directly to God through Christ if, and only if, she wears the prayer covering as a sign of her acceptance of her submission to man. In Christ she is restored spiritually, but in her Christian walk, she remains subject to man in accordance with divine order.

In a 1971 *Brethren Revival Fellowship Witness* article, James Myer writes that "Christian women must recognize that the head of the woman is the man." And in the article "Prayer Veil" (*The Brethren Encyclopedia*) by Harold Martin, Paul is quoted as saying "that women are to be submissive to the leadership of men, and veiling the head is a sign of the subjection of women to that order of leadership." Since Paul says that a woman's life is marked by prayer, "the veil is a symbol of prayer and submission."

I have been impressed that in recent years wearing or not wearing the veil has not been a matter of controversy. In most congregations and at Conferences, there seem to be feelings of respect and acceptance of each other whether veiled or unveiled. I remember a transition period for some who gave up the traditional covering but still felt that they should wear hats. As a boy I experienced how difficult it was in church to see what was happening up front because the sisters were wearing large, fancy hats. On one vacation trip in the East, my father, as usual, looked up one of our meetinghouses every Sunday morning. I remember one church where I was awestruck by the unity and simplicity of the veiled heads of all the women. I could see! I must confess that I liked them because my mother liked them and explained their use to me, though she quit wearing her covering when she was nearly the only one left who did.

The Order of Dress

"Do not be conformed to this world, but be transformed by the renewing of your minds, so that you may discern what is the will of God—what is good and acceptable and perfect" (Rom. 12:2).

Dress has been important—apparently so, for it takes up five large pages in *The Brethren Encyclopedia*. The manner of dress was not a main issue for Brethren in Europe or in colonial America. As refugees and pioneers on the frontier, simple attire was a necessity, a fact of life. They identified with the poor. Prescribed dress according to an order emerged in the nineteenth century. Emphases on simplicity were retained as uniformity increased. When Peter Nead, who was destined to be a leading voice of conservatives, first entered the church, he kept a somewhat stylish wardrobe, including a tall white hat that identified clergy. Although he was not disciplined, he was taken on a walk behind the barn by Brother Benjamin Bowman, who shared with him how much he was appreciated and presented him with a low-crown, black broad brim. It has been reported that Bowman said something like this: "Brother Nead, Brethren love you and would be pleased if you wear what is more in harmony with the humble profession you have made." Nead accepted the Brethren style of discipline and was even more admired.

It has been interesting to discover the rationale for the order of the garb. As I traveled in the church, I asked both those in the order and others to name symbolic meanings of plain dress. At times practices have been derived from cultural currents more than from obvious commandments of the New Testament. Instead of relying on theological and biblical proof texts and writings, I have attempted to discern convictions from conversations with brothers and sisters.

Simplicity of Lifestyles. I had an interesting conversation with a brother who was raised in a home that provided expensive clothing. Upon his conversion, he was challenged because he abandoned "simplicity" in the purchasing of expensive plain clothing. Since then, he says his life has been simplified in numbers and lower budgets and said that his friend could not fathom what his wardrobe was like before his conversion. More important, his lifestyle is less cluttered by not having to worry about and plan what he wears.

Our historians are aware that colonial Brethren dressed simply, for the most part, because they had no other choice. Today, we are seduced by consumerism, which leads us to keep buying clothes so that we have far more than we need. May our tradition inspire us to defy prevalent seductions of consumerism. Through our simplicity, may we also become more mindful of conditions in sweatshops. Amid complicated, busy, and multi-committed lives, our heritage symbols of simplicity may inspire us to focus more singularly on the Lord of Lords.

Priesthood of All Believers. A theologically informed defender of the order talked about clergy in other traditions who wear special garb that identifies who they are. He shared what I have learned from clergy who offer a rationale for the clerical garb. The answer has consistently been that their dress witnesses to being set apart for special ministries in the church. In this way they are part of a long and interesting history. One brother felt that to be a good explanation, for in our tradition all Christians are set apart for special witness and life for Christ. The special order expresses the priesthood of all believers.

Identity and Unity. Old German Baptist Brethren have responded that the garb identifies who they are to others and provides a sense of unity and equality in their community of faith. I have wondered whether on the American frontier, when Brethren were scattered in distant communities, if they were glad to have a symbol of identity. It may not be as peculiar as we think. Nurses, soldiers, athletic teams, the Amish, employees of corporations, and school children in Japan all wear clothing that identifies who they are— some with pride, some with resentment.

Witness and Testimony. Frequent responses have indicated that when you are identified so clearly, it influences your behavior in some situations where you might otherwise behave badly. Clergy often testify that in displaying their identity they are more approachable for those who are hurting. Some sense that simple styles constitute a similar witness to their faith.

Nonconformity. The text cited above from Romans 12 suggests that nonconformity is the reason given for the order more than any other virtue. Some sisters have shared how they had to dress differently after baptism and this helped them realize how being Christian should lead to being different about more important things. Others testify that the same experience led them to want to dress like other youth in the church whom they admired. My testimony is that to observe and learn about this stance helps me to understand and aspire to nonconformity in important personal and social issues that come from being a follower of the One who suffered and died on the cross for not conforming to many structures of his day.

Generally, members of our tradition ignore, are vaguely aware of, or like the above symbols. The symbols involve what we do and who we are more than what we think. When we participate in them, we may be tasting and responding to first fruits of the kingdom coming.

Chapter 11

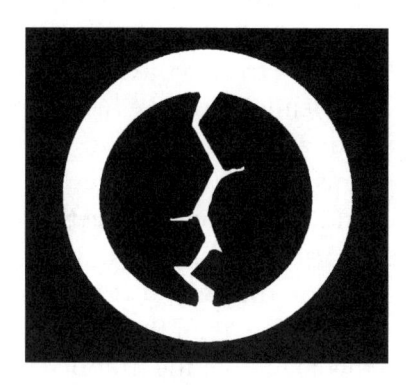

Unity and Dissension
How Brethren have dealt with differences

. . . bearing with one another in love making every effort to maintain the unity of the Spirit in the bond of peace.
—Ephesians 4:2-3

Most historical studies of Christianity encounter controversies, heresies, schisms, inquisitions, and a plethora of different theologies, movements, and missions. Anabaptist and pietist traditions, as well, have not escaped dissension and divisions.

This may explain why our forebears, who had to deal with disunity, included unity as one of four basic doctrines of Christ in an older version of the Brethren's Card. They anticipated contentious conflicts and inevitable differences. How the community of faith dealt with conflicted voices was important. For many decades ministers added two questions to baptismal vows. One question asked whether an aspirant before baptism would pledge never to drill or join military units. The other asked whether the candidate would promise to solve differences according to Matthew 18:15-20. One of the central responsibilities of deacons was to facilitate maintaining the unity of the Spirit in the bond of peace. When asked how Brethren differ from Mennonites, it has been alleged that Brethren treasure unity over truth. Mennonites more likely may savor truth over unity, whereas Brethren often compromise to maintain unity. In risking disunity Mennonites have held fast to what they regard to be true and right in risking disunity. Such an analysis may account for greater numbers of schisms among Mennonites. Among the Brethren I have perceived passions that impel us to stay together.

Thus, it may be helpful to examine how our fathers and mothers in the faith have dealt with differences. In a book focusing on theology, it may be difficult to justify issues that seem to deal with ethics more than theology. In our tradition, however, it is difficult to separate theology from the fruit of discipleship. Many in our tradition, for example, have been attracted to the widespread admiration of Dietrich Bonhoeffer because it is difficult to separate his life from his theology.

Ministries of Reconciliation

In attempting to list representative efforts to maintain unity of the Spirit in our tradition, I acknowledge that some attempts have failed, some have barely maintained unity, and some have been exemplary. It will be obvious that I have left out stories that may be more important than what I include. I confess that my choice and interpretations are subjective. When sisters and brothers disagree with my analyses, may the dialogue lead us to be more effective in finding ways to achieve reconciliation and maintain a bond of peace.

New Christian movements often begin with strict disciplines. This may explain why it is important for a persecuted illegal movement to know who is with them and against them. In adopting the ban, Mack maintained that genuine love requires strict discipline. He understood the ban not to be punishment, but what we name today as tough love directed toward restoration to full fellowship (Willoughby, *Counting the Cost* 74ff). The following stories deal with both exemplary and problematic ways to maintain unity in a spirit of love.

Exile and Exodus

Hacker Marital Affair. The first major conflict of the church occurred at Krefeld in Germany where a sizable group had emigrated. A previous chapter mentioned this story in order to understand its possible influence on church discipline. Here, the dispute that emerged when Wilhelm Hacker married the step-daughter of a Mennonite preacher is applied to ecclesiological ways to deal with conflict. Christian Liebe, who had suffered as an Anabaptist in the galleys of the king of Sicily, became one of the leaders of the church. He led a rigorist faction that placed Hacker in the ban. Johannas Naas and Peter Becker, who were friends of the young man, opposed the ban and approved the marriage.

An account of the dispute in the *Ephrata Chronicle* was probably biased due to the estrangement of the cloisters from Brethren leaders. However, their report that one hundred people at Krefeld recanted their decision to be baptized cannot be entirely discounted. Moreover, the account suggests that this particular ban led to the exodus to America and continued to wound and corrupt the church in the new environment. Durnbaugh and other historians have included economic factors, as well, that led to the first emigration of Brethren to America in 1719.

It would be positive to conjecture that those who first emigrated to America retained more of the love motifs of Radical Pietists. But it can't be denied that memories of the bad experience added to the sentiments of those settling in a new nation, and it may explain why the first love feast and baptisms did not occur until nearly four years later in 1723. We do know from Mennonite names of Brethren in colonial America that women married and converted sons of anabaptist neighbors to the new movement. As far as we know, this occurred without divisive conflict.

Anabaptists have a history of moving to another nation when their presence and beliefs are no longer accepted or when there are major disagreements between factions. As a result, they sometimes became a secluded, separate people. Yet their settling anew frequently led them to heed Jeremiah's advice to seek the welfare of the city wherever the Lord would send them (Jer. 29:7). Jesus advised his disciples to shake the dust off their feet and leave when they were not received (Mattt. 10:14). Likewise, in personal and congregational disputes, it may sometimes be salutary to suffer by leaving. Our forebears may have been motivated by the anticipation of living peaceably in establishing a renewed apostolic church.

Patience

Catherine Hummer's Visions. An unusual dispute in our early history focused on Catherine Hummer, a young sister who for several years had visions, signs, and trances. Her father, Peter Hummer, was a minister in the White Oak congregation. Together they engaged in special gatherings in other meetinghouses. Catherine testified to having visions of heavenly baptisms and joyful entrance into the kingdom of God. She talked with angels and confessed her sins and the sins of Brethren who could no longer love. I was taken by one of her visions that pictured members building walls to keep other people out. Sharing her mystical experiences created considerable excitement. And her pleased father reported many awakenings as a result of her visions.

Others were disturbed. Catherine wrote a letter to Alexander Mack telling him she was being persecuted especially by men because of her faithful testimonies. From the minutes of Annual Meeting in 1763, we read about efforts to maintain unity in love in this situation:

> *The undersigned brethren assembled here from their different places of residence in the fear of the Lord in heartfelt and compassionate brotherly love, in order to see how we might advise our in-God-beloved brethren in reference to the many astonishing occurrences and various transgressions that have occurred since the exercises, visions, and actions in connection with Sister Catherine Hummer.* (Durnbaugh, *The Brethren in Colonial America* 265. An excellent introduction to this happening is found on pages 259-66.)

The concluding minutes advised the Hummers against unnecessary and too frequent visits to congregations. The elders recommended practicing truth and honesty to avoid anything that would prevent unity of mind in Christ Jesus. They expressed in a closing statement that they could not "in the least give a cause for a separation for conscience' sake. Therefore we felt constrained not to criticize or judge this strange happening but rather urge everyone to Godlike impartiality and patience . . ." (266).

It is worth noting that in reviewing any rigid disciplinary actions throughout our history, we need to remain aware of numerous admonitions that advise Brethren to bear with one another and be patient with those judged to be deviant and sinful brothers and sisters.

I would add that Catherine only had visions when her boyfriend was present. After her wedding, Catherine no longer had visions. The Ephrata Cloisters were disappointed. Many Brethren were pleased. And many can ponder how getting married may stifle visionary gifts. This may explain why

Peter, in quoting Joel, noted how it was sons and daughters and young men who prophesy and see visions (Acts 2:17).

Protracted Responses

Revival Meetings. The word *protracted* entered Brethren life and thought in the mid-nineteenth century. The word refers to what our minutes call "methodistic" tendencies in revival meetings, when a verse or a chorus of a hymn would be repeated again and again to allow more time for encouraging folks to come forward and pray in relating to and accepting Christ. Traditional Brethren objected to emotionally charged conversions that often lacked counting the cost. The schisms in the 1880s provided threefold options of acceptance, rejection, or tolerance of revivalism.

Large portions of what was called the larger conservative body gradually accepted revival meetings. However, the call for conversions was usually less coercive and protracted than with other evangelistic traditions. Some congregations have successfully maintained them. But large portions of our churches have replaced revivals with other evangelistic and renewal endeavors.

Universal Restoration. In another example *protracted* refers to the long-time, subsequent consideration of a major issue among Brethren, universal restoration. This lesser known doctrine originated from pietist views of eternal salvation. Alexander Mack inherited radical pietist beliefs that divine love will bring all to a final blessed union with God for eternity. However, to be faithful to other biblical passages, Mack maintained a belief in hell for sinners after death and before eternal salvation. His views may have resembled some kind of purgatory, though that word was never mentioned. He advised against teaching views that could encourage sinful behavior. Mack's modified acceptance of the doctrine and his reluctance to preach it publicly provided the setting for many decades of both acceptance and rejection of this belief by Brethren.

From statements of their neighbors, there is sufficient evidence that the first Brethren in colonial America held to the doctrine of universal restoration. Early congregations in South Carolina, Texas, Arkansas, and Oregon adopted universalism, a belief that affirms all people who die will immediately be saved due to the atoning death of Jesus. Some remained faithful to Mack's teaching. All versions of the doctrine were supported by biblical texts such as Paul's statement: "for as all die in Adam, so all will be made alive in Christ" (1 Cor. 15:22). Many Brethren were perhaps influenced to accept these views because Elhanan Winchester (1751-1795) praised the Brethren in his book entitled *The Universal Restoration*. He had been a Baptist preacher who converted and became a zealous proponent for the Universalist denomination. In proving that the doctrine does not produce sinners, the author referred to the Tunkers, German Baptists, as such Christians as he had ever seen in doing the commands of Christ. He praised these people as being God's people "above any other in the world" (Durnbaugh, *The Brethren in Colonial America* 326).

Differences emerged when Brethren moved from universal restoration to universalism. There were many who rejected all versions of the doctrine. They agreed with later views of Brethren Revival Fellowship, who have based their disapproval on biblical passages that speak of God's judgment and the fate of hell. Through the years there have been both disciplinary actions and withdrawal of congregations in response to this issue. Differences with members in Oregon were settled when it was agreed that views on universal salvation would be kept private. Such was reflected in Annual Meeting minutes throughout the nineteenth century. In Article 30, the 1849 Meeting refused to approve public preaching of the doctrine of universal redemption. The following decisions represent a *few* and perhaps the most typical actions of Yearly Meeting. They seem, perhaps, to be trite statements that were possibly influenced by long-practiced consensus polity inherited from the Quakers.

1858—Art. 2: Is it according to the gospel of Christ for brethren, especially bishops, in speaking on the final destinies of the ungodly, to preach publicly that they shall be punished with everlasting destruction from the presence of the Lord, and privately teach that all will be restored everlastingly, whether they know God and obey the gospel of our Lord Jesus Christ or not? And if asked the question by an alien whether the devil himself will be saved make no reply?

Answer: We think the brethren should be careful not to contradict privately what they preach publicly.

Art. 3. Is it consistent to preach eternal punishment, and at the same time to peddle Winchester's Dialogues on Restoration? Tell us how it is.

Answer: If a brother preaches eternal punishment, it would be inconsistent for him to distribute Winchester's Dialogues on the Restoration.

1878—IX. We ask the Annual Meeting through the District Meeting to stop the Brethren in publishing and selling books in favor or against the doctrine of Universal Restoration.

Answer: We grant the request herein asked for.

The above answers were reaffirmed in 1902. The protracted nature of this issue is apparent in the answers that refuse to accept or reject beliefs. Instead, the church was concerned about maintaining integrity and unity.

The answers cleverly advised preachers not to affirm publicly what they did not believe or do privately. This was a ploy to gain agreement that Brethren should stop preaching or publishing views in favor of or against the doctrine of universal restoration.

For the most part, members have abided by this throughout the twentieth century. Due to the fact that it has been less controversial, less known, and publicly ignored, I will risk adding clever quotes that support one side or the other or do not reveal support for either polarity. Kirby Page led Bible Hours of the first National Youth Conference in 1954 with an overall theme that we should "never accept any idea of God that makes God less good than Jesus." In one of his presentations, he referred to Jesus' prayer to God to forgive the soldiers who were killing him for they did not know what they were doing. "If Jesus forgave his enemies on the cross," Kirby said, "how much more will God ultimately forgive all enemies." In those years, Nels Ferre, a prominent Swedish theologian, expressed his *agape* (love) theology in saying that "Heaven cannot be heaven as long as there is any one in hell."

Karl Barth's view of the atonement could lead to a universalist stance, but he draws back in saying that God's nature is such as to grant freedom of some to hold out forever and ever. A Roman Catholic author, John Burnaby, in his book entitled *Amor Dei*, says it another way: "Love never forces, and therefore there can be no certainty that it will overcome. But there may, and there must, be an unconquerable hope." And another from our brother William Beahm, former dean of Bethany: "Always think of the other person as capable for salvation and oneself as on the verge of going to hell."

According to Annual Conference, such statements are to be discussed privately. None have been accepted by consensus or votes of delegates. During many extended decades, our people have agreed to disagree about this issue. There have been no statements of the church to reject or accept a doctrine that has been with us from our beginnings. We have maintained unity by thinking and allowing others to think differently, and, for the most part, we have not publicly attempted to convert others to our views. Therefore, little has been written by Brethren on the subject. However, there is an excellent article on universalism by Michael Hodson in *The Brethren Encyclopedia*, 1291-93. And in 2001, Frank Ramirez wrote an essay entitled *Universal Restoration* for the Perspectives Essay Series published by Brethren Press.

Flexibility
Western Brethren and Feetwashing. Way out west in Illinois in the early decades, newly arrived and converted Brethren washed feet another way. Their practice was called the single mode, the way that practically all of our congregations do it today and the way our church historians judge it to have been done in Germany. But in the frontier days, the Brethren "back East" washed feet by the double mode. One washed the feet of several followed by one who dried feet with a towel. They reasoned that the double mode symbolized that you need more than one in the church to be servants of others. And Jesus washed more feet than one. Strong feelings existed about the mode of feetwashing, nearly leading to a schism. George Wolfe from Lancaster County moved to Kentucky and later became the first elder in Illinois. He faced discipline but avoided a division in assuring eastern Brethren that western folk would do it the eastern way wherever members of east and west gathered around the same tables.

The lesson in this example is that division was avoided when the church was flexible enough to allow a practice that was "not right" and "not like the Bible tells us" and deviated from "sacred" practices of the majority. And the flexibility made it possible for others to do feetwashing the "wrong" way, which ultimately became the way practically all of us do it as I write. If interested in pursuing this conflict, read chapter 7 in Jim Lehman's *The Old Brethren,* entitled "A Bold and Masterful Elder." He depicts Elder Wolfe to be one who "put himself under the church's discipline," yet was a brother who "was unduly accommodating while staunchly defending his own convictions" (188).

Proactivism
A Proactive District. In latter decades of the nineteenth century, it was controversial to send missionaries overseas. This was one of several issues that led to the early schisms. Old Orders were against sending professional ministers to places where they retained U. S. citizenship and their identities as Americans. They believed that missionaries should migrate, settle, and become citizens in the new land. Mission would mean learning to know their neighbors and inviting them to join their communities of faith. Progressives promoted missions. The German Baptists, the largest group identified as conservatives, were not of one mind. While the debate continued, the District of Illinois sent Christian Hope as a missionary to Denmark in 1876. This proactive act was not approved by the Big Meeting and was a test of what had been prohibited. It was not long before the district's missionary endeavors were accepted with enthusiasm by the majority of Brethren.

A Proactive Congregation. Serving as a home mission pastor in Iowa, I was urged by church leaders to add two bread and cup communions to our two love feasts. The proactive strategy assumed that if enough congregations would do the same, Annual Conference would at some time recommend the practice to all. I was surprised when my home mission congregation rejected the recommendation due to their enthusiasm for the love feast, which for many was a new experience. Moreover, we were required to fulfill other duties assigned by denomination staff at Elgin as mandated by Annual Conference documents.

This strategy did lead to the adoption of bread and cup communions in a church growth paper in 1958 to attract new members. Ironically, that year, 1958, is remembered as the zenith year of membership numbers in our denomination.

Whether for good or ill, many changes have their beginnings when congregations deviate from decisions of Annual Conference. Relative to Conference decisions, congregations have often been reminded to consider wishes and contributions of those of minority opinion in our desire to maintain unity in our life together in the bond of peace. Thus, we have tolerated many differences in congregational life throughout our history.

Inclusiveness

Biblical Inspiration and Authority. From today's perspective, it may be difficult to imagine that in 1977 many feared that a query seeking approval of biblical inerrancy would radically divide our church. As it turned out, a paper entitled "Biblical Inspiration and Authority" was overwhelmingly endorsed by the delegate body. Our purpose here is to learn from the process that occurred rather than consider the paper itself on the authority of the Bible. For that, one can read the 1977 Annual Conference Minutes or a booklet entitled *Biblical Inspiration and Authority: a study guide to the 1979 Annual Conference Paper* by Joan Deeter. (See also chapter 7 of this book.) Instead, we will interpret process and factors that led to a nearly unanimous decision.

First, the Standing Committee did a thorough job in recommending what was needed:

> *Inasmuch as some members . . . are raising concerns about the Brethren view of the inspiration and authority of the Bible, and because our denomination has been known for its affirmation, "We have no creed but the New Testament," we recommend that a committee of five be appointed [three from General Board, one chosen by Brethren Revival Fellowship and one by Bethany Seminary faculty]. . . .*

> *The committee should present representative positions held by Brethren today on the nature of the Bible as our authority in matters of faith and practice. Whatever consensus the committee is able to achieve on a Brethren position today should be stated in the paper. Finally, the committee should give some guidance on how we hold each other in love and fellowship when there exists a diversity of attitudes among us on the matter of the biblical inspiration and authority.* (Study guide, intro.)

In this case Standing Committee wisely observed that a paper prepared by a committee representing different views would more likely be received by the delegate body. Rick Gardner, the staff member on the committee, was instrumental in establishing the procedure for dealing with a difficult matter within the committee and then bringing the controversial issue to the larger body.

The first task was for each committee member to lead a Bible study of a text that might or might not be controversial. These Bible studies brought us together. We sought the best exegesis we could find from scholars and saints. We experienced that each one of us took the assignment and the Bible devotionally and seriously. These sessions provided a foundational orientation for the specific tasks given to us by the Conference.

Then we engaged in responding to specific historical and heritage assignments of Standing Committee. We discovered much on which we agreed. Then we came to basic differences, such as have often been dealt with by bringing both a minority and majority report to Conference as rules allow. The body usually votes for one or the other, which often results in a "win/lose" result for the delegates. Often the chosen paper is then amended in ways to include views that are set aside in the minority report.

Because we desired to bring a paper to Conference that was more inclusive, we listed in one column affirmations we all believed about inspiration, beliefs, and ways we interpret the Bible. In indented paragraphs relating to understandings we had in common, we defined areas on which we were not yet agreed. In doing this we included convictions and statements of all committee members and offered what has been called a win/win situation. We expressed honestly our agreements and disagreements. And we had a text that interpreted our differences in ways that attempted to be fair. This may not always be the best way to proceed, but it does represent a way to be inclusive and honestly present different views without a vote that sends one faction home as losers.

Win/Win

Abortion. It seemed that the controversies about abortion peaked in 1972, the year I was chosen to moderate the Annual Conference. Standing Committee was challenged by voices that felt it was foolish to waste time dealing with this explosive query. They judged opinions to be so set that almost everyone would leave thinking the same as when they came. A member of this honored body, a practicing physician, arose and with heartfelt demeanor said, "I am faced with this issue nearly every day. I want to know what my church believes."

Queries had come two years earlier, and in 1971 the committee was asked to rewrite its report with more conciseness and include specific suggestions that had emerged. The adopted paper in 1972 begins with biblical teachings about the sacredness of life and love for people. However, the committee humbly acknowledged that they had found few scriptural passages directly related to some of the questions, and for this reason it was difficult to be dogmatic in interpretations. Yet the paper emphasizes teachings of the Bible that say human life is a sacred gift from God. The final position statement clearly declares: "Brethren oppose abortion because it destroys fetal life."

It is impressive how thoroughly the committee discerned scriptural texts that helped provide possible answers to specific issues. For example, a story in Exodus 21:22-25 tells of a pregnant woman who had a miscarriage because she was injured by people who were fighting. The story suggests that those responsible should make amends to the husband. From this text it is possible to conclude that though the life of the fetus is precious it is not as precious as the life of the mother. In addition to allowing an abortion in order to save the life of a mother, the paper also supports a woman who would risk her life in order to save the fetus. The paper advises against coercing and compelling others to our way of thinking.

Likewise, the paper observes the failure of our society to help poor mothers with many children. If abortion would become illegal, the paper reveals compassion for poor women who would be victims of dangerous abortions, while wealthy women would have the means to obtain safer illegal abortions. The paper advocates that "Laws regarding abortion should embody protection of human life, protections of freedom of moral choice, and availability of good medical care." The committee approves Planned Parenthood educational efforts that strive to keep unmarried girls from wanting a baby. A Brethren woman employed by Planned Parenthood spent her days teaching against premarital sex and desires of young women to have a baby. She reported that she felt she was on the same side with some who spit and yelled at her every day she went to work.

Because of its compassionate attitudes toward the poor and concern for the lives of mothers, the paper appears in some situations to be pro-choice. At the same time, the paper is strongly pro-life in convincing Brethren that abortion is a sin. The dual position can be interpreted to be both pro-life and pro-choice, a position that seems to be impossible in our polarized culture. Yet most, not all, Brethren are at peace with these decisions. Though not entirely pleased, delegates on both sides who came with strong views left feeling that in some way their position was partly or fully represented in the Conference paper. The vote appeared to support this view.

Marriage and Divorce. The status and remarriage of divorced members remained a controversial issue through many decades of the twentieth century. Annual Conferences in 1933, 1964, and 1977 dealt thoroughly with these issues. The first Conference decisions were more traditional in affirming that marriage is a sacred covenant for life and remarriage was not permitted for one whose former spouse was still living. However, the 1977 Conference allowed exceptions if those involved were truly penitent and willing to confess failures.

Decisions of 1964 and 1967 can be treated together inasmuch as the entire earlier decision was included as part of the longer paper three years later. Both papers reflect how much divorce and remarriage remains a reality in our society. A majority of our membership, including pastors and leaders, has experienced failures of marriages among close and extended family members. In place of the long-held practices of putting legalistic pressure on a divorced member to remain single and accept a lifetime status of being a sinner, the paper quotes teachings of Matthew 19:9 and 1 Corinthians 7:15 to "recognize that not all marriages, even of persons who are members of the church, were truly ordained of God." In the first text Jesus provides an exception in the case of "unchastity," and in the second text, Paul gives this advice to a believer married to an unbeliever: "But if the unbelieving partner separates, let it be so; in such a case the brother or sister is not bound." This may agree with critiques of the long-honored marriage exclamation that "those whom God has joined together, let no man put asunder." Some respond that it is difficult to blame God for some couples who have gotten together in marriage.

The 1977 decision quotes Eugene Roop in a statement that applies to both divorce and remarriage: "To apply the biblical texts on divorce legalistically is to deny the spirit and tone of Christ's teaching. We all fall short of the expectations of God for us, but the gospel provides a way to confess our failure and find forgiveness" (*Brethren Life and Thought*, Summer 1976).

In Conference decisions dealing with the controversial issues of abortion and divorce, there were some who felt that Conference made a lose/lose rather than a win/win statement. They judged any approval of abortion to sanction killing precious, innocent lives. For some, to easily accept divorce and celebrate remarriage appears to compromise biblical and traditional teachings.

Both papers were accepted by sizable majorities, however, because they make it clear that our church opposes abortions and treasures the sanctity of a covenantal relationship with God and others in marriage. In dealing with failures and difficult choices, traditional views and literal biblical passages are overruled by the New Testament emphasis on forgiveness, love, and compassion. Our Lord modeled acceptance of sinners and redemption of newness of life for those who fail. It seems that most Brethren have lived out of these decisions. Coming to win/win conclusions seems to embody holding fast to basic biblical and traditional ethics while at the same time striving to be a loving, forgiving, and transforming people of God.

Pass It On

Flags on Church Grounds. Where and whether flags should be displayed has never been dealt with by Annual Conference. The 1990 Conference responded to a query about flags by refusing to deal with the issue. More fairly, it should be said that the delegates voted to pass concerns of the query on to congregations. Less fairly, it seems they returned an issue to congregations out of their own fears. Congregations and pastors who had been struggling with the issue were disappointed. They wanted theological and biblical studies to supplement their efforts to remain together in the spirit of unity. Since September 11, 2001, hindsight says that it would have been helpful to many if the church had pursued discernment on this issue.

Baptismal Practices. The last paper on baptism, in 1980, provided excellent clarification on how baptism relates to membership in the body of Christ. For the most part, the paper gives advice that implements traditional Brethren exegesis and views of baptism. It appears, however, that the majority of congregations have not given careful consideration to the issues highlighted in the paper in dealing with concerns of baptism of children too young for responsible participatory membership in congregations. Only a few have seriously attempted to investigate older Brethren or primitive Christian practices of having a ceremony and educating pre-teen children for such participation.

There is a tendency to be legalistic about controversial cultural issues that enter our lives. But some have actually shunned consideration of even the most basic issues suggested by the 1980 paper on baptism. It may preserve the peace to pass on or shun issues that are controversial; however, doing so tends to repress conflict and discussions in ways that eventually result in more discordant division or separation. As the body of Christ deals with dissension, we need to avoid shunning the views of others and the decisions of the church. Likewise, the body should avoid repressing and refusing to deal with fractures that need our attention.

When We Failed

The Big Schism (1880-83). The intent of this chapter has been to learn from ways Brethren have managed to stay together in times of dissension. During the past three hundred years, there have been numerous divisions when we have failed to apply what we have learned. One of those times was so major that we might learn from that experience as well. At the least, we may have a better understanding of our relatives in Brethren denominational streams.

What has been named the "Big Divide" jolted Brethren during the last half of the nineteenth century. Brethren lived with the intensified petitions of those who defended the "ancient order" and those who zealously advocated innovations in such things as paid ministry, dress, Sunday schools, and protracted revival meetings. During and between Conferences from 1880 through 1883, three factions labeled as Old Orders, Conservatives, and Progressives became three separate denominations, namely Old German Baptist Brethren, German Baptist Brethren (later named Church of the Brethren), and the Brethren Church.

The details of official visits, the platforms, petitions, resolutions, excommunications, personalities, and gatherings of the parties have been researched and judiciously written by Dale Stoffer in Part IV of his excellent book *Background and Development of Brethren Doctrines* (1650-1987) and by Donald Durnbaugh in chapter 14 ("Division in the Church") in *Fruit of the Vine*. Though rooted in the Progressive body, Stoffer's objectivity and fairness is apparent throughout his comprehensive treatment of issues and the story of the three-way schism.

> *The Old Order Brethren properly maintained the importance of the principles of community, nonconformity to the world, and a simple and a self-denying life style. Yet the danger in their position is found in legalizing the specific forms in which these principles are to be cast, thereby creating a rigid, closed system. The mission of the church became self-preservation rather than outreach to a needy world.*
>
> *The Progressives were correct in "criticizing the Conservatives for their near idolatry of the past," which the Progressives felt was hampering the*

church's freedom to develop new means for meeting the spiritual needs of society. The very real danger in the Progressive position was that the strong emphasis on individual freedom and adaptation to the modern world could lead to a loss of corporate unity and the exposure to every new wind of doctrine which would blow across the American religious scene. Holsinger and the Progressives can also be criticized for their lack of sensitivity to the unity of the Brotherhood and their impatient and radical reform methods.

The error of Conservatives was to be found in their abuse of their position of power at Annual Meeting and their use of the dialectic [Hence, while we are conservatives we are also progressive. D.B.] *for their own purposes. Though it may have been difficult to prevent the withdrawal of the Old Orders, leaders from both the Progressive and Conservative groups expressed their belief following the split that the division could have been avoided if greater forbearance and forgiveness had been exercised. It is true that the Conservative position was often vaguely defined with the result that the main body was censured by both extremes for deliberate inconsistency in playing both ends against the middle. Yet in fairness to the Conservatives, this ambiguity was frequently the result of trying to maintain creative balance between the Old Order and Progressive positions. At one extreme were the Old Order Brethren who tended to formalize the expression of the inner spirit, thereby making it dependent upon a specific "order." At the other extreme were the Progressives who, in their revolt against externalism and formalism, lost sight of the principle of mutual submission, for the sake of unity and brotherhood.* (156)

Most historians of the tradition have agreed with Stoffer that it would have been difficult to prevent separation of the Old Orders. With the growing acceptance of movements such as Sunday schools, it was increasingly impossible for the Conservatives to accept Old Order petitions brought to conference. Old Orders believed the church was drifting away from the apostolic order. Their firm adherence to the order in combination with the mood of the larger body undermined reconciliation. Hindsight does grant that their plain concerns were disrespectfully overruled. For example, the Old Order petition brought in 1881, the year of separation, was rejected because it had not come through a district.

Likewise, more recent historians have agreed with Stoffer that division of Conservatives (the present Church of the Brethren) and the Progressives (present Brethren Church) could have been avoided if greater forbearance and forgiveness had been exercised by leaders of Conference. The enthusiastic critical writings and activities of Henry Holsinger were no doubt difficult to deal with. Yet in crucial times near the end of the process, Holsinger asked for forgiveness and promised to remain in harmony with church practices and would not speak or write antagonistically to the order of Annual Meeting. After he was expelled, a group of Progressives met and recommended choosing a committee of twelve, six from each group, to meet and prepare a plan for general reconciliation. Such efforts were ignored or rejected. In excommunicating two sizable minorities, Annual Meeting then authorized that henceforth all baptized by Progressives and Old Orders be rebaptized. Though we were not there and there are many things we do not know, from today's perspective it has seemed that conservative forerunners of the Church of the Brethren lacked the long and treasured legacy of being a forgiving and patient people.

Since the schism, brothers and sisters in the larger body have continued to be open to cultural and religious trends and movements of the nineteenth and twentieth centuries. Another schism, named the Dunkard Brethren, emerged in 1926 from those who were disappointed that the church had not retained the conservative character claimed four decades earlier. However, the next chapter deals with debatable opinions and convictions that result when tossed to and fro and blown about by many winds of doctrine (Eph. 4:14).

Chapter 12

Tossed To and Fro by Winds of Doctrine

Theological, ecclesiastical, and cultural influences

We must no longer be children, tossed to and fro and blown about by every wind of doctrine, by people's trickery, by their craftiness in deceitful scheming. But speaking the truth in love, we must grow up in every way into him who is the head, into Christ, from whom the whole body, joined and knit together by every ligament with which it is equipped, as each part is working properly, promotes the body's growth in building itself up in love.
—Ephesians 4:14-16

We have noted how forebears of previous generations professed to be little children. Such humility did not keep members of the body from being open to the Spirit's gifts of wisdom and knowledge. Jesus teaches that a childlike heart is needed, but this does not mean that we should cultivate immaturity. Paul and other epistle writers recognized that members were not of one mind about circumcision or customs of eating. When Christians were taught to be of one mind and maintain unity in the bond of peace, the apostolic authors were not demanding uniformity of all lifestyles and beliefs. However, they strongly emphasized that every part of the body should speak the truth in love and be equipped to promote the body's growth in building itself up in love.

Brethren generally have accepted this advice to the Ephesians by giving priority to relational commandments over doctrinal propositions without denying the importance of both. From their beginnings Brethren have shared pietist concerns in rejecting bitter polemics of their time. They agreed that the Bible was often the vessel for proof texts to defend creeds rather than a resource for faith and life. They affirmed with the Pietists that there should be reformations of doctrine that result in reformation of lives.

The previous chapter dealt with ways Brethren have strived to stay together. This chapter deals with Brethren responses to specific theological movements and exegesis of texts. Like Christians of the first centuries, our good people have often resembled little children in being tossed to and fro by winds of doctrine due to trickery and deceit (Eph. 4:14-16).

Interactions with Theological Movements

Mystical Legacies from Radical Pietism
Streams of mysticism hover in a variety of ways over Brethren life. Mystical theology often focuses on special revelations, dated conversion experiences, individual salvation, and charismatic expressions of the Spirit. Some mystical currents have ascetic views that forbid "lust of the flesh." Such was the case when early Brethren related to dualistic legacies from Pietists who advocated celibacy as a higher spiritual attainment even for the married. Floyd Mallott, professor at Bethany, enjoyed writing a timeline for the period when Brethren vowed to practice continence. The *Ephrata Chronicle* reported it to be seven years after the first baptisms in 1708. Mallott winked as he walked to the board and marked the birth date of Alexander Mack, Jr., half

way through the experiment. It was not long before Brethren rejected rigid expressions of spirit-flesh dualism in their marriages.

More materialistic and worldly theologies stress life for others in the church and concerns for a better world. Through the years Brethren have been known for a this-world mysticism expressed in their loving care for the good earth. They have been a people attracted to service ministries on behalf of suffering, starving, and oppressed people. The emphasis on the goodness of creation and Paul's affirmation in 2 Corinthians 6:16 that "we are the temple of the living God" amplified their desire to be cleansed from "every defilement of body and of spirit" (7:1).

Without requiring total abstinence, the Yearly Meeting of 1804 advised against keeping a public tavern. That they were not entirely successful is indicated by a minute thirty-one years later that answered the same question with the phrase "Considered, as entirely unbecoming for brethren." In the last decades of the nineteenth century, many Brethren were attracted to a temperance movement that advocated abstinence from alcoholic beverages for all. As the movement grew and extended into the first decades of the twentieth century, many for the first time joined political movements to rid the nation of debauchery and drinking alcoholic beverages.

Unlike the Old Orders, the more progressive historical branches have substituted grape juice for wine in the love feast. Currently, moderation is more widely accepted and total abstinence has been recommended by Annual Conference though rarely used as a test of membership. Later Brethren temperance concerns against both growing and personal use of tobacco have joined public concerns for health and the environment. A growing sentiment today has come to mimic prejudices of my parents against smoking.

Alexander Mack desired to combine an inner mystical spirit with outward acceptance of communal and biblical authority and discipleship. In the twentieth century, we have experienced both tensions and synthesis between spiritual and material, faith and works, salvation and discipleship. Some of these tensions will surface in the following doctrinal expressions.

Liberalism and Fundamentalism
Fundamentalism emerged at the beginning of the twentieth century in reaction to prevailing liberal trends in mainline Protestantism. It was not long before Brethren were attracted to this movement because of its affirmations of authority of the Scriptures, faith and grace emphases, changed lives, eternal salvation, and lifestyles committed to personal ethics. At the same time, many Brethren appropriated existing liberal views that called attention to

the life and teachings of Jesus, public ethical concerns, tolerance and forbearance, and kingdom themes of peace and justice.

William Hordern, a Lutheran professor I was privileged to have as a teacher in graduate school, regarded Pietism as a root of both fundamentalism and liberalism. Pietist-sponsored devotional groups replaced scholastic, dogmatic polemics with biblical studies that were applied to daily living. And Pietism produced liberals such as Schleirmacher who replaced dogma with feelings and religious experience. Hordern's analysis may explain how plain Pennsylvania elders of a previous generation regularly turned their radio dial to "Fuller's Old Fashioned Revival Hour" and equally appreciated the radio sermons of Harry Emerson Fosdick, who became a candidate for the anti-Christ to some fundamentalists.

In twentieth-century denominational struggles, liberal leaders maintained control of most mainline church bodies. They disliked dogmatic minds and unlovely spirits who failed to share Apostle Paul's confession that we know in part and our knowledge is imperfect. Brethren leaders were concerned that discipleship emphases were sometimes supplanted by a docetic christology that so emphasized Christ's divinity as to neglect his humanity. Similarly, conservative winds of doctrine seemed to minimize weightier matters of the law mentioned by Jesus, such as justice and mercy.

In the first decade of the twentieth century, the fundamentalist movement benefitted from the efforts of two wealthy laymen who financed the publishing and wide distribution (250,000 recipients in the English-speaking world) of four volumes entitled *The Fundamentals*. Some Brethren identified with fundamentals of the faith as defined in these books and as listed in the second Brethren's Card. Other members preferred to be regarded as evangelicals or conservatives. All concerned conservatives believed that liberals did not believe enough about Jesus to give impetus to following the Jesus way. They also noted that liberals often possessed dogmatic minds and unlovely spirits. They judged that liberals overlooked the reality of sin. Grass roots conservatives were also disturbed by rapid adaptation to cultural values and lifestyles that were subversive to biblical authority and teachings.

Excellent sociological analyses by Carl Bowman and Don Fitzkee have documented the acculturation of Brethren to mainline and liberal American values (see bibliography). Values nurtured by consumerism and greed have been subversive to simple living, integrity, communal and family harmony, and discipleship to the Jesus way. Not as transparent is the theological acculturation of conservative Brethren. This becomes obvious in noting increasing identity with cultural currents that support capital punishment, lavish wealth resulting from greed, growing acceptance of the doctrine of redemptive violence, and a might makes right spirit of a militaristic culture that often reflects hatred toward the poor and outcasts of our society.

I was raised in a typical Brethren home that favored the party of Abraham Lincoln. My parents and the majority of our members would have identified more with Republicans and fundamentalists. At that time the majority of conservatives would have strongly opposed voting for Ronald Reagan, who was divorced, a movie star, and brought liquor back into the White House after it had been taken out by the previous president. Yet nearly thirty years later, conservatives had acculturated enough to regard Reagan favorably. All of which confirms we are a people, liberal and conservative, who are tossed to and fro by many winds of our culture. For example, strong prejudices against all movies gradually evaporated when TV sets were allowed in our homes.

Bethany professors, such as William Beahm and Floyd Mallott, imparted a love of the heritage. Identity with our heritage helped liberals avoid some of the pitfalls of modernism and softened the divisive character of fundamentalists. I often felt we could be comfortable with evangelical students and institutions because we shared basic ethical views and commitments to Christlike love. And we often could feel at home with mainline Protestant and Catholic traditions in our social commitments to justice and peace.

At Conferences, we have sung together with gusto "Take my hand and lead me, Father," written by our own William Beery, and Fosdick's hymn "God of grace and God of glory." Although there are many who are not entirely in agreement with our Brethren Revival Fellowship, they would nevertheless agree that most are warm, loving, and faithful disciples, unlike most television evangelists and Southern Baptist fundamentalists. It is quite remarkable that we have entrusted both so-called "liberals" and "conservatives" with leadership roles to serve all.

In the first years of the twenty-first century, we continue to be tossed to and fro by winds of right-wing conservatives who reject or ignore the teachings of Jesus, and by winds of post-modern currents and voices whose language games often seem confusing to the growing majority of our world's new Christians.

Neo-Orthodoxy

This neo-orthodoxy label is somewhat confusing. Literally it means a new old theology. Basically, it has been regarded as a revival and expression of the "old time religion." It has been said of twentieth-century theologies that they were created in Germany, corrected in Great Britain, and corrupted in America. This may apply to neo-orthodoxy, also known as crisis or dialectical theology. The crisis exists, according to Karl Barth, because we are not able to define our Christian faith through our reason and self-centered efforts. In discovering "the strange new world of the Bible," Barth believed that religion involves human efforts to find God. Christian faith, however, affirms that God finds us in the revelation of Christ. Christ is the Word that became flesh, not the Bible. He grants, however, that the Word, Christlike thinking, often comes alive for us in the Scriptures.

Consequently, Barth's commentary on Romans in 1919 inaugurated a theological current that departed from liberal theology's search for God through reason and experience. A cluster of theologians, such as Brunner, Tillich, and Bonhoeffer among many others, joined Barth with their own variations. It also may be necessary to add existential ingredients from Danish Søren Kierkegaard. Reinhold and Richard Niebuhr became somewhat deviant American counterparts with emphases on Christian ethics. Neo-Reformation became another identity label for this school that promoted renewed interest in the theology of sixteenth-century reformers, especially Luther and Calvin.

As a professor I enjoyed attempts to translate practical understandings of these theologians. I entered a graduate program in historical theology in 1956. Garrett Seminary, nestled in the center of Northwestern University, was saturated with a neo-orthodox ethos. I could not escape exposures that judged the doctrine of progress and optimistic humanism to be naive. The recovery of the doctrine of sin by Reinhold Niebuhr and the necessity of revelation accentuated the importance of sound biblical theology. What I gained personally was an ability to preach with integrity on biblical doctrines I had avoided as a pastor.

In the early sixties, I joined other faculty members at Bethany who shared similar graduate school orientations. Our Brethren heritage led us to allow students to develop their own theology, but they were required to be able to dialogue with a major theologian. This was no doubt a subtle way to enroll them in one of our classes. Warren Groff offered seminars on Barth, Don Miller on Tillich, and I chose Bonhoeffer because of the way he integrated reformation grace and faith themes with discipleship. His focus on the doctrine of the church was different enough but supporting enough of anabaptist ecclesiology to be intriguing. Students were free to choose other theologians from similar seminary offerings at Bethany or the Chicago cluster of seminaries.

I remain agnostic about how much this new orthodoxy trickled down to grass roots members. No doubt, some of the themes came through in faculty books, Christian education material, sermons of our graduates, and theologically literate members. Some reacted as I did at Garrett-Northwestern. The rhetoric often sounded like what I perceived to be a replay of the antinomian (against law) attacks of the reformers against anabaptist works righteousness. When I defended some ethical and pietist emphases of my heritage, however, they did not label me as an Anabaptist or Pietist. Rather they lumped me with those who were accused of being unreconstructed liberals.

There are more basic reasons why neo-orthodoxy was not appropriated in Dunkerdale. Neo-orthodox views of human nature rejected what was named a Greek dualism, which exalted and separated reason from our total being. The resulting commendable wholeness, nevertheless, seemed lacking to rank and file Christians due to its sophisticated intellectual environs.

In the language of Pietists, neo-orthodoxy seemed to be head more than heart religion. Incarnations of neglected emphases of what it takes to be a total person were to be found elsewhere in black churches, charismatic groups, liturgical high church revivals, and appropriation of dancing, music, and other artistic expressions. Exposure to neo-orthodoxy may be one factor in fostering the hunger for spirituality in anabaptist circles. The doctrine was often sound. Yet, it seems to be difficult to neatly plan communal worship that conjoins both head and heart religion.

Charismatic Movement

Neo-orthodoxy was a movement in which theologians desired that the church benefit from greater theological awareness and correctives to popular religiosity. Unlike these trickle-down wishes of professors, the charismatic movement rose from the bottom up. Theologians and seminarians were impelled to engage in exegetical and theological studies in order to be in conversation with grass roots concerns of zealous brothers and sisters. A movement that was an offspring of Pentecostalism cultivated enthusiastic gatherings in many denominations, including Roman Catholic circles. Charismatic winds blew in, bringing either renewal or division depending on the nature of the witness and receptivity of congregations.

In the '70s, when denominational staff requested I write a book on the issues generated by this movement, I wrote *Flamed by the Spirit* (1978), which included four biblical definitions of the Holy Spirit from Brethren perspectives. Since the four definitions appear in chapter 6 of this book, definitive explanations need not be repeated. Briefly, we will note both positive and negative responses to the charismatic movement. Joyful and enthusiastic expressions in worship helped to free up faith responses of our total beings. Those who felt that worship services were "cold" were helped by experiencing warm, genuine, communal manifestations of the Spirit. This has led many Brethren to feel more at home with Hispanic and black Christians.

The movement prodded others and me to engage in biblical studies about the Holy Spirit. At the same time, the charismatic winds led some to appropriate and redefine our anointing service.

Nevertheless, Brethren were moved to challenge what seemed to be faulty presuppositions. Though enthusiastic outward motions and praise seemed to enrich the worship for many, some Brethren believe that in our noisy environs there is a need for quietly listening to the still small voice of God. In preferring heart religion over head religion, some charismatics have minimized the aspect of the greatest commandment that calls us to love God with all our minds. Our members have also questioned whether the gift of tongues should be required as a test of the Spirit's presence. When speaking in tongues becomes the primary sign of being filled with the Spirit, those who do not speak in tongues have felt they are regarded to be second-class Christians. Concrete situations have led many to question seriously the assumption of some charismatics that there is a one-to-one relationship between how much faith one has and what God will do for you.

Some members left. Others have profited from experiences of freely responding to God with their feelings. As I write, contemporary praise services seem to be an expression of the strengths of Spirit-filled worship. Others are concerned that, in pietist language, we have new expressions of all heart and no head religion. Living in an age of increasing pluralism, many are accepting and rejoicing about the possibilities of learning from our differences. Charismatic influences will continue to hover over the Brethren. Therefore, it remains important to find common ground in our mutual allegiances to the Jesus way.

Millennial Winds and the Second Coming

It is difficult to think of any doctrine by which Brethren have been tossed to and fro more than doctrinal winds that interpret apocalyptic and eschatological texts. *Apocalyptic* literally means revelation. *Eschatology* refers to end times. As a noncreedal people, it is presumptuous and impossible for anyone to define our position for all. However, because we have a common respect for the teachings of Jesus and New Testament writers, it may be helpful to risk listening to contemporary voices. The best overview of our heritage is found in a variety of essays on end times in the winter/spring 2001 issue of *Brethren Life and Thought* that were contributed from a Forum for Religious Studies at Bridgewater College.

From this forum early winds affecting our heritage were revealed in an essay entitled "Early Brethren Eschatology: A Contribution to Brethren Beginnings." The author, Marcus Meier, added new insights about the influences of Radical Pietism, drawn from his doctrinal dissertation at Marburg University. We had been aware of the hope that emerged following terrible decades of war and famine. Following ages of God and Christ, as had been promised by medieval Joachim of Flora, many Pietists anticipated a new age of the Spirit. This third age of the Spirit would embody incarnations of love and peace.

Alexander Mack went on preaching missions with Hochmann von Hochenau, who frequently offered messages about the second coming of Christ. Today, we are told by many that we can prepare for Christ's coming by sending weapons to Israel. How different from Hochmann's advice that the way to get ready for Christ's coming is to love enemies and follow the way of Jesus. Meier reports that some set dates for the second coming. It was anticipated by most that his return would be in 1700. When Jesus did not come (the year 1708 was one among other new predictions), Hochmann experienced a deep personal change and withdrew to Schwarzenau to become a hermit, relinquishing outward concerns to search for God in his inner soul.

It is possible that Alexander Mack's eschatological expectations might have influenced the aforementioned period of celibacy. The first eight Brethren, including Mack, were led to establish a congregation in a period of failed and decreasing apocalyptic expectations. According to Meier, however, the first eight were primarily motivated by concerns to be obedient to all that Jesus had commanded. Now that Jesus had not returned, their mood was probably "let's have a church." They were in tune with the broader Pietist Reformation with the frequent wish for better times for the church and the world. They believed Jesus would be with them "to the end of the age" (Matt. 28:20).

As Brethren we should not be so fascinated with our own destiny and future of our world as to neglect why and how apocalyptic teachings were lived out by primitive Christians. As New Testament Christians, we believe we can be inspired in understanding books like Daniel and Revelation. Daniel was written to help and encourage people who suffered exile only to return home and experience multiple invasions and repressions by superpower civilizations of their day. The book highlights Daniel's faithfulness to Israel and his dreams for the future. Revelation was written from prison by a leader John. He wrote primarily to instill comfort in a persecuted people. He named Rome and its ruler as a beast who persecutes Christians.

In his book *The War on Terrorism*, Lee Griffith entitled a chapter "The Terror of God," in which he writes that Revelation is not a book about the end of the world. It is a book about terror defeated rather than terror inflicted. "Ninety-eight verses (of over four hundred) in the Apocalypse of John speak of catastrophe, and 150 refer to joy, consolation, brightness and hope" (205). Apocalyptic language is replete with metaphors, often images of animals. Jesus is represented as a victorious lamb whose sword is the Word of God coming out of its mouth. It has been conjectured that the apocalyptic language of Daniel and Revelation was written partly in code. The persecuted could understand it and were often comforted without revealing the real message to their persecutors.

Both Daniel and Revelation contain dreams, visions, and promises of God. The preacher in me wants to compare those dreams with Martin Luther King's famous dream. Among his hopes, King dreamed about the time when children would be judged by their character, not the color of their skin. Such a dream inspires, motivates, and gives hope to oppressed people.

Yet fulfillment of such holy, inspired dreams is not guaranteed. The fulfillment of a dream depends on those who say yes to the will of God who allows freedom. Many believe apocalyptic revelation of dreams in the Bible to be absolutely determined by God so as to eliminate the freedom God extends to believers to change the course of history.

Scholars have taught that apocalyptic promises influenced nearly all New Testament writers. For example, each beatitude combines a wisdom teaching with an apocalyptic promise. The merciful are blessed as those who will receive mercy. As Christians we are to hold fast to the promises of God while at the same time realizing that fulfillment of the promises will come from the first fruits of the kingdom by believers committed to the will of God

With Mack we need not literally believe that Christ will rule with his saints for a thousand years. Hedda Durnbaugh has discovered radical pietist apocalyptic views in the early hymnody of the Brethren. The hymns reflect victorious hopes without chiliastic or millennial elements. *Chilias* or *chiliastic* means one thousand in classical Greek. *Millennium* with its Latin roots refers to the same.

Whether literally believing in a millennium or symbolically regarding it to mean a long time, it is interesting to note how important time is to the varieties of views about end times in recent centuries. The number seems to be more important and taken more literally than "seventy times seven" in Jesus' answer to Peter's query about how many times we are to forgive one who sins against us (Matt. 18:21-22). Commentators advise that numerals in Revelation are to be understood symbolically and not literally. The thousand years represents the martyrs' reign with Christ.

Yet, apocalyptic language has been taken more literally by millions in the nineteenth, twentieth, and now the twenty-first century. In the early and middle 1800s, waves of revivalism flowed with the western expansion, resulting in phenomenal church growth and inspiring missionaries to preach the gospel to the ends of the earth. Charles Finney, one of the most popular revivalists of the pre-Civil War period, commissioned each convert who accepted Jesus as Lord and Savior to join abolitionist, peace, temperance, and women's rights societies. All embodied a millennialist spirit, believing in the coming ideal society that had been symbolized by a thousand years in Revelation 20. It seemed obvious that when increasing masses of people accepted Christ, the world would become better. Views of Finney and others were named "postmillennial" because of their conviction that Christ would return after an age of peace and prosperity. Postmillennial expectations were in accord with social gospel movements of the twentieth century.

In the nineteenth century, however, postmillennial optimism was challenged by premillennial expectations. During the Civil War period, some evangelicals began to give up their belief that they should or could change the world. They discerned a relationship between events in their time and prophecies they judged to be *the* biblical apocalypse. They found texts that offered disclosures of catastrophic events that would herald the imminent coming of Christ.

These expectations gave rise to three chiliastic or premillennial movements. The Plymouth Brethren in England, led by John Nelson Darby in Great Britain in the 1830s, were the first to translate metaphorical language of Paul to literally predict a rapture in which living believers would be caught up in the air to be rejoined with dead believers before the seven-year period of tribulation that would precede warfare ushering in the millennial kingdom (1 Thess. 4:17).

Oxford University Press's *Scofield Reference Bible,* mostly unchanged since its publication in 1902, merged with Darby's dispensational view of history. This Scofield Bible has continued to be one of the most widely used reference books in conservative Protestantism. The Bible includes comments at the bottom of its pages that include events related to the rapture. Many readers regard Scofield's added commentary to be equally as true as the biblical text. Dispensational views support the belief that teachings of the Sermon on the Mount do not apply to us, but are written to be observed in the millennium after Jesus returns. For some, certain political realities must be present before this final salvation of Christians can occur. For example, the state of Israel must be in place so that Jews will have accepted Christ. There are several interpretations of this order; some believe such events will occur before while others believe during or after the rapture.

A second movement includes many Adventist groups, the largest being the Seventh-Day Adventist denomination. It was a farmer, William Miller, a man with much charisma, who with his followers had Americans counting the days waiting for his prediction of the second coming of Jesus in 1944. When other dates likewise did not happen, small groups that maintained the faith led a movement that has grown to be a major denomination.

A third group, named Russelites after their founder and better known as Jehovah Witnesses, emerged in the last decades of the nineteenth century with different emphases, but of similar expectations. Professor Mallott reported that the founder was influenced by the writings of a Brethren elder, though the story remains undocumented.

In years after the Civil War, a Baptist preacher, William Thurman, converted to the Dunker persuasion. He got into more trouble with the church by advocating the single mode of washing feet (the way we do it today) than being a convinced premillennialist. On several occasions after predicting a date, he would gather Brethren in Virginia and adjoining states to a hill to await the second coming. I have always guessed that they knew that Christ would choose the most beautiful place, the Shenandoah Valley. Don Durnbaugh has an even better version you can read in *Fruit of the Vine* (180-83).

When I first studied premillennial movements in seminary, I never dreamed that Hal Lindsey's *The Late Great Planet Earth* would sell over fifteen million copies and a subsequent Left Behind movement focusing on the rapture would sell many times more copies of movies and books. In my teaching I have usually strived to discover a rationale or reasons for such a worldly success. And I try to discern what is good about a movement, along with critiques offered by others and myself. When students still persist in their seeking, I reveal some of my prejudices and the judgments of others whom I respect.

I have articulated that the power of the movement may be seen in the simple logic derived from common impressions of our kind of world. I note the following presuppositions. First, the world is getting worse, not better. Daily newspapers document this. Second, with so many evil forces, we feel helpless. There is not much we can do to make it better. Third, glory hallelujah, God can and will. The worse things get, the nearer we are to the time when Jesus will return and usher in the perfect kingdom on earth. Premillennialists probably were more accurate in sensing the movement of history than liberals who predicted that the twentieth century would be a Christian century of peace, justice, and plenty for all. Their biblical realism teaches them that things often do get worse before they can get better. We cannot easily roll up our sleeves and build the kingdom of God on earth.

Yet Adventists engage in many medical and charitable enterprises. Many who have been oppressed, violated by terrible structures, or who have lost loved ones in wars are consoled and attracted to movements that are certain about possibilities of an imminent, wonderful kingdom ushered in by the return of our Lord. In preparing for the return of Jesus, many adopt more healthful and sensible lifestyles. Often there are sincere desires and fulfilling ministries devoted to saving others from the wrath to come.

The following criticism will not apply to all who hold premillenial views. My intention is to point out some views that seem to fall short of reflecting the mind of Christ:

Pretends to know more than Jesus knows. *After appropriating some well-known apocalyptic sayings, Jesus indicates that he does not know the time or the hour (Mark 13:32). When I have read about the movements in contemporary literature, I am surprised at how much of what is predicted cannot be found in the Bible.*

Subverts the doctrine of the goodness of God's creation. *Some religious and political leaders have believed that war and even a nuclear holocaust are a part of God's plan. An eschatology of despair tends to lock God outside of history. The sign of the rainbow and the story of redemption point to God's intention to redeem rather than condemn the world. John 3:17 certainly verifies this.*

Denies Christian freedom. *In troubled times, premillennial teaching caters to our desire to nail everything down. We hanker to have details of the future that tell exactly what will happen. We are reluctant to walk by faith. In terms of our personal destiny, Brethren and other Christians have rejected the idea of predestination. We have assumed that we are free to say yes or no to God's saving grace. But many who espouse freedom of choice in their personal lives accept predestinarian schemes in determining big events of war and injustice. Such is true both for those who believe nuclear holocaust is the will of God and for those who believe that God will not let it happen. Our faith affirms that God's providential care works through people instead of denying human freedom.*

Placing the kingdom of God entirely in the future. *Some, not all, premillennialists ignore the teachings of Jesus that the kingdom is among us both now and in the future. Biblical faith advises that we can participate in the first fruit of the kingdom now. The prayer Jesus taught us to pray seems to assume that the kingdom can come on earth. The earlier reference to Martin Luther King's dream sermon can be compared with biblical dreams that can be obeyed, disobeyed, or changed in the future by humans. Fulfillment of visions and dreams is biblical and sacred. We are free to make a difference now in participating in the fruit of the kingdom coming.*

Too easily makes good news out of bad news. *A popular singer testified that his spine tingles in ecstasy as he thinks of being raptured out of this world to meet Jesus in the sky, even as he looks down and sees millions perishing in a nuclear holocaust. Instead of weeping compassionately, some seem to rejoice in bad news that proves biblical prophecies will be fulfilled. Our Lord wept when he contemplated the destruction of Jerusalem, and cried out: "If you, even you, had only recognized on this day the things that make for peace!" (Luke 19:42).*

Jesus Against the Rapture is the name of a book written by New Testament scholar Robert Jewett (see bibliography). One of his chapters refers to the time when Pharisees and Sadducees came to test Jesus in asking him for a sign. He answered: "An evil and adulterous generation asks for a sign, but no sign will be given to it except the sign of Jonah" (Matt. 16:4). Through lenses of our tradition, and in reading carefully, we can deduce that the sign of Jonah was a withered bush that led the Lord to teach Jonah to love his enemies (Jonah 4:6-11).

Whither are the Brethren with these winds of doctrine? Some still feel it right to be postmillennial, regardless of the barrage of evil in the world. Other brothers and sisters identify with one or more premillennial predictions. Some modify their beliefs based on their Brethren heritage. For example, the Sermon on the Mount is for us today and not just for the time when Jesus comes again. Apologetically, I introduce another word here—*amillennialism*. This word has often been explained by Augustine's rejection of a future millennium in assuming that the thousand years symbolically designates the age of the church between Christ's resurrection and his final coming.

This third word, amillennialism, may help in any summary of our tradition. Though Brethren have been tossed to and fro by many winds, essays from the Bridgewater conference that quote influential members, past and present, may suggest some majority sentiments. Many Brethren who affirm premillennial views do not place them at the center of their faith as others do. As seen in a few of our past and present leaders, the amillennial tendencies of our tradition accentuate living the faith now.

We have noted that Alexander Mack's eschatological expectations were connected to his admonishment to be obedient to all that Jesus commanded. In colonial America, before millennial proposals of the next century, Mack's concerns were extended to include mystical forebodings of present and future manifestations of the age of the Spirit. In the nineteenth century, Peter Nead influenced many Brethren to accept versions of premillennialism. Henry Kurtz spoke against wasting time in discerning when Christ will return. Instead, he wrote that "We should be content to trust in God with childlike faith, that in his care all things are well." Galen Royer may have represented the missionary movement in 1899 with an optimistic hope that all nations will be won to Christ (William Kostlevy, "Eschatology, Mission and American Destiny," *Brethren Life and Thought,* Winter/Spring 2001). Emanuel Hoff, one of the founders of Bethany, placed Revelation in the context of persecution of Christians. This leads us to likewise refuse to worship the state. From her study of authors and leaders in the early twentieth century, Christina Bucher believes that even those who manifested influences from premillennialism, Darbyite dispensationalism, and historical biblical scholarship would likely support a later president of Bethany, D. W. Kurtz, who concluded: "God will take care of the future. Let us do his will in the living present" (*BLT,* Winter/Spring 2001).

Other Doctrinal Winds

Not less important, but less treated, a multitude of theologies seemed to have appeared following the dominance of neo-orthodoxy. Partly because of their Brethren Service experiences, many were drawn to what was named *secular theology,* which co-opted themes from Bonhoeffer's prison letters. As Christ was the man for others, so the church exists for others. Bonhoeffer appropriated what he believed to be basic with Barth, namely, that in Christ God became worldly, deeply concerned for the world.

Brethren identification with victims of war, conjoined with struggles for justice, led many to resonate with a variety of *liberation theologies and movements*. The views drew heavily from prophetic books of the Old Testament.

Women have appropriated many motifs from feminist theologians. They have ably interpreted scriptural passages and doctrines in ways that redefine their roles and challenge authority patterns in the church. In local and global experiences, women have often identified with victims of persecution and oppression.

It was not difficult for one who appreciates Barth, such as Warren Groff, to appropriate *narrative theology*. Brethren have always conveyed theological truths by telling stories. The various theological pursuits grow, perhaps, out of the challenge to understand our increasingly pluralist context.

Because we were birthed by a people who committed civil disobedience, we declare that we were not satisfied to remain with the majority. As a result we are occasionally given credit along with others for the advent of religious freedom and separation of church and state, and this too has been a source of Brethren doing theology.

The word *radical* attached to our tradition has bothered some and been treasured by others. Those who propose to accept it point out that the word can lead us to redefine the roots of our faith that facilitate biblical views of nonconformity. In response to Death of God theologians who claimed to be radical, I responded in the early seventies with an article in *The Christian Century,* which led two publishers to ask me for a book. In writing *The Christian Revolutionary,* I defined as a more radical stance a returning to New Testament roots of our faith. I maintained that to do so would lead more to radical discontinuities with cultural currents of greed and violence than to accommodations with contemporary agnosticism. The book had some impact beyond Brethren circles, especially among many who identified with concerns of the evangelical left. I confess that the Christian revolutionary was dressed up in anabaptist clothing. In defining a radical stance in this way, I have discerned that we may be both conservative and liberal, sectarian and ecumenical.

What about deconstructionist moods that might be somewhat prevalent in contemporary theology as I write? One reaction is to think that this is what our forebears were about in our beginnings. Their refusal to exalt unchangeable creeds and their emphasis on Spirit openness to new light may describe attitudes of postmodern theology. This chapter gives a nod of appreciation to pluralism. Our love theology, which is applied to our life together, should not hinder the call to love others. Postmodernism seems to favor artistic expressions, proverbs, diversity, acknowledgment of other ways of living and believing. Our focus on simplicity grants that it is not altogether clear what postmodernism is or how to express the same in more simple language. The best article I have read speaks of America's quintessential postmodern proverb as being "Different Strokes for Different Folks." This essay by Alice McKenzie epitomizes the best and worst implications of postmodernism for Christian faith communities in its acknowledgment of diverse experiences of human communities and moral relativism (*Theology Today,* Vol. 53, No. 2, 201-212).

Recovery of the Brethren Vision

In James McClendon's second volume, *Doctrine,* he identifies his small "b" baptist theology in proposing it as a third way that is neither Protestant nor Catholic. This view by a major theologian may give credence to the blowing-in-the-wind movement that was dedicated to recovering our heritage. Here we need not be repetitious due to extensive reviews of Pietism and Anabaptism in chapter two. Rather, we tell the story that empowered the wind of the recovery.

In the 1950s, Donald Durnbaugh served with many in Brethren Service programs directed by M. R. Zigler. Durnbaugh's contribution to hands-on service programs in Europe led to deciphering early archival and manuscript documents related to the early Brethren. He was aided by the linguistic acumen of his new Austrian wife and prodded by Zigler's historical interests.

Amid the legacy of fundamentalism, liberalism, and the growing influence of neo-orthodoxy, Durnbaugh became the Harold Bender of the Brethren. Mennonite historian Bender has continually been credited with recovering the anabapatist vision. Durnbaugh's source book of early documents in *European Origins of the Brethren* appeared in 1958 in connection with the 250th anniversary of the church. That same year Durnbaugh wrote two Bender-like papers delineating "The Genius of the Brethren." They are available in the winter and spring issues of *Brethren Life and Thought,* 1959. The first essay concludes that Brethren should be considered primarily to be in the anabaptist tradition. He emphasizes that they departed from Pietism, though he grants that some elements of Radical Pietism clung to them. The second essay surfaced two major themes of restitutionism and obedient discipleship. Discipleship themes influenced peace concerns.

The 250th anniversary celebrations, the source book, and Durnbaugh's articles precipitated the first theological study conference in a 1960 meeting at North Manchester, Indiana. Participants gathered around the topic "The Church, the Churches, and the Church of the Brethren." Major papers prepared by separate study groups before the conference were made available in the summer 1961 issue of *Brethren Life and Thought.* My contribution to the conference and journal drew heavily from my recent doctrinal dissertation that focused on Pietism. During that time I had accepted a faculty position at Bethany as an anabaptist pietist associate of Durnbaugh, who joined the seminary the same year. In our first years, members of the seminary community organized times when the two of us would debate whether we were more anabaptist or pietist. Through the years I have identified more with Anabaptism than earlier, and Durnbaugh came to recognize more influences of Radical Pietism.

As a seminary student, I was prepared for recovery through joint classes of General Conference Mennonite and Bethany Seminaries, which were both located in Chicago. I remember one class when a Mennonite rose to speak and looked directly at the Brethren. He reminded us to wake up to who we are as he held up an anabaptist book. And Mennonites saw to it that anabaptist collections invaded our library. It would be remiss not to mention the resources and influence of individuals from all Brethren groups who have been responsible, along with Don Durnbaugh, for the three (soon to be four) volumes of *The Brethren Encyclopedia* and other heritage books in their publications. The recovery also has been stimulated by the continuation of the periodical *Brethren Life and Thought* and the establishment in 1986 of the

Young Center for the Study of Anabaptist and Pietist Groups on the campus of Elizabethtown College. Another Brethren-Mennonite Heritage Center has emerged in the Shenandoah Valley.

It is difficult to measure the impact on the Brethren of this significant recovery and discussion of basic motifs. In more than three decades of teaching at Bethany, most of the years with Durnbaugh, students had a positive interest in our heritage, with few exceptions. They often expressed alienation from their church experience, however, because of its lack of faithfulness to that heritage. Their interest was reinforced in the years when Anabaptism was threatening to become another theological fad in mainline theological schools (primarily during the '60s and '70s). However, the majority of our members often appear to be ignorant of basic ingredients of the recovery. Heritage books often join the Bible as icons to be revered only to be left on the shelf apart from shaping our personal, family, and congregational lives.

Yet our heritage remains for many a blessed ingredient in tossing us two and fro. In conclusion, we might consider the value of our biblical and theological moorings in our periodicals and church school classes. We can summarize Brethren responses to winds of doctrine by quoting from the Annual Conference paper on "Biblical Inspiration and Authority." The following quotes come from the section on "Holding One Another in Love and Fellowship."

> *In spite of an essential unity, diversity is God's pattern in creation. God's delight in variety is expressed in countless ways (Ps. 104). To those who walk in the Spirit, varieties of gifts are given (1 Cor. 12:4). Conformity is humanity's pattern. It is the way of the world to try to force individuals into a uniform mold.* (29)
>
> *However, Christian freedom does not imply an unchecked individualism. Our Anabaptist heritage teaches that no one enters the kingdom apart from one's brothers and sisters.* (30)

Christian love requires:
- *that we acknowledge the integrity and worth of those brothers and sisters with whom we cannot totally agree.*
- *that we behave in ways that build up the church.*
- *that we be obedient to Jesus Christ.*
- *that we not attempt to gloss over our differences, but that we face them honestly and work at resolving them "with patience, forbearing one another in love, eager to maintain the unity of the Spirit in the bond of peace" (Eph. 4:23).*

- *that we hold before us the goal of "being in full accord and of one mind" (Phil. 2:2).*

What a challenge from our Annual Conference! For we are being tossed to and fro and blown about by every wind of doctrine. Blow winds blow! Let us throw away doctrines that prevent us from walking in the steps of Jesus. May the winds blow us to manifestations of his love and fulfillment of our baptismal vows.

Chapter 13

Heritage of Peace
Still a peace church?

Zechariah, father of John the Baptist, prophesied that his son would prepare the way for a Savior who would "guide our feet into the way of peace."
—Luke 1:79b

With little debate, delegates to the Portland Annual Conference in 1991 adopted the most biblically based, comprehensive, radical, and practical statement on peacemaking in our history ("Peacemaking, The Call of God in History," Minutes of the 205th Annual Conference). This transpired during the first Gulf War against Iraq. Twelve years later in 2003, a few weeks after the second invasion of Iraq, delegates at Boise, Idaho, overwhelmingly voted for the resolution "Call for a Living Peace Church." Co-sponsored by On Earth Peace and the Church of the Brethren General Board, the resolution resolved "to follow Jesus in seeking together an active Christian peace witness in our congregations and districts."

In major worship services at these wartime Conferences, preachers often failed to apply our biblical heritage either to those who supported the war or to the nonconformists who defied the war in a culture that glorified it with patriotic fervor. To be fair to those who plan our large family reunions, however, our Conferences frequently include insight sessions, Bible study electives, and meals that feature speakers and discussions on peace concerns. Yet the paradox of the status of our peace witness continues to surface in our Conference experiences. Without exception throughout our history, official declarations of our pacifist heritage have been affirmed almost unanimously. At the same time, our best sociologists have gathered data indicating that a sizable majority of our members are either indifferent to or oppose our peace position. The best and most comprehensive research has been done by Carl Bowman in *Brethren Society, The Cultural Transformation of a Peculiar People* (1995).

Our Peace Heritage

Early Brethren commitments to obey Christ-centered teachings occurred in the context of dismal social and economic conditions. The destructive Thirty Years War (1618-1648), in which at least one-third of the population perished, was likely one factor that led a local ruler to allow illegal refugees to settle at Schwarzenau. Unfortunately, the end of the war did not bring peace to the Germanys. Alexander Mack remembered as a boy how neighboring peasants grew weary of armies from France plundering their fields. In *Fruit of the Vine*, Durnbaugh concludes, "The period when the Brethren emerged was thus one of continual warfare. It is not surprising that from the beginning they took a firm stand against war and violence" (3).

Antiwar sentiments were part of the Pietist Reformation within the church. Prevailing moral decadence prompted Spener and Francke, spiritual leaders of the movement, to espouse persuasive love in dealing with heretics and encouraged rulers to strive for a better and peaceful world. Jacob Boehme (1575-1624), who has been regarded as the ideological father of Radical Pietism, advised Christians to refuse to participate in the wars of Babel. In dividing history of the world into six ages, he believed a seventh age of peace and unity to be near.

Such influences led Hochmann von Hochenau, a friend and evangelistic associate of Alexander Mack, to preach that Christ's call rejects military service if conscripted. Our early forebears read histories of Gottfried Arnold (1666-1714), whose pacifist beliefs were kindled by his love for pacifist

Christians of the first three centuries. He was one of the first to write favorably of the nonresistant Anabaptists, noting a tragic event that occurred when Prussian recruiting officers rushed into his church and seized all the young men who were present. Our early ancestors retained radical pietist notions about a powerful in-breaking of the Spirit for an age of peace and justice. Such emphases on the Spirit made it easier for Brethren to adjust to Quaker life and thought in William Penn's colony.

Other winds of doctrine emerged when eight Radical Pietists decided to be baptized and start a church against the advice of their beloved Hochmann. In this act they embodied discipleship and obedience theology of the anabaptist branch of the sixteenth-century Radical Reformation. An Inspirationist neighbor, Ludwig Gruber, asked Mack to compare his movement with the Mennonites. Though Mack referred to the Mennonites as "deteriorated" Baptists, he added that it would indeed be desirable if the whole world were full of them. For the Baptist seed was better than the seed of Luther, Calvin, and Catholics who "go publicly to war and slaughter one another by the thousands" (Durnbaugh, *European Origins of the Brethren* 343).

From this milieu Brethren believed that any laws requiring military service or oaths opposed the will of God. Andreas Boni, one of the first eight to be baptized, had already defied legal expectations in his refusal to bear weapons associated with citizenship in Switzerland. He was arrested for appearing without the customary side arms when he attended the infant baptism of his cousin's child (90-95).

The story about the tall Brethren elder John Naas has been popular from our beginnings. The following is one version of a story that has been handed down to verify the pacifism of our founders: Recruiting officers captured and tortured Naas. Then they dragged him before the king of Prussia. "Tell me, why will you not enlist with me?" inquired the king.

"Because," said Naas, "I have already, long ago enlisted into one of the noblest and best of enrollments, and I would not, and indeed could not, become a traitor to Him."

"Why, to whom, then? Who is your captain?" asked the astonished king.

"My captain," replied Naas, "is the great Prince Immanuel, our Lord Jesus Christ. I have espoused his cause and therefore cannot, and will not, forsake him."

"Neither will I then that you should," answered the king, who presented him with a handsome gold coin as a reward for his faithfulness to his Lord.

We know this story from the children's book entitled *The Tall Man* and an article by A. H. Cassel in *The Brethren Family Almanac*, 1871 (24). The name John Naas may have been attached to an earlier account recorded in the 1700s by a Quaker historian, Samuel Smith. Instead of Naas, the hero was named John Fisher (see *Biblical Pacifism,* 14-15, for an earlier version). Whoever he was, he was purely anabaptist in regarding obedience to Jesus as a priority.

A primary claim to the centrality of early pacifist views rests in the context of our founding mothers and fathers. The church was birthed by Radical Pietists who absorbed the pacifism of the writings and preaching of that movement. In launching illegal baptisms, the first eight adopted the ecclesiology and Christ-centered obedient and nonresistance theology of Anabaptism via the Mennonites. This occurred only a few years before they settled in the new world where they supported and were governed by this-world, one-kingdom Quakers. In striving to be peacemaking children of God whom Jesus called blessed, Brethren were saturated by cultural mores of a threefold pacifist environment. Consequently, in their first growing years, Brethren were pacifists without needing to figure it out. But this threefold legacy was destined to change, reflecting a variety of expressions of one or more of this Pietist, Anabaptist, Quaker heritage.

Interpretations and Changes in Our Pacifist Witness

Early views reveal the centrality given to the peaceable example of Jesus, his commandment to love enemies, the resultant refusal to engage in warfare, and baptisms that result in ministries of love and reconciliation in the community of faith. It remains difficult to fully understand how and why Brethren have changed, abandoned, or remained faithful to this heritage. The most cited book of our pacifist history was written by Rufus Bowman, who was president during my student years at Bethany. At that time his book, *The Church of the Brethren and War, 1708-1941,* had just come off the press. In the first edition of *Biblical Pacifism* (chapters 2 and 3), I trace the history of our peace heritage and variations of the peace church tradition. Bowman's accounts end with the beginning of World War II. My analyses end shortly before the end of the Cold War with the Soviet Union. A more updated historical account is found in Jeff Bach's article entitled "Our Conscience Is Bound: A Survey of the Brethren Peace Witness" in *Brethren Life and Thought* (Fall 2000, 157-197).

Bach's extensive research provides new stories and updated interpretations from the seven-year French and Indian War (1756-1763), the American Revolution (1775-1783), the War of 1812, the Civil War (1861-1865), and major wars of the twentieth century. Bach shares his own prejudices and conclusions. In risking the same, I want to be fair in presenting events and conclusions learned from Jeff Bach, Carl Bowman, and others.

Acceptance and Rejections of Pacifist Statements

Official corporate bodies have without exception affirmed the Christ-centered pacifist heritage of our tradition. There is much data that validate the importance of the decisions.

French and Indian War and Indian Massacres (1756-1763)

Peaceful communities in colonial America faced their first real trials during the French and Indian War and Indian massacres that occurred in the last decades of the eighteenth century. One tragic situation was cited by U. J. Jones, historian of the Pennsylvania Commonwealth, who wrote in detail of the massacre of Brethren by the Indians at Morrison's Cove. He describes the Brethren as strict nonresistants who "not only refused to take up arms to repel the savage marauders and prevent the inhuman slaughter of women and children. But they refused in the most positive manner to pay a dollar to support those who were willing to take up arms to defend their homes and their firesides, until wrung from them by the stern mandates of the law, from which there was no appeal" (Rufus Bowman 74).

From his sources Bach discovered that during these frontier, warlike skirmishes, some Brethren and Mennonites did take up arms against their attackers.

Revolutionary War (1775-1783)

With patriotic fervor emerging to support the Revolutionary War, Mennonite and Brethren elders submitted a joint petition appealing for liberty to allow their people to abide by their nonresistance stance. The English translation of the petition was handed to the Pennsylvania assembly on November 7, 1775. It began by thanking God and the assembly for granting liberty of conscience as had William Penn to those who "are persuaded in their conscience to love enemies and not resist evil. . . . " Then the petition offered counsel to their own people.

> *The advice to those who do not find Freedom of conscience to take up arms, that they ought to be helpful to those in need and distressed circumstances, we receive with cheerfulness towards all men of what station they may be—it being our principle to feed the Hungry and give the Thirsty Drink—we have dedicated ourselves to serve all men in everything that can be helpful to the preservation of Men's Lives, but we find no Freedom in giving, or doing, or assisting in any thing by which Men's Lives are destroyed or hurt.* (Rufus Bowman 80)

It is noteworthy that Mennonites and Brethren were working together. It is also interesting that very early in our history we declared a strong service stance in responding that as Christians we are dedicated to serving all people in everything that can preserve lives, while at the same time refusing to assist in anything that destroys lives. This service theme has remained integral to our peace position and continues to be basic to both traditions today.

Hatred toward those who refused to participate in the rebellion against England continued to grow. The assembly required all males who refused to bear arms to contribute an amount of money equivalent to the time others gave for military drills. In a spirit of intense patriotism, the assembly required an oath of allegiance from each male above the age of fifteen. The oath renounced allegiance to George the Third and declared faithful allegiance to the new Commonwealth of Pennsylvania.

Annual Meeting forbade Brethren to take this oath to a new country, no doubt because they regarded the colonial government to be one of the best the world had ever known. If they took the oath to the revolutionary government, it could mean that a brother would be deprived of the kiss of fellowship and breaking bread with loved ones who supported the colonial government. It was for his refusal to take this oath that Elder Christopher Sauer, Jr., saw his press and property, estimated at $150,000, confiscated and destroyed. He was arrested, suffered humiliating treatment, and until his death was a poor man taking refuge among the Brethren.

Other Brethren were not as faithful. The Big Meeting at Conestoga in 1780 forbade members to pay the "substitute money," which would support someone else to take their place in the rebel army. Contrary to the decision of the Big Meeting, there were members who took oaths and paid money as demanded. We know this because the next Annual Meeting in 1781 again recommended that the men stand up for their principles, but they allowed that when Brethren were threatened and coerced to pay or fight, paying a tax would not be considered a sin. The body decided to leave such a difficult decision to the conscience of members who faced the dilemma of whether or not to take an oath to the new government.

A decade later (1785), the Yearly Meeting responded to a brother who was advocating war on the basis of 1 Peter 2:13-14. The answer advised Christians to live as free people who nevertheless honor everyone including believers and the emperor.

So we hope the dear brother will not take it amiss when we, from all these passages of Scripture, and especially from the words of Peter, cannot see or find any liberty to use any sword, but only the sword of the Spirit, which is the word of God, by which we cast down imaginations and every high thing that exalted itself against the knowledge of God, and bring into captivity every thought to the obedience of Christ, as Paul says (2 Cor. 10:5).

War of 1812

Bach concludes that "Brethren entered the nineteenth century with a strongly biblical pacifism shaped by following the example of Jesus" (165). Generally Brethren remained firm in their opposition to participation in war during the war with England from 1812-1815 and with Mexico in 1845. In 1822 it was finally decided after several attempts without success, that young men should not "take the liberty to go on muster grounds (a gathering of troops) or take part in the festivities of Independence day." The number of times this came to Conference divulges that some young Brethren were defying the advice of the church. In the War of 1812, Bach traces possible participation in military service by two members in Ohio (166). The 1848 Yearly Meeting ruled that candidates seeking baptism be asked to accept "defenselessness," the church's peace teaching. For decades new members were asked to promise not to engage in warfare and to deal with conflicts in the church according to Matthew 18.

Civil War (1861-1865)

In years before the Civil War, Brethren Conferences opposed slavery. Northern Brethren had a built-in bias for the Union. In the South the abolitionist stance, which was strongly held by John Kline, seemed to be consistent with pacifist convictions. Southern Brethren opposed slavery and secession because they desired to maintain fellowship with brothers and sisters in the North. This created an ongoing faithfulness to teachings against war. Brethren suffered more in the South. Some fled west and north as refugees.

William Thurman, a Baptist convert, was eventually disfellowshiped because he proposed that our present single mode of feetwashing replace the double mode that was prevalent in the East at that time. Likewise, he was tolerated but not widely followed when his premillennial views led minorities on several occasions to join him in awaiting the second coming of Jesus. He also wrote a pamphlet entitled "Non-Resistance," which gained wider acceptance among the Brethren. Instead of getting him in trouble, it may have influenced passages in a petition presented to the Confederate Congress signed by more than one hundred advocates of peace. Its purpose was to appeal for support of an exemption law for conscientious objectors. A short portion of his pamphlet appears here:

> *In war there is a continual retaliation, returning of evil for evil. But the Christian can "recompense to no men evil for evil" (Rom. XII:17 [KJV]). Hence cannot go to war. In war men avenge the evils imposed by other nations, which the Christian is forbidden to do. "Avenge not yourselves, but rather give place unto wrath."*
>
> *In war men overcome their enemies by pouring on them more evil than they are enabled to return or withstand.*
>
> *But the little flock of Christ must take a path, leading just in the opposite direction: they must "overcome evil with good" (Rom. XII:21 [KJV]).* (Rufus Bowman 141-142)

We have seen that Brethren welcomed alternate humanitarian services during the American Revolution. However, the assembly of the Confederate commonwealth required conscientious objectors to pay taxes to cover expenses of a soldier as an alternative to military service. Later, there were movements to elicit the promise that the payment would be used to help victims of warfare. There were variations of such alternatives in the North during the war: the friendly attitude of President Lincoln toward conscientious objectors, the need for good farmers to produce food, and the North's superior military strength combined to provide more comfortable exemptions for conscientious objectors. At first these were provided by individual states such as Indiana and Ohio. Exempted individuals were required to pay $200. Later, the Federal Act of 1863 provided payment of $300 for expenses of substitutes.

A year later, due to the opposition of the Society of Friends, there was a greater recognition of conscience. When drafted, draftees from peace churches would be considered noncombatants and were assigned hospital duty or an assignment to care for freed slaves. They could be exempted from such responsibilities by paying $300. Another possibility that made this payment easier on the conscience was the provision that the money would be used for the benefit of "sick and wounded soldiers," rather than the hiring of military substitutes.

Though the sympathies and prayers of the peace churches were mostly for the Union cause in the Civil War, Rufus Bowman reported that Brethren experienced fewer defections from their peace stance than Quakers, Mennonites, and Amish. However, caught up in the patriotic fervor, some young men from historic pacifist churches entered the army on both sides of the Civil War. In all of the peace churches, there had been a dearth of pacifist teaching for several generations preceding the war. (See more extensive treatment of the Civil War in my *Biblical Pacifism*, 1986 edition, 22-26).

The church entered the twentieth century with a sense of optimism due to their growth and because many enthusiastically believed they were entering a Christian century. The following are selections from a peace tract published by the Brethren's Tracts and Pamphlet committee in 1900, titled "Christ and War" by Daniel Vaniman.

> Christ, its author, says, "Love your enemies." War says, "Hate them."
> Christ says, "Do them good." War says, "Do them harm."
> Christ says, "Pray for them." War says, "Slay them."
> Christ says, "I come not to destroy men's lives but to save them." War says, "I come to destroy men's lives, and for this purpose I want the most effectual weapons. . . ."
> Paul says, "If thine enemy hunger, feed him." War says, "Starve him."
> Paul says, "If he thirst, give him drink." War says, "Destroy his wells, cut off his supplies of every kind."
> Paul says, "We wrestle not against flesh and blood." War says, "We do wrestle against flesh and blood. Crowd them to the wall and into the last ditch; utterly destroy them if they don't submit.

Such Christ-centered biblical quotes were supplemented by the tone of a 1910 resolution of Annual Conference that called on "the entire membership to activity to the cause of peace."

World War I (1917-1918)

Brethren were not prepared for World War I, and the government was unprepared for conscientious objectors. The draft law of May 18, 1917, freed pacifists from combatant service. Yet, they were required to join the army. As soldiers, they were promised roles limited to noncombatant duties. These promises were often forgotten, and members of peace churches were threatened and coerced to drill and wear military uniforms. Confusion abounded and many questions emerged. What do you do with a small group of COs in training? Do they drill or wear a uniform? What is and what is not noncombatant service?

A special session of Standing Committee was called to meet at Goshen, Indiana, in January 1918. After expressing their love for our country, their willingness to cooperate in constructive ways, and commending the loyal Brethren who were in camps for their firm stand against participating in acts of war, they agreed on the following statement that would be distributed to all pastors and camps:

We further urge our brethren not to enlist in any service which would, in any way, compromise our time-honored position in relation to war; also that they refrain from wearing the military uniform. The tenets of the church forbid military drilling, or learning the arts of war, or doing anything which contributes to the destruction of human life or property.

Six months later, after the statement had circulated in the camps, J. M. Henry, pastor of the Washington, D. C. congregation and member of the Central Service Committee, was called into the office of Dr. Keppel, a third assistant of war, who read the following: *"The United States Government charges the officers of the Goshen Conference and the authors of the Goshen Statement as guilty of treasonable intent in obstructing the select draft law."* This could mean two years in prison and/or a $10,000 fine for each of the three church officials charged with "attempting to incite inaction, disloyalty, mutiny, and refusal to do duty in the military forces of the United States" (*Gospel Messenger,* July 27, 1918). Henry had forty-eight hours to prepare an answer. Henry called two other members of the committee to Washington. After prayer and much discussion, a judge kept them from going to prison when they pledged to use their influence with the Church of the Brethren to discontinue the distribution of the statement.

As a result, the Goshen Statement was recalled from the mails, and camp visitors were urged not to use it in the military camps. Since then, many have wished that the committee would have refused the threats, which might have been a bluff, by professing their determination to go to prison rather than renounce the will of the church and their commitment to the Prince of Peace. Steadfast faithfulness to Christ and the church could have greatly enhanced our witness to peace in the twentieth century. Some have felt we have never recovered from this.

Between Wars

The good and bad experiences of war produced peace leaders such as Dan West and M. R. Zigler, who were influenced by the example of Quakers during World War I. Through summer camps, caravans, workcamps, Sunday schools, and the General Welfare Board, the church was motivated to attempt its first programs in peace education and action. The Board of Christian Education appointed a Peace Commission which served until 1934, when Manchester College faculty were requested to serve in this capacity as peace educators.

Somewhat independently Dan West launched a movement in the early '30s to enlist "One Hundred Dunkers for Peace" and to organize key youth who would be trained as peace workers. They would help enlist "Twenty Thousand Dunkers for Peace" to sign a pacifist pledge. Annual Conference of 1935 may have upstaged the actual execution of the plan by ambitiously adopting the slogan "Two Hundred Thousand Dunkers for Peace." Our famous labor leader, Kermit Eby, advocated applying strategies of peacemaking to labor and racial disputes. At the same time Brethren were deeply involved in relief work in Spain and China. This provided the context for the church's approval of the Heifer Project, a movement dreamed by Dan West when offering humanitarian relief in the midst of the Spanish Civil War (1936-1939).

Few Conferences during this period passed into history without strong pronouncements on peace. In statements from 1932-1941, all war was declared to be sin "unconditionally and always." The major peace statement in 1970 at Lincoln, Nebraska, involved changes that were passionately debated and will be discussed later. Yet, Christ-centered bases were not abandoned. The 1918 Conference stated, "We believe that war or any participation in war is wrong and incompatible with the spirit, example and teachings of Jesus Christ." And in 1948 the Conference advised,

> *Love your enemies, do good to those who hate you, bless those who curse you, pray for those who abuse you. To him who strikes you on the cheek, offer the other also . . . (Luke 6:27, 28). . . . So whatever you wish that men would do to you, do so to them, for this is the law and the prophets (Matt. 7:12). . . . Put your sword back into its place; for all who take the sword will perish by the sword (Matt. 26:52).*

Such Conference statements substantiate that Christ-centered biblical texts have permeated the decisions of the body. We will examine decisions that are obviously different in the twentieth century. Some regard these decisions as constituting major theological distancing from traditional beliefs. Others insist that we have added previously neglected biblical themes to fit a different cultural context.

World War II (1941-1945)

Data reveals that Brethren have rejected our peace heritage in every war since we migrated to America. The difference between earlier centuries and the twentieth century is that in the latter the defectors constitute a sizable majority. Remembering the unfortunate experience of the special Goshen decision in World War I, M. R Zigler was motivated to prepare for something better when contemplating alternatives in the advent of World War II. He gathered leaders of other peace churches to make a deal with Selective Service to provide special provisions for all secular and religious objectors to war. The alternative was called the Civilian Public Service program or CPS (1940-1947). The church operated a series of base camps for supervised work in forestry and soil conservation. The government made the rules and specified programs of work. The peace churches paid the bills. By the end of the war, Brethren had contributed $1,300,000 to support the camps.

Later, the government allowed CPS men to work on detached service projects at mental hospitals, in medical experimentation, in public health, and in agriculture efforts. The experiment in human starvation at the University of Minnesota and the parachuting smokejumper units that fought forest fires were sensational projects that made heroes for this teenager. Projects of doubtful worth and the usual red tape of government regulations motivated church leaders to be more determined to devise a better system if ever again confronted with conscription.

During World War II the percentage of our young men who chose to take the oath for military service instead of participating in CPS has frequently been estimated to be somewhere between eighty and ninety percent. The draft was reinstated during the Korean and Vietnam Wars in the '50s, '60s, and early '70s. With even better provisions for conscientious objectors and the unpopular war in Vietnam, the numbers of conscientious objectors increased more than twofold from World War II.

Civil Rights Movement, Korea, and Vietnam

Official and lay participation by Brethren in the civil rights movement led to greater impetus and commitment to our peace testimony. After experiencing Reinhold Niebuhr's criticisms of nonviolent resistance movements, Martin Luther King provided specific examples of how biblical emphases on suffering love and overcoming evil with good, in which biblical themes were sung and preached, actually could make a difference for greater justice.

In 1948 Congress voted in a new Selective Service law, which surprisingly exempted COs. But in 1951 Congress required two years of civilian service and offered a broad range of possible projects including some Brethren Volunteer Service assignments already in operation due to the Conference decision to institute BVS in 1948. The draft continued through the Korean and Vietnam Wars from 1951 to 1973 when President Nixon ended the draft. The alternatives permitted draftees to choose projects that were generally approved by draft boards. The church had the authority to accept or reject applicants to its programs. This constituted one of the most liberal provisions for conscientious objectors in the history of conscription for war.

However, some youth chose a more radical stance of complete resistance to the draft system. They shared strong antiwar sentiments of the time. Draft boards would not grant selective service objectors from just war traditions the same privileges granted to members of peace churches. Some went underground, were sent to jail, or escaped to Canada or Sweden. Some Brethren resisters were also sent to jail. Others were required to participate in humanitarian programs. Only a few, facing a sympathetic judge, were freed from all alternatives or penalties. Throughout this period, our draft resisters identified with other non-cooperators. A few Brethren went to jail in order to identify with those who were denied privileges extended to members of an historical peace church.

Annual Conference in 1957 introduced favorable support for Brethren who joined military units. Thirteen years later, a more extensive paper reacted to draft resistance. This 1970 Conference slightly modified what had gone before with more definite degrees of approval of the choice of draftees. This Conference paper did not use the word *conscience*. It did repeat the earlier statement of support, respect, and desire to remain in fellowship with those who choose military service. But the church *commended* to its members both alternative service and nonviolent opposition to the draft. In an environment of strong emotions for and against the Vietnam War, a long fervent debate centered on approving draft resistance that was illegal and chastised. The most debated departures from previous statements appear below:

> *The church pledges its support and continuing fellowship to all of our draft-age members who face conscription. We recognize that some feel obligated to render full or noncombative military service and we respect all who make such a decision.*
>
> *We commend to all of draft age, their parents, counselors, and fellow members the alternative positions of (1) Alternative Service as conscientious objectors engaging in constructive civilian work, or (2) open, nonviolent noncooperation with the system of conscription. The church pledges itself to renew and redouble its effort to interpret to the membership of the church at all levels of the church's life these positions which we believe are in harmony with the style of life set forth in the gospel and as expressed in the historic faith and witness of our church.*

There were so many non-cooperators with the draft that the legal justice system's inability to process such a huge backlog of cases contributed to the end of the draft by the Nixon administration in 1973, which Congress ended officially in 1974.

There is another category that has been overlooked in speaking of alternatives to the draft. Roman Catholic polity maintains an historic position that forbids clerics and members of religious orders to bear arms. They believe that the hands that have shed blood can never be permitted to handle the sacred bread and wine. Through many centuries governing powers have been persuaded to give exemptions for priests. When Luther heard that the Swiss reformer Huldreich Zwingli was killed in a battle against Catholics, he responded that it served him right, for he should have been doing what pastors are called to do.

This explains why Protestants who are ordained or are preparing for ordination have shared the same exemptions in conscription laws. Because of the position of our church and the governmental requirements for church approval, very few Brethren have taken military oaths in order to serve as chaplains. Some of our largest enrollments at Bethany Seminary occurred during World War II and the extended years of the Vietnam tragedy. I remember how I was talked out of entering civilian public service by college administrators near the end of World War II, who negotiated with my draft board to secure exemptions for those preparing for the ministry.

As I write, there are bills in Congress to revive the draft. These would replace or accompany a professional army recruited from volunteers. Many who voluntarily join the military come from poverty situations; they often join for financial reasons and opportunities for a college education. Currently, those who advocate a universal draft believe it might lead those in power to be more reluctant to send soldiers into harm's way if their own sons and daughters were subject to conscription. Between wars and when there is no draft, excellent volunteer service programs modeled after Brethren Volunteer Service attract fewer Brethren. Yet BVS orientation sessions prepare volunteers for projects related to peace and justice concerns, and the program continues to offer quality projects for Brethren, non-Brethren, and international youth. The units have at times served the requirements of German conscientious objectors.

Thinking About the Decline of Our Peace Heritage

Both sociologists and historical theologians have given reasons for the changing views and status of our peace witness. They have concluded that the church has moved from a corporate ethic to an individualistic ethic. They rightly observe that authority has shifted from communities gathered around scripture seeking the mind of Christ to individual conscience. Aforementioned schisms in the 1880s led the church in this direction. These differences resulted from opinions about the authority of Annual

Meeting. Old Orders remained nonresistors. Progressives left the decision up to the individual.

The larger body of conservatives, Church of the Brethren, has been influenced by individualist currents in our culture. The acculturation was similar to that of the progressives, advocating such things as Sunday schools, paid pastors, and overseas missions. However, the conservatives were more attracted to peace emphases that were present in Finney Revivalism and social gospel movements. The progressives, now referred to as the Brethren Church, have been influenced more by conservative evangelical theological movements, few of which have pacifist convictions.

Vocational Pacifism

Acculturation and tolerance views of the larger body of the big schism led some to believe the peace witness to be for some but not for all. This has been named vocational pacifism.

> *We declare again that our members should neither participate in war nor learn the art of war. It is recognized, however, that not all members will hold the beliefs which the church recommends. Some will feel conscientiously obligated to render full military service and others noncombatant military service. Some, on the other hand, may feel compelled to refuse to even register under a conscription law. Since the church desires to maintain fellowship with all who sincerely follow the guidance of conscience, it will respect such decisions, in spite of its disappointment that its message has not been taught better or comprehended more fully.* (1957 Annual Conference Statement on War 4)

When a sister or brother has proposed leaving decisions of choosing military service to the conscience of youth, I have chided: "What if a young women wants to be employed where she will likely be tempted to be a call girl to earn money for college? Would you say to her, 'Our church opposes prostitution, but we will support you wherever your conscience leads you'?" If supporting one's conscience means approval for whatever the individual conscience decides, I share the critique of those who favor the corporate ethic, even as I want to promote programs and mentors that bind the conscience with the community of faith.

Nevertheless, in addition to Bach's basic reasons listed above, it is interesting to add reasons World War II Brethren veterans have given for joining the army. The following list comes from a survey by Rufus Bowman in *Seventy Times Seven:* "Duty to country, social pressure, the economic problem, inadequate peace teaching, the feeling that the war was forced on them, indifference to the church and lack of sympathy with the C.O. position" (45).

We do need to examine why and how young men and women have related to conscription. In doing this we need to consider questioning the moral absolutes of a substantial number of our members. Sociologists call it acculturation. The old Brethren saw it as "getting worldly." Rufus Bowman argued that individual consciences were more influenced by the ethic of our culture than by the collective ethic of the church. Floyd Mallott gave it an economic flavor. In class he pontificated that when the "Dunker couple first climbed into their Model T Ford and started down the highway, it was not long before the broad brim hat flew off, then the bonnet . . . then many of their peculiar practices, and finally the nonresistant peace testimony" (*The Brethren Encyclopedia* 784).

We can also say that in Christian education we have failed to teach our corporate peace witness. We have noted how Brethren have been unprepared for war because of our failure to witness for peace between wars. This quietism was overcome only when our own sons were threatened with military service. Only Christian Hope, our first missionary to Denmark, shared the peace witness with those who became Brethren and migrated to America partly because of compulsory military service laws in their home country. Our missionaries to India, China, and Nigeria, for the most part, failed to share biblical peace teachings. Perhaps, this was due to the peaceful conduct of the newly converted societies. Nigerian students at Bethany shared that when their sons began to enlist in the army during their Civil War (1967-1970), they were told by American Brethren: "Going to war is something that we do not do!" They reported that Nigerians felt like responding, "Now you tell us this! Why didn't you tell us this earlier?" Realizing that movements of reconciliation are urgently needed if Christians and Muslims are to live together peacefully, Nigerians are now interested in our peace position.

Affluence and cultural beliefs can contribute to the failures of our peace witness. Both of these are engineered by a media that promotes religious and cultural views that foster consumerism and militarism. A visit to the beautiful Shenandoah Valley reminded me of our peace leaders, such as John Kline, M. R. Zigler, and Rufus Bowman, who had been nurtured there, and I wondered how so many in the present generation could have lost the peace witness. A discerning young pastor put it this way: "Our culture and government have done a more effective job convincing us that the good life consists of possessions defended by the military than we have in preaching that our security lies with Jesus and his gospel."

We can also point to the influence of media preachers and fundamentalist neighbors who are exclusively concerned about saving souls from this world, but avoid the biblical Hebraic and Jesus heritage of praying that the kingdom come on earth as in heaven. We can also blame the demise of our peace position on our colleges. Our tradition has been regarded as problematic in that our strong theology of love and a spirit of tolerance sometimes work against emphases on discipleship derived from the teachings of Jesus.

Carl Bowman's "Brethren Profile Study" reveals that only a third of the membership agrees with the old Dunker premise that it is wrong to help in any war by fighting (*Brethren Society* 391). I was privileged to be on a committee that supervised Jeff Copp's dissertation entitled "What Pastors Experience in Their Congregations as They Represent the Peace Position in the Church of the Brethren" (D.Min., Lancaster Theological Seminary, May 2004). His study reveals that ninety-two percent of our pastors are not satisfied with the present state of our peace position for different reasons. It was clear from the data that the number of congregations engaged in some form of witnessing for peace is small in comparison to the number of congregations that are not.

Before I make the case that we still are a peace church, I need to join in confessing the realities of the data documented above. At Bethany we would frequently experience a student nurtured in a Brethren congregation, who testified that he or she had never heard of our peace position before coming to Bethany. In Copp's survey, pastors were asked what they would like to see happen with the peace position. Approximately thirty-five percent would like the position to be modified to better reflect divergences of opinion in the church. Nine percent would like to see the position dropped. That leaves fifty-six percent of pastors who want the peace position reclaimed as a part of our anabaptist-pietist heritage.

As stated before, the data reveal that Brethren have had defectors from our peace heritage in every war since we migrated to America. The difference between earlier centuries and the twentieth is that in the latter the defectors constitute a sizable majority. Jeff Bach observes that especially during World War II "the Brethren no longer had a church that expected its members to act on its rhetoric" (178).

The Case for Being a Peace Church

Everyone who takes our peace position seriously should appreciate the research and conclusions of our academicians. Their findings have not eliminated their love for Christ and the church. Their realistic conclusions challenge my assumptions and disturb my dreams. Yet they provide assessments that stimulate my efforts to make a case that the Church of the Brethren can still claim to be a peace church.

Most of the data used to measure degrees of faithfulness to our peace heritage have focused on percentages of young men who have joined the armed services. I first questioned this way of determining faithfulness in a conversation with others comparing ages for baptism with the age for confirmation in other traditions. A United Church of Christ seminarian commented that in increasing the age for confirmation, newly confirmed youth depart very soon afterward to attend institutions of higher education and years pass before they appear for the christening (baptism) of their new baby. In response, I asked, "Think of a favorite doctrine that identifies your tradition and tell me whether you would judge the status of that doctrine by surveying eighteen-year-old members and men in their early twenties?"

To this she replied: "Absolutely not!"

Do we judge whether we are a peace church by what one age group does? Or do we determine it in the corporate setting? I respect this anabaptist legacy. Brethren congregations and districts endeavor to confirm basic decisions by sending a query to Annual Conference. Standing Committee, a smaller representative body from districts, devises a process for dealing with the query. If the query is accepted, the Conference often selects a committee to engage in study sessions. They attempt to bring back a paper derived from consensus and to return with their statement the next year. Their conclusions have been guided by our biblical and theological heritage. The committee may be asked to engage in another year of study, but, finally, the paper may be presented for discussion, amendments, and votes of the delegates. The process works from the bottom up, and all are encouraged to be open to the guidance of the Holy Spirit.

Without exception, such collective decision-making has resulted in a near consensus affirmation of our historic peace heritage. I ask, when individualism permeates our culture, why not focus on a long existing corporate ethic? Kermit Eby, a labor union leader and later professor at the University of Chicago, maintained his love for our heritage in writing and speaking about Baugo Church of the Brethren, his home church in Indiana. He is reported to have said: "Brethren boys leave and join the army. When they come home, their congregation sends them to Conference. There they vote for our peace position."

Jeff Bach's essay maintains that World War II revealed Brethren to be rhetorical pacifists, meaning that although the church professed pacifism, most of our members did not embody it in their beliefs and life. To be fair to Bach, he is not saying this only about eighteen-year-olds. Rhetoric without incarnation is like worshiping the Bible without taking it down from the shelf to read. He is right.

We could say the same about many beliefs and practices. Corporately our people would say that we are a New Testament church in which members are biblically literate. We could affirm it with a consensus vote. However, a survey might reveal widespread biblical illiterateness. It is my view that in spite of missing the mark, we should strive for greater integrity through our corporate affirmations, inspiring representative members to sanction our beliefs at the one unique place—Annual Conference—where Brethren meet to renew their covenant with one another (see preface to Henry Kurtz's *Brethren's Encyclopedia*).

Likewise, it can be misleading to dwell on realistic assessments of our lack of faithfulness to our peace position in World War II without looking at the larger picture. Even if only ten to twenty percent of our members were visible, active pacifists, we could count from ten to twenty-five thousand Brethren peacemakers. Existentially, I find it difficult to echo that we are no longer a peace church. My personal pacifist convictions began in junior high days during World War II. My family belonged to a peace church. I was nurtured by my pastor and a Sunday school teacher who was a conscientious objector. I was influenced by my experiences at Brethren camps, a summer work camp, and in bull sessions at McPherson College. These all strengthened my fledgling ideals.

I remember many who suffered as they lived out their pacifist witness. Brethren paid for CPS camps and risked enmity for their convictions. Their witness inspired groups in most of our congregations to make peace and love enemies through many Brethren Service programs during and after World War II. Many participated in activities that witnessed to biblical pacifist commandments to love enemies and overcome evil with good. The Bible tells us that often it is only a few who enter the narrow gate that leads to life (Matt. 7:13). That can be true at the same time that many others along the way are willing to consider the grace that can be empowered even in "weakness" (2 Cor. 12:8-9).

Pietist Conscience and Anabaptist Communalism

"The inner word" was somewhat similar to professions of a personal conscience that defines right from wrong, and Alexander Mack accepted the possibilities of divine leadings and mystical experiences. His long association with Pietists led him to both reject *and* retain individualist aspects of that heritage. Pietism emphasized the worth and sacredness of every person. Many were persecuted for even small deviations from the creeds. Brethren remained in prison when they could have been freed simply by not insisting that good works be part of the creed stating that we are saved by faith alone.

This led one time to saying that it may be possible for one person with Christ and extensive identification with our biblical heritage to be right over against an entire congregation or empire.

I have joined others who critique Martin Brumbaugh's often quoted phrase that Brethren believe there should be "no force in religion." He articulated this in agreeing with a growing opposition to contemporary expressions of church discipline. In doing so, he misrepresented the phrase that historically was used to defend Christians from coercive acts of the state. Although I agree with many of his critics, my pietist impulses have led me to have some empathy for applications of the phrase. When we oppose and/or experience coercion of the state, we may be influenced to have a more tolerant attitude toward brothers or sisters who disagree with us. Our pietist heritage might partially explain why Brethren preceded Mennonites in departing from numerous and stricter measures of church discipline. We have learned that the first Yearly Meeting decided to refuse to pay substitute money while at the same time they left the decision to the "conscience" of the members.

Yet, Mack added important modifications to his acceptance of a presence of the inner word. He insisted that the inner word needs to be checked by the outer word of the Scriptures and corporate views of the community of faith. From previous chapters we repeat that the pietist openness to new light must be checked by what Anabaptists have named the rule of Paul: "Let two or three prophets speak and let the others weigh what is said" (1 Cor. 14:29). So it is with our conscience. We can respect the conscience of those who differ, but we believe that conscience needs to be nurtured by heritage, biblical faith, and other members of the body of Christ. I continue to agree with Carl Bowman's suggestion that tensions existing between Anabaptism and Pietism can also be viewed as mutually reinforcing currents.

A pastor kept me up late during a visit in order to share his story for the first time with someone he guessed might be sympathetic. He spoke of being a Mennonite facing conscription during World War II. Without consulting with him, his ministers worked out details of his alternative assignment to the draft. They arranged an appointment and told him where he would be going and what he would be doing. We might say it was his individualist conscience that rejected what they had planned. They had failed to consider his thinking and wishes. His anger hastened his leaving the church and joining the Marine Corps. It did not take long for him to realize he was in the wrong place. He was awakened at night by fists slugging him in the stomach. Officers stepped on his hands and fingers when he was ordered to crawl on the ground. He came to believe that these and other violent acts and language were designed to make him into an angry fighting animal. He suffered much and was lucky to be released after a few months at war's end. When he returned to his home community, he joined the Church of the Brethren, because he knew they taught the peace position but also allowed more freedom to the individual to participate in deciding one's destiny.

Had this young man been able to absorb the communal ethic, he might have ended up in a better place by exploring other possibilities in talking with friends, his family, and the ministers. It is obvious that he may have been motivated to follow his conscience in an attempt to punish and expose his ruling elders. At the same time, we can believe that the church could have better applied their corporate ethic by including him in decisions about his future.

In his studies, Jeff Copp concludes that requiring allegiance to the peace position as a test of membership is not feasible for many today. But in an effort to restore our corporate ethic, he recommends that all church membership classes make it clear with dialogue and strong convictions that candidates are joining a congregation and denomination in which peacemaking and pacifist nonconformity will continue to be our corporate ethic.

In summary, we can speak of our position as being one of conscientious objection to war. Through the centuries we have petitioned the powers to respect the conscience of our members. In this way conscience can be a good word if the conscience has been nurtured to embody corporate ethics derived in obedience to New Testament biblical faith centered on the life and teachings of Jesus.

Departures from Biblical Nonresistance

Some Brethren who honor our heritage share concerns that faithfulness to our peace heritage has suffered from some views that have moved us away from nineteenth-century nonresistance. This is the case with Jeff Bach who empathizes so well with the convictions of German Baptist Brethren and other conservatives. I share his analyses at the same time I differ in evaluating what changes are consistent with or divergent from our New Testament heritage.

Quaker Influences

From their experiences in World War I, M. R. Zigler, Dan West, Gladdys Muir, and others appropriated ideas from service programs of American Friends Service Committee to launch major Brethren Service programs of the church. Friends (Quakers) might appropriately be called the charismatics (the Spirit-led believers) of the pacifist tradition. They have believed the presence, power, and authority of Jesus through the Holy Spirit to be basic to their testimony. They declared to King Charles II in 1770 that the Spirit of Christ "will never move them to fight and war with outward weapons, neither for the kingdom of Christ nor for kingdoms of this world." The living Christ takes away the hatred and pride that provide occasions for war.

Friends refer to the Lamb's war in the Book of Revelation, which contains the news of conflict in which evil will be overcome and a new heaven and new earth will be established. Christ wants to enlist his people to fight in the Lamb's war, which can be defined as every struggle against evil in human history until God in mercy brings history to the peaceable kingdom promised in Isaiah and described in the last book of the Bible. This war is waged with nonviolent, loving weapons symbolized by the Lamb. To participate, we need to allow ourselves to be perfected by the Holy Spirit in the confidence that the Lord is at work in this thick night of darkness.

Quaker-like influences were evident in colonial America where Brethren voted for Quakers and inherited the consensus-making polity of their yearly meeting. I agree with Don Durnbaugh that in the twentieth century Quaker influences modified nineteenth-century nonresistant views that embodied a strong anabaptist flavor. Rather than completely departing from the past, the Brethren may have been appropriating some of their colonial peace heritage. Brethren may, at times, be perplexed at what seems to be naive optimism of the Quakers or their absolute confidence of being led by the Holy Spirit. They embody some of the same differences and polarities as we. Nevertheless, it is questionable how much their influence has led us to forsake our heritage. It may be sustained by our pietist heritage that teaches us to be open to new light as it breaks forth from the Word. Bach depicts Muir, first professor of peace studies in our colleges, as believing she was connecting with the Brethren peace heritage, when in reality it was her interest in Quaker spirituality. This is partly true, yet our peace heritage may not, or perhaps has not, been completely lacking of Quaker spirituality.

Optimistic Humanism

Bach accurately observes that both inside and outside our institutions, Brethren were afflicted with theology and movements that were not grounded in Christ-centered biblical faith. He records that Jacob Funk in 1910 drew arguments from the international peace movement in his book *War and Peace*. Bach discovered there was an absence of focus on Jesus and the Bible. Instead, Funk defined war as the negation of love and justice. I am more likely to defend Brother Funk in believing that he assumed that Brethren were already aware of many affirmations of love and justice in the Bible.

Every generation adopts beliefs from environs that seem to be right and friendly. The following Conference decision supports Bach's critique in its optimism about the advent of a better world. Adopted at the 1935 Conference at Winona Lake, Indiana, the statement mingles anabaptist themes with more politically oriented ones. It declared that "war is incompatible with the spirit, example, and teachings of Jesus." Apart from a few references like this, the paper adds a different, new flavor:

> We believe that war is not inevitable. Those beliefs are not based upon a peculiar peace doctrine of our own; they arise from our application of Christian standards to all human relations, whether individual, group, class, or national. To settle conflicts in any of these relationships by war is not efficient, not constructive, not permanent, and certainly not Christian. We believe that nonviolence, motivated by goodwill, is more powerful than the sword, making possible the survival of both parties, while warfare insures the ultimate destruction of both. (Minutes of Annual Conference, 1923-1944, 110-111)

In addition to the demise of the influence of the corporate ethic, Jeff Bach suggests that church peace leaders and peace studies programs at Brethren colleges distanced themselves from a pacifism with christological and biblical bases. However, one wonders why Bach ignores the more pessimistic visions of the future by fundamentalists and premillennialists that have often undermined our peace heritage while claiming to be biblical.

In our daily work, we can no longer avoid associating with unbelievers. Paul even allows a believer to accept an unbeliever's invitation to a meal (1 Cor. 10:27). With the following example, I have answered those who criticize joining secular humanists in peacemaking. Suppose I see a little girl drowning in the river and an atheist happens to join me in saving her life. Afterwards, when we are resting together, I will ask him why he risked his life for this little girl. Then I can share my Christian faith in the sacredness of life. Mennonite Thomas R. Yoder Neufelt speaks of sharing peace and justice concerns with lovers of peace who are not believers in Christ. He relates that, for those of us who have not forgotten our roots, "to find collaborators in the work of peace beyond the borders of the church is a bright sign of God's peaceable presence in our world" (*The Conrad Grebel Review*, Winter 2003, 58).

I have often shared the faith views of Jacques Ellul with young humanist peacemakers. If we love people because they are naturally good and they respond otherwise, we can easily become disillusioned liberals. However, if the foundation of our love is that God has loved us even when we have been unworthy of his love, then we can keep on loving another whether successful or not. Peacemaking with unbelievers can provide evangelistic opportunities to witness to our faith.

Nonresistant Vocational Pacifism

Bach consistently depicts Brethren as having a strong biblical pacifism shaped by following the example of Jesus. He adds that "They did not see the Christian ethic as one by which to rule a government, nor to expect of all humanity" ("Our Conscience Is Bound," *Brethren Life and Thought,* Fall 2000, 165). Another slightly different expression of the above statement comes from their European context: "The Brethren did not expect this behavior of everyone everywhere, nor did they seek to impose it on governing powers" (159). Later, Bach seems to critique twentieth-century Brethren pacifists for not maintaining the same stance. Accurate statements about the past can be used to support contemporary vocational pacifist views that believe the teachings of Jesus to be for Christians, not for governments. It has been named a two-kingdom theory. Jesus as Lord of the pacifist church constitutes one kingdom. The other kingdom is the state: "The sword is an ordering outside the perfection of Christ" (Schleitheim Confession). Many Mennonites, however, insist this view is not scriptural.

I have appreciated another anabaptist, two-kingdom vision. The first is defined by Jesus in responding to the question, When will the kingdom come? He answers, "The kingdom of God is among you" (Luke 17:20-21). The New Testament writers interpret this by promising that we can participate and embody the first fruits of the kingdom coming. This promise has influenced anabaptist teaching that we are to live in our present kingdom as if the future kingdom of God has already come. Many sincerely agree with the two-kingdom view expressed, perhaps at its worst, by an elder of a Mennonite community during a visit by Brethren youth. He stressed that their sons would never be soldiers, yet rejoiced that American soldiers were in Vietnam defending all of us from communism.

One obvious response is to realize how the early context in Europe differed from ours. Then they lived under governments that regarded Brethren as criminals guilty of civil disobedience for baptizing those already baptized as infants. This certainly would not be the same relationship that Brethren have often experienced in America. In Europe Brethren related to the powers by shaking the dust from their feet and emigrating to a colony where they voted for and supported a government that was attempting to rule in ways consistent with the teachings of Jesus.

John Howard Yoder, with others, has taught us that older versions of Romans 13 probably led our ancestors to believe that God *ordained* the powers to wield the sword. Yoder adds that more accurate translations of original Greek would be that God *orders* and can work through the powers. Likewise, when the passage clearly says we should be subject to the powers, we can understand that to be subject is different than mere obedience. We are taught in Acts 5:29 that we are to obey God, not man. Those who are in charge of our democracy tell us they want to know what we believe. We can be subject to them by telling them what we believe. Being Anabaptists we cannot *force* them to do what we say. The anabaptist word is that we can and should *witness* to our faith. Like Jesus, we can witness to others as we put on the spirit of love. We are free to share what we think is best for our nation. In a democracy, what we say may not be accepted. We may experience nonconformist sensitivities that serve to transform our minds to know the will of God (Rom. 12:2).

Reinhold Niebuhr, a Christian ethicist, provides an interesting case study. After disclaiming his pacifist position, he still granted that Jesus was a nonresistant pacifist. He sanctioned war when he believed force was necessary to ensure justice in defeating evil powers. He believed it to be good to have pacifists who exemplify the Jesus way of love, for they provide a plumb line to test which is the lesser of two evils. He admired Amish and Mennonites who strive to live peaceful lives. He did not appreciate, however, Quakers who were trying to tell the government what to do.

During the few years before he died, Niebuhr and his followers changed their views somewhat. In thinking of the possibility of a nuclear war, they came to believe that war would no longer be the lesser evil, but likely the greatest evil. In their critique of pacifists who advocated nonviolence, they judged their actions to not be consistent with the nonresistant Jesus. They changed their views in light of the success of the civil rights movement. King achieved some greater justice by his willingness to suffer rather than to inflict suffering on others. The movement's nonresistant stance involved resistance that seemed to be supported by Pauline teachings to overcome evil with good.

Scholars like John Howard Yoder taught many about the politics of Jesus who had social concerns as well as personal ones. Jesus embodied the worldly theology of Isaiah about the heavenly kingdom of peace and justice coming on earth. Walter Wink has made a strong case for Jesus' third way, which is neither flight nor fight, but nonresistant, nonviolent engagement. In the beginning of our Lord's ministry, his evangel (good news) included releasing captives, freeing the oppressed, and bringing good news to the poor (Luke 4:18-19). In proclaiming the year of the Lord's favor, Jesus was referring to the Jubilee year of the Lord, which promised economic justice. And his teaching leads us to believe that the golden text of John 3:16 on personal salvation needs to be supplemented by John 3:17, the call to participate in God's purpose in redemption, not condemnation, of the world.

This chapter has endeavored to explore a history of our peace heritage that includes significant issues and honest differences with others who have explored our heritage. It may have focused too much on corporate decisions made by what many regard as our annual extended family gathering. We are aware that grass roots Brethren have not always agreed with these decisions. And we can say with some integrity that we are not the peace church we would like to be. At the same time, we still use "we" language when we talk about our rich heritage. It does seem that while our peace heritage is less absorbed by most members, it is more respected by other ecumenical Christians and large numbers of lovers of peace.

Chapter 14

Whither Brethren?
Peacefully, simply, together

Finally, beloved, whatever is true, whatever is honorable, whatever is just, whatever is pure, whatever is pleasing, whatever is commendable, if there is any excellence and if there is anything worthy of praise, think about these things. Keep on doing the things that you have learned and received and heard and seen in me, and the God of peace will be with you.
—Philippians 4:8-9

As I have traveled throughout our denomination, I have frequently been asked, What is happening to us? Where are we headed? These inquiries bring to mind some of the questions raised in the stirring Louisville Conference in 1966. The annual gathering was deciding whether or not to join the Consultation on Church Union (COCU). The Fraternal Relations Committee, now the Committee on Interchurch Relations, had prepared the following question for consideration: "Are Brethren willing to see a 'peace position' as part of the total witness of a new church, but not as yet central and primary?"

Some eighty percent of the delegates voted for the committee's recommendation against joining. We still could have maintained our observer status. As a member of the committee and one of our representatives to COCU, I recall my passionate speech to the body. I believed this rejection would only be compelling if our denomination would revive our peace witness and make it central in our life and thought. We probably could have worked out other differences in belief and practice more readily than gaining acceptance of our peace heritage. I remembered the opinion of a German theologian, Otto Piper. He reminded us that our peace witness is the only justification we have to continue to exist as a denomination.

J. Denny Weaver is raising this same challenge to Mennonites. He points out that Mennonites have a list of good beliefs in which peace is but one. He advocates, however, that Mennonites be a peace church in which New Testament views of peace are central and permeate the life and thought of the church. In many ways I agree with Denny and Zechariah, father of John the Baptist, who, filled with the Spirit, proclaimed his son would prepare the way for a Savior who would "guide our feet into the way of peace" (Luke 1:79).

A movement entitled "Every Church a Peace Church" has evolved out of the New Call to Peacemaking movement of the three historic peace churches. I heartily support it. As a part of this dream, I join all who advocate that every Brethren congregation be a peace church. Unlike many others, I cannot predict the future. But I can envision a future church that is more consistent with the teachings of our Lord. For this reason I want to test how our peace church heritage can be central and how it might shape theological precepts of our faith. My attempt to apply anabaptist themes to controversial doctrines will likely evoke some disagreement. Hopefully, in our tradition we can discuss them together in helping each other to be "rightly explaining the word of truth" (2 Tim. 2:15).

Theological Issues for a Peace Church

Here I propose that we deal with three theological issues that intrude on peacemakers. In order to do this, we will deal with issues of consistency and interpretations of ancient and present doctrines. Our purpose will be to introduce new possibilities and recognize that other answers may likewise claim biblical roots.

Is God Nonviolent?

As members of a tradition that calls us to follow the nonresistant or nonviolent resistance of Jesus, it behooves us to deal with texts that mention the terror, wrath, or vengeance of God. How do we answer the question, Is God nonviolent? This question was also the title of an issue of a Mennonite publication, *The Conrad Grebel Review* (Winter 2003). The stimulating articles motivated me to both justify and test their novel thoughts by doing additional research.

Lee Griffith's chapter entitled "The Terror of God," in his book *The War on Terrorism and the Terror of God,* depicts the terror of God's love to be the victory over all terrorism. This means that the resurrection was and continues to be the terror of God. Like Quakers he refers to the war of the Lamb, which in Revelation depicts the victory of Jesus over the powers, the meek over evil. Referring to ten kings with the beast, John of Patmos writes: "They will make war on the Lamb, and the Lamb will conquer them . . ." (Rev. 17:14). Griffith concludes, "Revelation is not a book about the end of the world. Its ultimate vision is not one of destruction, but one of re-creation in the new heaven and new earth" (215). In similar ways King's civil rights struggle offers a sign that suffering love can overcome prejudicial hatred. Griffith answers our question with a rhetorical question: "How can we claim that Jesus is nonresistant but God is not?"

John Howard Yoder's definition of the wrath of God supplements Griffith's exegesis. He concedes he is not offering just a Mennonite view in simply describing hell as a condition of wanting to be left alone. Likewise, God's wrath is the fact that one can disobey God if he or she wants to. It is the freedom of the will to choose wrong. If we so choose, God will let us do it. The Bible names this the wrath of God. God's love allows the freedom of the beloved to reject love. When we turn away from the love of God and God's creation, we become slaves to our self-centeredness. It is only when we are open to divine manifestations of love that we are free to be for others. A much longer definition is found in Yoder's essay "The Wrath of God and the Love of God," which has circulated since being read at an International Fellowship of Reconciliation Conference in England in 1956.

This works in various ways, as found among articles of The *Conrad Grebel Review.* When people or participants in a community or nation turn their backs on the most precious gifts of divine creativity to humankind, the consequences of God's judgment and wrath come through forces who hate our insensibilities and oppressive selfish structures. God's permissiveness will not physically punish us, but God's ultimate will can come through violent responses of those who have been violated.

In an article in the *Review*, Mary Schertz writes about events of September 11, 2001, as a "judgment upon this country's reliance on militarism and consumerism and on the reality that we are big and powerful enough to turn a deaf ear on global concerns for poverty, the environment, and political and economic oppression." She adds that our response of "additional violence of war in bombing Afghanistan and a deaf ear to global protest just as surely falls under God's judgment and wrath as do the actions of the pilots who drove the hijacked airliners into the World Trade Center. In both cases, human beings are relying on something or someone other than God, and such decisions invite the wrath of God" (34-35).

In Matthew 25:31-46, a favorite passage of Brethren about serving the least of these, a judgment and warning were given metaphorically in apocalyptic language to folk who felt they might be living in the last days. The Son of Man, Jesus, was taking the place of a king to the nations. I journeyed to the library to find a commentary on this in *The New Interpreter's Bible*. I learned that this was intended to be pastoral advice to early Christians. At the same time it may have been an appeal to the nations to treat Christian missionaries more decently. In separating sheep from the goats, nothing was said about grace, justification, or forgiveness of sins. What counts is whether believers or nations act with loving care for needy people. Here we find popular Brethren views about what constitutes the wrath of God.

While in the library, I looked up Romans 12 understandings of the vengeance of God. The apostle advised that we should never avenge ourselves. For "Vengeance is mine, I will repay, says the Lord" (12:19). In place of vengeance, Paul says the way to act is to feed the hungry and give drink to thirsty enemies. This is an example of overcoming evil with good. Paul adds that in doing this we "heap burning coals on their heads" (Rom. 12:14-21). This metaphor was likely given to point to the wrath of burning shame of remorse for having treated someone so badly. In refusing vengeance that belongs to God, it may have the effect of turning others' hearts. It teaches that the way to overthrow evil is to take its force and give back goodness instead.

Anabaptist Views of the Atonement

My teachers stressed the crucifixion to be so important, so mysterious, that no one theory of the atonement can do it justice. This view may apply to my relating possible pacifist understandings to three historic theories of the atonement. I owe the idea of "anabaptizing" (my word) atonement theories to James McClendon, Jr., in *Doctrine*, the second volume of his *Systematic Theology*. Atonement means "at-one-ment." It involves how we get right with God and God's good creation. McClendon was a major theologian who was raised Southern Baptist, taught mostly at an Episcopal seminary, and ended his last years as a member of the Church of the Brethren after being converted to Anabaptism by John Howard Yoder. The following three theories of atonement point to ways God gets right with us or, as mentioned, we get right with God.

The Ransom Theory. Bishop Irenaeus of France, in the late second century, developed an atonement theory from Paul's references to Christ being the second Adam. Adam had yielded to Satan's trickery by doing wrong. The second Adam put it right. So Christ frees us by defeating Satan. In primitive, sketched illustrations, God put Jesus on a hook to catch the Devil. Augustine later said the same. He declared that the cross of the Lord became a trap for the Devil; the death of the Lord was the food that ensnared Satan.

If we understand this at all, the death of Jesus on the cross leads to victories over evil. Luther extended this in frequently claiming that Christ's death defeated death, sin, and the devil. In these ransom atonement theories, crucifixion is bound with resurrection to complete the whole story. In recent centuries Scandinavian theologians have named this theory Christus-victor to point to victories over evil through Jesus' sacrifice on the cross. Rene Girard, French-American anthropologist and Christian, notes that Jesus was crucified as a scapegoat (John 11:50-51). The Renard school reasons that Jesus, whose life and teaching utterly opposed violence, brought an end to violence for all who would follow him. For McClendon, Jesus' death signals the end of the kingdom of violence and is thus, ironically, a sacrifice to end all sacrifice. "The resurrection was God's sign of self-identification with Jesus who had taken the nonviolent way of the cross" (*Doctrine* 233-236).

Saul was present and approved the stoning of Stephen who cried out the words of Jesus that their sins not be held against them. Saul continued to breathe threats of murder against the disciples of Jesus. Yet, on the Damascus road, he was blinded by lightning and heard a voice of the Lord asking why he was being persecuted. For three days Saul was without sight. His victory came when hands were laid on him out of his experience to join a nonviolent movement. He became a voice proclaiming love as the greatest doctrine and virtue in the world. He advocated the nonviolent way of Jesus of overcoming evil with good (Acts 8–9). Christ's victory over the powers heralds the triumph of communities that are socially relevant even when outwardly diminutive and despised. Such expresses the power of suffering love that is basic to anabaptist-pacifist views of the atonement.

Satisfaction or Penal Theory. In the last years of the eleventh century, views of tricking the devil and Christ's role of defeating evil dropped out of the picture. Anselm, a devout monk who ended his life as Archbishop of Canterbury, focused on the restoration of relationships between humanity and God. His views of the atonement were meant to reform monetary practices of penance. He reasoned that humans have dishonored God in breaking their obligations. We owe God a debt. Though God in his mercy would like to forgive us, God's honor requires justice. Only Christ, who is human and divine, in suffering and giving his life can satisfy divine legal demands of both mercy and justice. Though Anselm's logic is difficult for modern minds, the substitutionary theory has become one of the popular fundamentals among conservative Christians. The message is clear: Jesus paid the supreme price. Our sins are forgiven. We are saved and heavenward bound.

A couple of generations after Anselm's death, Abelard rejected the view that Christ's suffering pays off our debt to the world. "How cruel and wicked it seems," he wrote, "that anyone should demand the blood of an innocent person as the price for anything." This recalls the story about the little boy who in Sunday school listened to the penal view. At home, he told his mother that he hated God, but loved this guy Jesus. The legal demand of God that requires the death of his Son is often contrasted with the forgiving love of Jesus to those who killed him. This seems to deny the nature and unity of the trinity. Anabaptists believe that Jesus is like God and that we can never accept any view of God that makes God less good and loving than Jesus. One can anabaptize this view of the atonement with a satisfaction theory that sees in the Jesus story what really satisfied God. Jesus' way was God's way to respond to evil in the world. God was pleased and satisfied that Jesus chose the way of suffering love on the cross.

Example of Divine Love. The third theory is one we trace back to Abelard who lived in the early decades of the twelfth century. He is best known for his famous love story with Heloise. Central to his views about atonement was his belief that in life and death Christ embodied the appearance of God's love. His commentary on Romans articulates his views on atonement.

> [I]n teaching us by word and example even unto death—[Christ] has more fully bound us to himself by love: with the result that our hearts should be enkindled by such a gift of divine grace, and true charity should not now shrink from enduring anything for him. (William Placher, *A History of Christian Theology* 145)

Abelard's theory advocates that Christ lived and died in order to show us how to live by his words and example. For many this limits the work of Christ to an ethical teaching. But Jesus acted to change human lives. The incarnation of God's transforming grace and forgiveness through Jesus' crucifixion empowered disciples to follow the Jesus way. This may not tell the entire story. But it was essential to New Testament authors and later anabaptist confessions. The following is one among other texts that support Abelard's theory: "For to this you have been called, because Christ suffered for you, leaving you an example, so that you should follow in his steps" (1 Pet. 2:21).

For Our Sins. The above perspectives on three historical views of the atonement seem to minimize texts that inform us that while we were yet sinners Christ died for us (Rom. 5:6-11). It was in reading *God Was in Christ* by D. M. Baillie that I realized that all accounts of the incarnation and atonement were written long after the crucifixion event. Instead of assuming that such timely events were planned by God, it is more likely that from a distance early Christian writers discerned the Spirit and nature of God working through the event. Otherwise, all participants in the crucifixion and resurrection of Christ would not be free human beings, but puppets doing what God led them to do. Such would mean that those who killed Jesus were doing God a favor.

One critique of the way Anselm's theory has been used is to point out that God was seen to be a penal, forgiving God in the Hebrew Bible. God was able to forgive sins before Christ's death on the cross.

In looking back, however, the authors could discern manifestations of the will of God. In other words, it was and is possible to discern the presence of the Spirit of God in history. This can be the case with Anselm's satisfaction theory. We can discern what happened on the cross to be a story about the forgiving love for all. Yet Anabaptists have found it difficult to believe that God required the death of his Son and that Christians can ignore the way of the cross because Jesus paid it all. Other Christians, however, would feel that many contemporary Anabaptists neglect that Jesus died for our sins.

I learned about a family's tragedy that may relate to how God works through an event not desired and planned by God. This story has been helpful in thinking about the atonement. A good father was hit by a drunken driver and paralyzed for life. Most members of his large family were typical materialists, busy in their self-centered ways to outdo others and rise to the top. Their self-centered lives often created jealousy and alienation within the family circle. Ultimately the tragedy brought them together. When their dad needed help, they re-examined their priorities. Having drifted from Christ and the church, they related anew to the church family and discovered it to be a blessing for all of them. From good feelings in new experiences and warm relationships of being with and for others, they began to look back on the tragedy as an event in which they discerned the presence and work of

God. But God certainly did not approve of drunk drivers crippling others for life. We have noted that wrath is biblically defined as God letting a tragedy like this happen in the freedom given to all of us as sinners. The family experienced the Spirit of God at work through and following the tragedy. Their sins were forgiven through Christlike suffering being present in the community of faith.

The Christian God of love did not desire to have his own Son killed. The wrath mentioned in Romans 5 can be described as God allowing it to happen through all involved in the passion story. For Christian dogma has agreed that the forgiving love of God was present as reported in the Hebrew Bible. But they saw in the crucifixion and resurrection the forgiving and suffering presence of God forgiving those who participated in the crucifixion and radically changing the lives of all who were involved in that event. Transforming events make Christians aware that Christ died for our sins when we participate in the fruit of his death, resurrection, and the Spirit's presence in our lives. Romans 5 shows that we absorb the message of salvation when we receive Christlike love and forgiveness. This inspires us to respond with tough or patient love to forgive our enemies and to be ministers of reconciliation of the nonviolent Christ.

These three theories of the atonement may be related to definitions of grace by anabaptist theologians. For Catholic traditions, they reason, grace is substance, something available in the mass and to all of us in a variety of ways. For Protestants, grace is favor, God's forgiving love for our sins. More stressed by Anabaptists is the theme that grace is that creative love whereby the Spirit of God's love can flow through the community of faith. The above redemptive scheme has circulated in anabaptist circles. Such a formula here is not meant by itself as an invalidation of other more complete and favorable interpretations of Catholic and Protestant traditions.

Biblical Nonresistance and/or Nonviolent Resistance?

In peace church traditions, there have emerged differences between those who espouse nonresistance and those who advocate nonviolent resistance. Both sides believe that Christians should refuse to participate in warfare that involves killing. Both perspectives maintain that ethical teachings of the Sermon on the Mount should be applicable to our life together in communities of faith.

Nonresistance. Nonresisters strive to be faithful to Jesus' command in the Sermon on the Mount teachings "to resist not evil" (Matt. 5:38-42). They identify with streams of Anabaptism such as the Amish and Old Order plain groups that trace their roots back to the sixteenth-century Schleitheim

Confession. The confession acknowledges that outside the perfection of Christ, God has ordered the sword to punish the wicked and protect the good. In seeking conversations with the powers, they resisted being identified with being wicked and sought to be identified with the good.

Most contemporary adherents of this position identify with the label of biblical nonresistance to differentiate their position from what they name secular or humanist pacifism. They advocate that Christians should suffer patiently. They believe coercive and manipulative tactics of many demonstrations, boycotts, and protests fail to model a witness to peace.

Many, not all, of this persuasion adopt a two-kingdom view, often referred to as church-world dualism. Simply, the doctrine proposes that the ideal way of *agape* love taught and modeled by Jesus is only possible for those who are members of redeemed communities of faith. Christians cannot expect unredeemed humanity to endure or advocate responses of suffering love. They would agree with the above confession that God has ordained the sword to preserve order in the world. Most nonresisters will refrain from voting or holding public offices. Fewer numbers maintain that to work for peace may defy God's will because Jesus predicted there will be wars and rumors of wars.

When black brothers and sisters at Chicago's First Church of the Brethren were singing freedom songs of the civil rights movement, Brethren from lush farmlands admonished them to suffer patiently in love. Was this advice a valid reference to or a caricature of nonresistance? The same questions are being asked in reference to many who have been abused by members of their own families.

Nonviolent Resistance. Those who espouse nonviolent resistance believe that to be faithful to biblical mandates to seek justice, it is necessary to resist evil. However, Christians are to resist in the most loving and nonviolent way possible. Such has been the contribution of Walter Wink. Through intensive study of varieties of biblical texts, he insists that Jesus' advice to "turn the other cheek" and "go the second mile" are acts of resistance. This requires that when we resist, we do not resist in kind. Our response needs to reflect the Pauline counsel to "overcome evil with good" (Rom. 12:17-21).

For some nonviolent resisters, the word *pacifism* disturbs them when it is interpreted as passivity. Instead, they understand that pacifism literally means to make peace. Viewpoints are kindred to traditional Quakerism with its one-kingdom doctrine that proclaims Christ to be Lord over all. This provides the basis for Quaker insistence on speaking the truth to power. Likewise, nonviolent resisters of many varieties draw heavily on the philosophy and strategies of Gandhi and Martin Luther King, Jr. In one so-called nonviolent demonstration, the chant of the demonstrators called police "pigs." One has to ask if this is consistent with Christian nonviolent strategy.

Intertwined Nonresistance and Resistance. These differences seem to focus on ways those who claim to be peacemakers respond to enemies. Peace church theologians could describe many virtues and pitfalls of each position. In writing a transition from one chapter to another in *Biblical Pacifism,* I wrote, "Nonresistance pacifism has much to preserve, while the pacifism of nonviolent resistance has much to add" (chapters 1-2, 2002 ed.). Then I found an article that said it better: "Resistance and Nonresistance: The Two Legs of the Biblical Peace Stance" by Thomas R. Yoder Neufeld in *The Conrad Grebel Review* (Winter 2003). The author maintains that these two, nonresistance and resistance, vulnerable suffering and victorious struggling, Good Friday and Easter, go together. They are intertwined in the Jesus story of the Gospels and the letters. He adds, "It is equally important not simply to collapse them into each other; for there is value in keeping both polarities alive in our minds . . ." (69).

The following admonitions and stories may help to discern the necessity of including both. Likewise, a biblical case can be made for binding these "two legs" together. Neufeld believes that nonresistance is less about strategy than character. He quotes the following Pauline passage to emphasize that "Our experience of grace needs to find its complement in our offer of grace to our enemies" (71).

> *We also boast in our sufferings, knowing that suffering produces endurance, and endurance produces character, and character produces hope, and hope does not disappoint us, because God's love has been poured into our hearts through the Holy Spirit that has been given to us.* (Rom. 5:3-5)

To this wonderful proof text for nonresistance he adds one of many for nonviolent resistance.

> *For our struggle is not against enemies of blood and flesh, but against the rulers, against the authorities, against the cosmic powers of this present darkness, against the spiritual forces of evil in the heavenly places.* (Eph. 6:12)

The above texts can be intertwined. Right character is necessary in our call and struggles against cosmic powers and rulers; for they need to be resisted by overcoming evil with good.

In looking again at the influential Schleitheim Confession, a few that signed it had participated two years before in a demonstration, crying out "Woe to Zurich" in imitating Jonah's shout to call the inhabitants to repent. They branded Zwingli as the dragon of John's Revelation. In threatening banishment, the town council had required immediate baptism of all children. As authors of the first anabaptist tract on nonresistance, they were resisting Christendom's declaration of death for all who participated in establishing congregations of baptized believers.

Another symbol of nonresistant pacifism has been Anabaptist Dirk Willems. His story and icon is found in the *Martyrs Mirror*. Hotly pursued by a thief-catcher, Willems ran for his life over the ice. When his pursuer broke through the ice, Willems turned around and saved his persecutor's life. Willems was captured, imprisoned, and burned at the stake. The picture of Dirk saving the life of his enemy is most revered by Amish and others to teach their people to be nonresistant followers of Jesus. To support our thesis, Dirk's running away from the evil intent of his pursuer can be considered as an act of resistance. Anabaptists have given us memorable examples of Christlike behavior in refusing to do to others what was being done to them.

Adin Ballou, a New England abolitionist raised as a Baptist, published a book in 1846 entitled *Christian Non-Resistance*. Replete with biblical texts, the book that later influenced both Tolstoy and Gandhi cured my notion that Anabaptists have been the sole progenitors of biblical nonresistance. Consistent with the title, Ballou discusses the "resist not evil" text. He argues that nonresistance does not imply passivity. He asserts that we should resist flood, tornadoes, temptations, and the devil. He anticipates Walter Wink in maintaining that turning the other cheek in reality embodies both nonresistance and resistance. He says that the difference between nonresistance and Christian nonresistance is that the latter adds that we are to "overcome evil with good" (Rom. 12:21).

Ballou espoused a neo-anabaptist view. Since the United States Constitution and government support war, capital punishment, and slavery, he believed it wrong for anyone to vote or swear to support the Constitution. When Christians by example influence multitudes to renounce this idolatry, others will join us and all will be pleased to vote. Yet Ballou engaged in active demonstrations of love. He organized marches in which blacks and whites linked arms and engaged in civil disobedience by walking down the streets together. His life serves as an excellent example of the intertwining stances of peacemakers. The polarity between personal evangelism and social responsibility may be eliminated by intertwining nonresistance and nonviolent resistance.

I experienced this intertwining in a civil rights march in Chicago with Dr. King. We were questioned and only accepted to join the march if we were committed to nonresistance. We had to promise that if a brick was thrown at us, we could not throw it back. If anyone yelled profanities our way, we were required to keep the peace. If we were attacked physically, we could not fight but only kneel in praying and singing. Yet, the purpose of the march was an endeavor to resist the exclusion of blacks and other ethnic groups from purchasing homes in the suburbs.

Finally, I report a more recent event through an e-mail from a former student. He related how Muslims were encouraged by the Indonesian army to burn Christian churches. Women were raped and there were other acts of violence. After relating these terrible events, he added a footnote: "Just like the early Christians. Because we responded with love, some Muslims are becoming Christians."

This story reminds me of concluding statements by Mennonite Neufeld that focus on evangelism. "The very highest form of resistance is evangelism." He continues: "If evangelism does not awaken us from the deep slumber of imperial fantasies and callousness regarding our enemies, it is not yet the gospel of peace that Christ preached, lived, and died for (Eph. 2:13-18). If evangelism does not call us out of a culture of enmity and greed, it is not yet the good news of the Christ who said no to the promise of plenty, security, and power." It has been difficult at Conference to listen to voices separate the two by regretting that we hear so many speeches about peace, but none about evangelism. Perhaps our definitions of evangelism and peace have not been deep enough to show that our witness to peace is our evangelism and our evangelism includes our commitment to peace.

Communal Dreams for Peace Churches

"How very good and pleasant it is when kindred live together in unity!"(Ps. 133:1). "Peacefully, Simply, Together" conveys who we are at our best. In this book on theology, doctrinal issues have been extensively related to living *peacefully*. It is imperative for a peace church to do this *together*. Emil Brunner, a Reformed theologian, has maintained that in the New Testament *ekklesia* (church) is never conceived as an institution or building. In the first centuries, *ekklesia* identified a fellowship of believers who met in house churches.

Brethren have been labeled as primitivists because of their desire to restore the life and Spirit of Christ in apostolic caring and sharing communities known for their love for one another. Biblical accounts reveal that early Christians were not without conflicts and serious disagreements. They were, nevertheless, commissioned to be a peace church in which cultural divisions between Greeks and Jews were reconciled. New Testament epistles reveal that Christians created one humanity in place of two. And this was not always easy.

This restorationist vision has been compatible to Brethren. The looking backward becomes an integral part of our looking forward. But we now try to live in the first era of human history in which we lack the benefits of a larger family. Today in our messed-up world, there are growing signs of widespread hunger for models of community. Because the nuclear family and single-parent families have not been able to bear all the needs carried by the extended family of the past, there exists this deep hunger for community. We have and need to have more such models of peacefulness in our nuclear and extended families, congregations, and denomination.

Many are rightly concerned about our withering numbers, down considerably from our largest membership of over 200,000 when we celebrated our 250th anniversary. Many congregations fail to proclaim our peace witness for fear of losing members. During the extended Vietnam War, the numbers of Mennonites remained steadier than was the case with us. I believe this was due to their more unapologetic pacifist stance. We have many who wish to adopt mega-church evangelism techniques. Though their methods are often successful, our emphasis, instead, should be on growth in faithfulness more than in numbers. On one hand, we might lose some members, but because of the present and future need to overcome violence and hatred in our world, my hunch is that we might gain more members by inviting others to participate in Christlike, loving, and caring communities, while actively placing our peace heritage at the center of our life together.

Prophetic Confessions of Peacemakers

"The time is fulfilled, and the kingdom of God has come near; repent, and believe in the good news" (Mark1:15). Though it is important to accept God's peace in our hearts and in our relationships in communities of faith, we are ordained to proclaim peace in our global environment. If evangelism does not summon people to nonresistant and nonviolent resistance to hatred and violence in our world, we have not extended the invitation to follow Jesus.

In beginning his ministry, Jesus called his listeners to repentance in pronouncing that the kingdom was near. John the Baptist and Peter, in the wilderness and at Pentecost, called people to repent. Ezekiel prophesied to people who worshiped idols and engaged in violent acts. He called his people to "cast away" all their transgressions and get "a new heart and a new spirit" (Ezek. 18:31). I write three years after the 9/11 terrorist attacks, and I believe that as a peace church we need to call our citizens to repentance. We need to begin with ourselves. It is difficult to believe we can bring peace into the world as long as Americans believe our nation has done nothing wrong.

Our nation has not focused on definitions of terrorism. Perhaps this is because we have only applied that name to others. We have experienced in our nation the illegal and terrible acts of terrorists. Terrorism is defined as violent attacks that kill innocent civilians for purposes of political and national interests. In traveling before 9/11, my friends in other countries confronted us: "You Americans have never been bombed. If you had, you would know how terrible it is. And you surely would quit bombing other countries." I always felt that if we had experienced violence on our shores, many Americans would confess our terrible deeds to other peoples in the world. How wrong I was! Contrary to all virtues and wonders associated with America, our nation, led by Democrats and Republicans, has killed more innocent civilians than any other nation on earth. We have bombed twenty nations since World War II, killing millions of civilians.

We are the only nation that has committed acts of terror with three weapons of mass destruction—namely, *chemical* poisons made from depleted uranium from bombs dropped in Yugoslavia and Iraq. They are responsible for hundreds who have suffered cancerous deaths. And our own soldiers have been exposed to depleted uranium and other toxic waste from the first Gulf War, a fact not fully reported by our media. *Biological* weapons have destroyed forests and fields of food. America is the only nation to have employed *nuclear* weapons when they dropped one bomb each on Hiroshima and Nagasaki killing thousands of innocent Japanese women, children, and senior citizens. Beyond that, thousands of children have been crippled for life and some killed by our use of land mines. We are demanding that some nations cease acquiring or attempting to make nuclear weapons at the same time we are spending billions of dollars to research and prepare to make smaller nuclear weapons we can more likely use. And our culture is permeated with an ancient Manichean heresy named by early Christians. Its philosophy radically divides good so as to reside with one side, our side, and allow all evil to entirely engulf others.

I write shortly before the 2004 election. It has been eleven years since Arab terrorists made an explosive-laden attack with a truck on the World Trade Center. Eight years ago a similar terrorist attack by two young Americans made and delivered a bomb that destroyed the federal building in Oklahoma City, killing 168 of our people including many children. Timothy McVeigh, an ex-soldier, confessed he was thrilled in doing the same as he did in Iraq.

Three years after the most recent attack on the World Trade Center in New York on September 11, 2001, newspapers have acknowledged that our nation has spent more than $1 billion to duplicate the way terrorists have successfully used similar truck bombings. And they report that there is no defense against a terrorist barreling down the street with a truck bomb (article by Spencer Hsu and Sari Horwitz, *The Washington Post,* Aug. 8, 2004).

Jesus warns against eye-for-an-eye strategies. Yet these have been used to satisfy vengeance demanded by Americans. In reporting that there is "virtually no defense," the analysis of the *Post* gave no answers. In an article in *Fellowship,* my brother posed the question: "Can the U. S. build a new approach to Defense?" He expressed hope that the ideals of our country include the ability to make friends. Paul did teach that "God chose what is foolish in the world to shame the wise . . . and what is weak in the world to shame the strong (1 Cor. 1:27). The Sunday school answer would be simply to make friends, not more enemies.

There is a negative version that is increasingly articulated by many who are concerned, namely, that the violence and length of the invasion of Iraq has greatly increased the numbers of terrorists and enemies. It may be our calling to participate in and pass on concrete ways to love our enemies in overcoming evil with good. As I write I learn of Brethren Christian peacemakers who are teaching nonviolent strategies and philosophy to Muslims in Iraq.

I share a personal experience from an opportunity to participate in a World Council of Churches conference in the District of Columbia eleven months after 9/11. They planned the conference in order to expose American Christians to what Christians worldwide were thinking about the war against terrorism. The purpose was to deal with the gap between how Christians in the world judged the war and how congregations in America were thinking. Around the circle they all responded that members of their congregations met to pray for our country. They reported an outpouring of love for America. However, without exception, all reported that America blew it. We lost an opportunity when we bombed Afghanistan. The thought of the most powerful and wealthy nation bombing the poorest nation in the world that had for years suffered so severely was difficult for them to understand. They all agreed their countries would have cooperated in police and ground actions to punish those who were guilty of gross terrorist acts.

These Christians seemed to be aware of documents that revealed America's intention to rule the world. These documents revealed both the rhetoric and manifestations of a Pax Americana, a new Rome. They expressed more fear of America's power than fear of terrorists. For them, our seeking to understand the cause of terrorism did not justify it. They realized that there is no one nation or cluster of powers that can measure up to the military prowess of America.

Guerrilla warfare, like what has appeared in Iraq, seems to be another option that Christians cannot accept. There seems to be a growing interest in nonviolent ways as the only Christian way to resist misused power in the world. In this context I mentioned the idea of a confessing church. I was surprised with the speeches and interest it aroused. In light of "Whither Brethren" envisioning, I could imagine portions of the Church of the Brethren joining a worldwide confessing church that would advocate the nonviolent ways of our Lord. My hope for our nation is that this will not be necessary. I pray that our nation will turn away from primarily using military strategies and bombs in dealing with terrorism.

Future Hopes for a Pacifist Church

"Your kingdom come, your will be done, on earth as it is in heaven" (Matt. 6:10). "Peacefully, Simply, Together." Kierkegaard and other Christian saints have defined simplicity as willing one thing—that is, reducing the clutter of possessions, activities, or commitments to what is singularly most basic. This fits pragmatic Brethren notions of the simple life. For our future, I am proposing we focus on being a peace church. This choice or passion need not be the only thing we are about, but it could highlight who we are as Brethren. It would simplify our predictions of the future. Instead of premillennial schemes, predictions of futurologists, or scientific discoveries of changes, we Brethren could simply desire to feast on the first fruits of what God wants in the future kingdom. We realize we are not there yet, but we would participate now in kingdom themes of peace, love, and acts for greater justice.

When I read prophetic predictions about the future from those describing the details of the second coming or warning us about being left behind, I am certain I have not learned as much about the end times as I have about the dreams and beliefs of brothers and sisters in Christ. It seems that every generation has popular voices that predict times and data about a future that never arrives. Let us instead choose a dream like Martin Luther King's. He dreamed that children will be judged by their character, not by the color of their skin. From my bias this dream has divine approval. Yet it will or will not actually happen apart from humankind who have inherited God's freedom. Rather than attacking terrorists or the enemies of our own government and vassals, our simplicity is to live out our nonresistance in response to the overwhelming wealth of God's mercy and love (Eph. 2:4). We can live so as to allow that love and grace to increase our hunger for offering that grace and love to our broken world.

My unquenchable hope is that Brethren will respond to the moving of the spirit of peacemaking with justice. Their devotion to the peaceable kingdom has nurtured my faith, my hope. I am being led to give up my messianic compulsion to save our peace stance. I have faith that much of what we were called out by God to be is still alive. I have faith that the church of discipleship and peace for which God called out our people will survive in concrete witnessing communities of faith. The peace witness will continue to be basic to Christians as long as Christians live on this planet. Thus, I no longer feel called to save the Church of the Brethren in order to save the peace witness or to save this witness as the major justification we have for continuing to exist as a denomination.

Still, I not only love my heritage, I love the Brethren. My roots are deep in this community of faith. Freed from having to save our church, I am freer to call all of us as Brethren to be a part of what God is doing. God calls us to participate in redeeming and reconciling activity in the lives of people in the world that God loves. And in so losing our lives, God's forgiving and enabling grace may even save us as messengers for the kingdom coming.

Bibliography

This bibliography does not offer an exhaustive list of resources. It includes a list of books and articles cited in this study and additional ones that have influenced the author or are considered important. Some are annotated. A more complete but dated bibliography can be found in Donald Durnbaugh and Lawrence W. Shultz's "A Brethren Theology," *Brethren Life and Thought* (Winter/Spring 1964).

BE is the abbreviated form of *The Brethren Encyclopedia*, edited by Donald F. Durnbaugh. Philadelphia, Pa.; Oak Brook, Ill.: The Brethren Encyclopedia Inc., 1983.

BLT is the abbreviated form of *Brethren Life and Thought,* available from Bethany Theological Seminary, 1955ff.

Anabaptism in Outline: Selected Primary Sources. Edited by Walter Klassen. Scottdale, Pa.: Herald Press, 1981.

Arnold, Gottfried. *Die Ersten Liebe Der Gemeinen Jesu Christi Das ist, Wahre Abbildung Der Ersten Christen.* Franckfurt am Mayn: Gottlieb Friedeburgs Buchhandlung, 1696. History of early Christians read by first Brethren.

_____. *Unpartheyische Kirchen-Historie*, 3 vols. Franckfurt am Mayn: Thomas Fritsch, 1699-1700. Impartial history of the church that considers heretical movements to be manifestations of the true church.

Aukerman, Dale. *Darkening Valley: A Biblical Perspective on Nuclear War.* New York: The Seabury Press, 1981. A devotional and prophetic book by a Brethren saint.

Bach, Jeff. "Our Conscience Is Bound: A Survey of the Brethren Peace Witness." *BLT*, Fall 2000. Updated and excellent survey, which I appreciated, appropriated, and critiqued.

Baillie, D. M. *God Was in Christ.* London: Faber and Faber Limited, 1961. A classic essay on incarnation and atonement.

Baillie, Gil. *Violence Unveiled: Humanity at the Crossroads.* New York: Crossroad, 1995. A novel and excellent interpretation of violence and the sacred in Rene Girard's school of social analysis.

Bonhoeffer, Dietrich. *Sanctorum Communio: Theological Study of the Sociology of the Church* (Dietrich Bonhoeffer Works, Vol. 1). Edited by Clifford Green. Minneapolis: Augsburg Fortress, 1996.

_____. *Discipleship* (Dietrich Bonhoeffer Works, Vol. 4). Edited by Geffrey Kelly and John Godsey. Minneapolis: Augsburg Fortress, 1996. Especially relevant is his commentary on the Sermon on the Mount.

_____. *Life Together: Prayerbook of the Bible* (Dietrich Bonhoeffer Works, Vol. 5). Minneapolis: Augsburg Fortress, 1996. A classic, beautiful essay that articulates theology of communities of faith.

Bowman, Carl F. *Brethren Society: The Cultural Transformation of a "Peculiar People."* Baltimore: The Johns Hopkins University Press, 1995. A wonderful revealing and needed study by a sociologist who loves our heritage.

Bowman, Rufus. *The Church of the Brethren and War.* Elgin, Ill.: Brethren Publishing House, 1944. The first historical study of our peace witness by a Brethren leader who prophetically proclaimed what he believed during World War II.

Brethren in Transition: 20th-century directions and dilemmas. Edited by Emmert F. Bittinger. Symposium of Forum for Religion Studies. Bridgewater College, Bridgewater: Penobscot Press, 1992. Variety of authors and subjects.

Brown, Dale W. *Brethren and Pacifism.* Elgin, Ill.: Brethren Press, 1970. Written during the Vietnam War.

_____. *The Christian Revolutionary.* Grand Rapids: Eerdmans, 1971. Rooted in gospel for evangelical and other "radicals." With anabaptist flavor.

_____. *Understanding Pietism.* Grand Rapids: Eerdmans, 1978. Nappanee, Ind.: Evangel Publishing House, 1996 rev. ed. Introductory book for many pietist traditions.

_____. *Flamed by the Spirit. Biblical Definitions of the Holy Spirit, A Brethren Perspective.* Elgin, Ill.: Brethren Press, 1978.

_____. *Biblical Pacifism.* Elgin, Ill.: Brethren Press, 1986. 2003 second ed. Evangel Press, Herald Press, and Brethren Press, 2003. Changed focus in second edition from historic peace churches to ecumenical peace and justice concerns rooted in scriptures.

Brumbaugh, Martin G. *A History of the German Baptist Brethren in Europe and America.* Elgin, Ill.: House Church of the Brethren, 1899. Governor of Pennsylvania who created theme "no force in religion."

Deeter, Joan, ed. *Biblical Inspiration and Authority, a study guide to the 1979 Annual Conference paper.* Elgin, Ill: Brethren Press, 1980.

Durnbaugh, Donald. *European Origins of the Brethren.* Elgin, Ill.: Brethren Press, 1958. A Brethren source book.

———. *The Brethren in Colonial America.* Elgin, Ill.: Brethren Press, 1967. Both source books provide valuable primary and secondary sources of development of life and faith of early Brethren. The most referenced books by Brethren historians.

———. *Fruit of the Vine: A History of the Brethren,* 1708-1995. Elgin, Ill.: Brethren Press, 1996. Durnbaugh is by far our greatest historian who has served to recover our heritage.

———. *Pragmatic Prophet: The Life of Michael Robert Zigler.* Elgin, Ill: Brethren Press, 1989. A classic biography of a revered Brethren saint in the context that invites us to be present in family, community, church, and brotherhood life of rural Brethren in early decades of the twentieth century. Reads like a novel.

———. "The Descent of 'Dissent.'" *BLT,* Spring 1974. Don has written more books than listed and hundreds of articles. This article is my favorite because I learned many things I did not know.

Eby, Kermit. *For Brethren Only.* Elgin, Ill.: Brethren Publishing House, 1958. Labor leader and professor of social sciences, U. of Chicago. Reminiscences of home church at Baugo.

Eller, Vernard. *In Place of Sacraments.* Elgin, Ill.: Brethren Press, 1972. A significant introduction to ordinances and anti-sacramental views.

Fitzkee, Donald R. *Moving Toward the Mainstream.* Intercourse, Pa.: Good Books, 1995. Helpful in discerning changes among Brethren in the twentieth century.

Franklin, Benjamin. *Autobiography.* New York: P.F. Collier & Son, 1909.

Frantz, Edward. *Basic Belief.* Elgin, Ill.: Brethren Publishing House, 1943. Easily read presentation of basic beliefs by an editor of *The Gospel Messenger.*

Funk, Benjamin. *Life of John Kline.* Elgin, Ill.: Brethren Publishing House, 1964. Classic diary of our famous martyr.

Gish, Arthur G. *The New Left and Christian Radicalism.* Grand Rapids: Eerdmans, 1970.

Griffith, Lee. *The War on Terrorism and the Terror of God.* Grand Rapids: Eerdmans, 2002. Unusually perceptive book written before 9-11-01.

Groff, Warren. "Christology," *BE,* Vol. 1. Helpful theological essay.

Jacobs, Henry. "Symbol, Symbolical Books," *Lutheran Cyclopedia.* Concordia Publishing House, 1954, 1975.

Kreider, J. Kenneth. *A Cup of Cold Water: The Story of Brethren Service.* Elgin, Ill.: Brethren Press, 2001. Complete and inspiring.

Kurtz, D. W., S. S. Blough, C. C. Ellis. *Studies in Doctrine and Devotion.* Elgin, Ill.: Brethren Publishing House, 9th printing, 1950. Bestseller for years. Amazing that Brethren who differed theologically could agree in a book treasured by most Brethren at that time.

Kurtz, Henry, ed. *The Brethren's Encyclopedia.* Columbiana, Ohio: (published by author), 1867. Interesting, due to personal footnotes to Minutes of Annual Meeting.

Lehman, James H. *The Old Brethren.* Elgin, Ill.: Brethren Press, 1976. Written by a storyteller. Heritage ethos infuses stories of fascinating and interesting characters.

Longenecker, Stephen. *Piety and Tolerance: Pennsylvania German Religion, 1700-1850.* Metuchen, N.J.: Scarecrow Press, 1994. Our colonial ancestors were more tolerant, cooperative, and ecumenical than many have thought.

Mallott, Floyd E. *Studies in Brethren History.* Elgin, Ill.: Brethren Publishing House, 1954. Mallott's enthusiastic teaching enlivened our identity with our tradition.

Martyrs Mirror: The Story of Fifteen Centuries of Christian Martyrdom from the Time of Christ to A.D. 1660. Contains largest numbers of sixteenth-century anabaptist martyrs. Includes stories, letters, faith, and testimonies.

McClendon, James. *Systematic Theology.* Nashville: Abingdon Press. Vol. 1, *Ethics,* 1986. Vol. 2, *Doctrine,* 1994. Vol. 3, *Witness,* 2000.

Miller, R. H. *The Doctrine of the Brethren Defended*. Indianapolis: Printing and Publishing House Print, 1876. By popular and respected leader.

Minutes of the Annual Meeting, Annual Conference, can be ordered from the Annual Conference office, Elgin, Illinois. You can find more recent minutes in church and Brethren college and seminary libraries. Brethren Historical Library and Archives at Elgin will help you. Decisions have been identified by place and date.

Moore, J. H. *The New Testament Doctrines*. Elgin, Ill.: Brethren Publishing House, 1915. Another clear, brief, and popular presentation by an editor of *Messenger*.

Nead, Peter. *Theological Writings on Various Subjects; or a Vindication of Primitive Christianity as Recorded in the Word of God*. Dayton: B.F. Ellis, 1850.

On Earth Peace. Edited by Donald Durnbaugh. Elgin, Ill.: Brethren Press, 1978. Presentations on war/peace between peace churches and European churches.

Pietists: Selected Writings. Edited by Peter C. Erb. The Classics of Western Spirituality. New York and Ramsey, Toronto: Paulist Press, 1983. Primary sources.

Plecher, William C. *A History of Christian Theology*. Louisville, London: Westminster John Knox Press, 1983.

Ramirez, Frank. *Universal Restoration* (Perspectives Essay Series). Elgin, Ill.: Brethren Press, 2001.

Sappington, Roger E. *The Brethren in the New Nation*. Elgin, Ill.: Brethren Press, 1976.

———. *The Brethren in Industrial America*. Elgin, Ill.: Brethren Press, 1985. Source books 3 and 4 after source books by Durnbaugh.

Sattler, Gary. *Nobler Than the Angels, Lower Than a Worm: The Pietist View of the Individual in the Writings of Heinrich Muller and August Hermann Francke*. Lanham, New York; London: University Press of America, 1989.

The Schleitheim Confession. Edited and translated by John Howard Yoder. Scottdale, Pa.: Herald Press, 1977.

Spener, Philip Jacob. *Pia Desideria* (Pious Wishes for the Church). Philadelphia: Fortress Press, 1964. Desired marks of the church for a reformation of life.

Snyder, Graydon F. and Kenneth M. Shaffer. *Texts in Transit*. Elgin, Ill.: Brethren Press, 1976 and 1991. Biblical texts related to Brethren life and thought.

Stoffer, Dale R. *Background and Development of Brethren Doctrines, 1650-1987*. No. 1, Brethren Encyclopedia Monograph Series. Philadelphia: The Brethren Encyclopedia, Inc., 1989. Most thorough history of Brethren doctrines from large portions of author's dissertation at Fuller Theological Seminary.

Willoughby, William G. *Counting the Cost: The Life of Alexander Mack*. Elgin, Ill.: Brethren Press, 1979. The only biography we have of one of first founders.

_____. *The Beliefs of the Early Brethren 1706-1735*. Philadelphia: The Brethren Encyclopedia, Inc., 1999.

Wink, Walter. *Engaging the Powers*. Minneapolis: Augsburg Fortress, 1992. His major peace and powers book.

_____. The *Powers that Be: Theology for a New Millennium*. New York: Doubleday, 1998. A popular summary of the three powers books.

Yesterday and Today. Edited by Donald Durnbaugh. Elgin, Ill.: Brethren Press, 1986, 2nd ed. This symposium was requested by a bishop in Germany for a series on churches.

Yoder, John Howard. *For the Nations: Essays Public and Private*. Grand Rapids: Eerdmans, 1997. One of last books of many by this Mennonite scholar.

_____. *The Politics of Jesus*. Grand Rapids: Eerdmans, 1997, 2nd ed. The most popular and helpful book that influenced several major theologians.

Index

abortion, 28, 40, 134, 136, 165-166, 167
abstinence, 173
agape meal, 129, 130
American Friends Service Committe, 211
American Revolution. *See* Revolutionary War.
amillennialism, 184
Amish, 4, 26, 66, 198, 215, 224, 227
Anabaptism, definition of, 18-20
anabaptist discipleship, 26-27
Anglican, 6, 36. *See also* Episcopal.
Annual Conference Decision 1979 (Bible), 96-98. *See also* Biblical Inspiration and Authority.
anointing, 116, 125, 132-138; services of, 38, 178
apocalypticism, 46, 178-185
Apocrypha, 99
Apostles Creed, 7
apostolic creeds, 6-7
apostolic succession, 16-17, 36. *See also* Chicago Quadrilateral.
Arndt, Johann, 3
Arnold, Gottfried, 22, 24, 55-56, 75-76, 104, 192-193
Athanasian Creed, 3
atheist, 59, 213
Bach, Jeff, 194-195, 197, 205, 207-208, 211-214
Baillie, D. M., 223
baptism, 17-20, 78, 83-84, 92, 111-117, 120-126, 167, 197; believers baptism, 23-24, 56, 193-194, 227; first baptism, 28; infant, 6, 23, 25, 38, 53-54
Barth, Marcus, 110-112
Beahm, William, *x*, 135, 161, 175
Becker, Peter, 157
Beery, William, 175
Believers Church, 23, 50, 71-72
BEM (Baptism, Eucharist, and Ministry), 6, 114. *See also* Chicago Quadrilateral.
Bernard of Clairvaux, 15-16, 67
Bible, 36, 38, 51, 70; abortion in, 165; Holy Spirit in, 75-93; inspiration and authority, 95-107, 163-164; nonresistance/nonviolent resistance, 224-226; oaths, 141
"Biblical Inspiration and Authority," 98, 163-164, 188
Big Divide, 168

birth of Anabaptist movement, 20
Bittinger, Emmert, *x*
Blough, S. S., *x*
Boehme, Jacob, 3, 22, 103, 192
Bohemian Brethren, 11, 17
Bonhoeffer, Dietrich, 31, 33, 36, 37, 44, 56-57, 112, 117, 130, 131, 142, 156, 176, 185
Boni, Andreas, 193
Bowman, Benjamin, 153
Bowman, Carl, 20, 174, 192, 194, 207, 210
Bowman, Rufus, 106, 136, 194, 195, 198, 205, 206
Bowman, Warren D., 136
bread and cup communion, 127, 129, 131, 163
Brethren Revival Fellowship, 152, 160, 163, 175
Brethren Volunteer Service, 202, 204
Brethren's Card, 7, 8, 9, 12, 67, 89, 140, 155, 174
Brumbaugh, M. G., 23, 127, 210
Brunner, Emil, 35-36, 63-64, 176, 228
Buber, Martin, 63-64
Burnaby, John, 161
Calvin, John, 6, 36, 100, 176, 193
Calvinists, 4, 35, 100, 115
charismatic movement, 177-178
Chicago Quadrilateral, 6, 36
christology, 61, 65, 68-71, 174
Christus-victor, 221
church membership, 45, 123, 125, 211
civil rights movement, 79, 202, 215, 225
Civil War, 181-182, 194, 197-198, 201, 206
Civilian Public Service, 202, 204
cleansing, 129
Collegiants, 17
commandments, 12, 25, 27, 65, 120-121, 128, 139, 140, 142, 209
Commissioning Spirit for Mission, 92-93
Communicorp, 64
communion, 25, 40, 78, 111-131, 145
community, 28, 37-38, 47, 83
conflict transformation, 42, 45
Conrad Grebel Review, The, 69, 213, 219, 226
consecration of children and parents, 125

conservatives, 10, 40, 70, 97, 153, 162, 168-169, 174-175, 205
Consultation on Church Union (COCU), 217
conversion, 16, 24, 54-55, 69, 71, 83, 91-92, 121-122, 153
covenant, 37-41, 104-105, 116, 122, 209
creation, doctrine of, 50-51, 59
Creation-Fall-Restoration, 58
Daniel, Book of, 179-180
deconstructionist, 186
Denck, Hans, 53, 103
Dentler, Larry, 151-152
Diognetus, 146
discernment, 6, 59, 86, 124, 131, 167
discipleship, 19, 26-27, 45, 65-66, 95, 121, 126, 142, 156, 173-174, 176, 187, 193
dispensationalism, 185
divorce, 166-167
Dominican Republic, 79
Dompelaars, 17, 120
double mode. *See* feetwashing.
Dunkard Brethren, 170
Dunkers, 17, 32, 78, 120, 122, 126, 200-201
Durnbaugh, Donald, *ix, xiii,* 17, 78, 168, 182, 186-187, 212
Durnbaugh, Hedwig, 76, 180
Dutch Arminian Party, 17
Eastern Orthodox tradition, 81, 134
Eberly, William, *x*
Eby, Kermit, 201, 208
ecclesiology, 24-25, 31-32, 47-48, 113, 176, 194
ecumenical, 6-7, 19, 28-29, 71, 186
Edict of Milan, 23
Eller, Vernard, *x*, 19-20, 95, 111, 114, 117
Ellis, C. C., *x*
Ellul, Jacques, 213
end times, 46, 178, 180, 232
Episcopal, 6, 64, 114, 221
eucharist, 6, 110-112, 114, 129, 131, 149
Evangelical Covenant Church, 18
extreme unction, 110, 134
Fall and Redemption, 58
feetwashing, 15, 125, 128-130, 149; double mode, 162, 197; single mode, 127, 162, 182, 197
Felbinger, Jeremias, 17
fellowship meal. *See* agape meal.
Fellowship of the Spirit, 83, 93
feminist theologians (feminism), 185
Finney, Charles, 145, 181, 205
Fitzkee, Don, 174
flags, 34, 167
Flamed by the Spirit, 77, 177
Formula of Concord, 3
Fosdick, Harry Emerson, 29, 174, 175
Fox, George, 67

Fox, Matthew, 52
Francis of Assisi, 16, 51, 67
Francke, August Hermann, 3, 21-22, 54-56, 101, 192
Franklin, Benjamin, 2-3
Frantz, Edward, *x*, 15
Frantz, Michael, *x*, 25, 38
Fraternal Relations Committee, 217
Freemasonry, 144
French and Indian War, 194-195
Friends. *See* Quakers.
fruits of the Spirit, 27, 88-92
Fuller's Old Fashioned Revival Hour, 29, 174
fundamentalism, 28, 173, 174, 187
fundamentalists, 5, 13, 29, 102, 174, 175, 213
Gardner, Rick, 164
Gemeinschaft, 28, 35, 126
gifts of the Spirit, 80, 85-88
Girard, Rene, 221
Goshen Statement, 199-200
great awakenings, 28, 57
Grebel, Conrad, 20, 69, 213, 219, 226
Green, Michael, 82
Griffith, Lee, 179, 219
Hacker Marital Affair, 42, 157
Hacker, Johann, 42
Heifer International, 128, 201
hermeneutic, anabaptist communal, 101-103
hermeneutics, Brethren, 100
Hochenau, Hochmann von, 179, 192
Hochmann, Ernest Christopher, 22, 23, 25, 46, 179, 192-193
Hoffert, Gordon, 141
Hoffmann, Melchior, 53
holy kiss, 25, 43, 120, 131-132, 148-149
Holy Spirit, *x,* 4, 27, 37, 56, 75-93, 101-102, 120-121, 124, 177-178, 211-212, 226
Hope, Christian, 162, 206
Hordern, William, 137, 174
Horning, Estella, 79
Huguenot, 104
humanism, 59, 176, 212
humility, 15, 28, 66, 67, 129, 131, 172
Hummer, Catherine, 158-159
Huss, John, 17
Hussites, 111
Hut, Hans, 51
image of God, 51, 56, 58
Indian Massacres, 195
inner word, 53, 63, 103, 104, 105, 209, 210
Inspirationalists, 104, 193
integrity, 143, 145, 160, 174, 176, 188, 209, 216
Islam, 62, 81, 106
Joachim of Flora, 179
Kierkegaard, Soren, 95, 111, 176, 232

King, Martin Luther, Jr., 57, 180, 183, 202, 225, 232
Kline, John, 25, 83, 197, 206
Korea, 202
Krefeld, 42, 157
Kurtz, D. W., *x*, 185
Kurtz, Henry, *x*, 40, 97, 98, 106, 145, 151, 184, 209
Laeuchli, Samuel, 111-112
Lamb's war, 212, 219
Lambeth Quadrilateral. *See* Chicago Quadrilateral.
lawsuits, 147-148
Lead, Jane, 25
legalism, 58, 87, 140
Lehman, James, *xi*, 162
liberal, 10, 29, 42, 70, 87, 97, 102, 173-175, 182, 186
liberalism, 28, 173-174, 187
liberation theology, 28, 185
Liebe, Christian, 5, 42, 157
Lincoln, Abraham, 175, 198
Lindsey, Hal, 182
Longenecker, Stephen, 28
Lord's Supper, 17, 42, 110-111, 115, 126-127, 129
love feast, 25, 38-39, 47, 75, 78, 106, 116-117, 119, 126-132, 157, 163, 173
Luther, Martin, *ix*, *xi*, 3, 21, 27, 36, 53, 96, 99-100, 104, 110, 114, 123, 128, 139, 140, 176, 193, 204, 221
Mack, Alexander, Jr., *x*, 53, 54, 106, 122, 130, 172
Mack, Alexander, Sr., 14, 17
Mallott, Floyd, 15, 16, 35, 61, 67, 84, 91, 104, 172, 175, 182, 206
manna, 119
Manz, Felix, 20
marriage, 78, 113, 146, 166-167, 173; Hacker affair, 42, 157
Martin, Harold, 152
Martyrs Mirror, 5, 26, 90, 227
Matthew 18, 28, 38, 45, 147, 156, 197
May, Melanie, 7
McClendon, James Wm., *xi*, *xii*, 78, 79, 83, 102, 186, 220, 221
meetinghouse(s), *vi*, 32, 35, 51, 78, 126, 132, 152, 158
Meier, Marcus, 178-179
Mennonites, 41, 71, 86, 101, 214-215, 218-219, 228; compared with Brethren, 14, 18, 24, 69, 78, 115, 148, 156, 187-188, 193-196, 198, 210, 229; confessions of faith, 11; Hacker affair, 42, 157; *Martyrs Mirror*, 26.
messianic banquet, 130
Methodism, 21, 91

Methodists, 27
Meyer, Lauree Hersch, 7
millennium, 180, 181, 184, 240
Miller, D. L., *x*, 14
Miller, Donald, 176
Miller, R. H., *x*
Miller, William, 181
Ministries of Reconciliation, 156
miracles, 85, 86, 136-137
modernism, 28, 175, 186
Moore, J. H., *x*
moralism, 140
Morse, Kenneth, *x*, 76
Mow, Anna, 25, 105, 150
Murray, Andy, 143, 144
Muslims, 62, 206, 228, 231
Myer, James, 152
mysticism, 15-16, 67, 71, 76, 103, 114, 172, 173
Naas, Johann, 42, 157
narrative theology, 11, 28, 185
National Youth Conference, 72, 76, 161
Nead, Peter, *x*, 14, 46, 65, 152, 153, 184
neo-orthodoxy, 28, 58, 175, 177, 185, 187
neo-reformation, 176
Neufelt, Thomas R. Yoder, 213
Nicene Creed, 23
Niebuhr, Reinhold, 57, 102, 176, 202, 215
Nigeria, 206
No creed but the New Testament, 10, 11, 96, 104, 107
non-litigation, 147
nonconformity, 1, 28, 30, 41, 92, 140, 154, 168, 186, 211
nonresistance, 26, 27, 194-195, 211, 224-228, 232
nonviolent God, 59, 219, 221, 224
nonviolent resistance, 27, 148, 202, 215, 219, 224-227, 229, 231-232
oaths, *xiii*, 6, 16, 141-142, 145-146, 196, 204
Old Order Brethren, 162, 168-170, 173, 205, 224
On Earth Peace, 191
ordinances, 10, 109, 110, 112, 117, 120, 125, 127
ordination, 83, 122, 124, 149, 204
Original Sin, 49-58
Orthodox, 6, 81-82, 99-100, 110, 112, 114, 117, 123, 134, 176
outer word, 82, 103, 104, 210
Page, Kirby, 72, 161
passing the salutation, 131
Paul, Apostle, 150, 174
"Peacefully, Simply, Together," 12, 217, 228, 232
"Peacemaking: the Call of God in History," 1991, 191

Penn, William, 195
Pentecost, 37, 39, 77, 80, 83, 92, 116, 121, 229
Pentecostalism, 85, 177
Pentecostals, 78, 79-80, 84, 88
Peter, Apostle, 15-16, 69, 83, 110, 121-122, 129, 159, 180, 196, 229
Philadelphian Society, 25
Philips, Dirk, 53, 71
Pia Desideria (*Pious Wishes for the Church*), 3, 5, 21
Pietism, definition of, 21-23
Pietist Justification, 26
Pietist Reformation, 3, 179, 192
Pietists, 6, 18-19, 21-24, 26-27, 55-56, 58, 79, 81, 88, 92, 101, 103, 157, 172, 177, 179, 193-194, 209
Piper, Otto, 218
plain dress, 152-154
Plymouth Brethren, 181
postmillennialism, 181-184
postmodernism, 186
prayer coverings, 149-152
premillenialism, 28, 182-185
Presbyterian, 37, 50, 114
priesthood of all believers, 13, 81, 83, 112, 122, 131, 153, 154
primitivism, 24
pro-choice, 166
pro-life, 166
progressives, 162, 168-170, 205
Protestant scholasticism, 4
puberty, 125
Quakerism, 21, 225
Quakers, 6, 7, 25, 41, 52, 53, 68, 78, 88, 112, 113, 115, 143, 160, 194, 198, 200, 211, 212, 215, 219
Quinter, James, *x*
Quran, 62, 106
Radical Pietism, 3, 19, 22, 25, 27, 103, 140, 172, 179, 187, 192
Radical Reformation, 17, 18, 26, 54, 92, 120, 193
ransom atonement theories, 221
Reagan, Ronald, 175
reconciliation, 34, 43, 45, 92, 132, 133, 138, 156, 169, 170, 194, 206, 219, 224
recovery of the Brethren vision, 186-189
Reformed tradition, 10, 35, 36, 106
regeneration, 21, 26-27, 122, 129
restitutionism, 24, 187
Revelation, Book of, 88, 99, 179, 180-181, 185, 212, 219
revivalism, 28, 145, 159, 180, 205
Revolutionary War, 194-195, 198
Riedemann, Peter, 47
Roman Catholics, 4, 6, 35, 112-113, 117, 134

Roop, Eugene, 166
Royer, Galen, 185
Rule of Paul, 86, 101, 210
sacrament, 4, 15, 36, 53, 110, 112-115, 128, 131
sacrament, mystery, 36, 109-113
sacramentalism, 110, 112
sacramentarianism, 110-112
sacraments, 6, 36, 99, 109, 128, 131, 134
Sanctification, 26-27, 80, 88, 91, 122, 129-130
Sappington, Roger E., 9-10
Satan, 42, 53, 221
Satisfaction or Penal Theory, 221-222
Sauer, Christopher, *x*, 2, 196
Saul, 83, 221
Schertz, Mary, 220
Schleitheim Confession, 214, 224, 227
Schwarzenau, 17, 24-25, 42, 46, 104, 111, 130, 179, 192
Scofield Reference Bible, 181
second coming, 46, 178-185, 197, 232
secret societies, 144-146
secular theology, 185
separate people, 145-146, 157
Seventh-Day Adventist, 181-182
Sharp, S. Z., 151
Simons, Menno, 46, 53, 71, 99, 103
single mode. *See* feetwashing.
Snyder, Graydon, 150-151
Socinian, 17
Solingen Brethren, 5, 17
Spener, Philip Jacob, 3, 4, 6, 11-12, 21-22, 27, 55, 101, 104, 192
Spirit, 75-93. *See also* fruit of the Spirit and gifts of the Spirit.
spiritualism, 25
Standing Committee, 39-40, 97, 163-165, 199, 208
Stassen, Glen, 143
Stoffer, Dale, *x*, 168-169
Symbolical Books, 3-4
symbols, 3, 25, 27, 76, 112, 116-117, 122, 139-154
systematic theology, *x*, *xi*, 35, 101, 220
temperance movement, 173
the trinity, 18, 23, 37, 63, 77, 81-83, 222
The War on Terrorism ("The Terror of God"), 179, 219
theology of love, 25-26, 207
theology of the cross, 26
Thirty Years' War, 4
Tillich, Paul, 101, 116, 140, 176
transignification, 115
Treaty of Westphalia, 5
trine immersion, 124
Trinity, doctrine of, 37, 81-82

True Christianity, 3
Unitarian, 17
universal restoration, 26, 39, 159, 160, 161
universal salvation, 160
universalism, 28, 159-161
unpardonable sin, 87-88
Vatican II, 99, 112-113
vengeance of God, 43, 219-220
Vietnam, 52, 69, 202-204, 214, 229
Visser D'Hooft, W. A., 130
vocational pacifism, 205-207, 214-216
Waldensians, 16
Waldo, Peter, 16-17
War of 1812, 194, 197
Weaver, J. Denny, 218
Wesley, John, 11, 27, 54, 57, 91, 92
West, Dan, 107, 200-201, 211
Wieand, A. C., 151

Willems, Dirk, 26, 227
Willoughby, William, *x*, 17, 156
Winchester, Elhanan, 159, 160
Wohlfahrt, Michael, 2
Wolfe, George, 162
World War I, 199, 200-201, 211
World War II, 194, 201-202, 204-205, 207-210, 230
wrath of God, 219, 220
Zechariah, 96, 191, 218
Ziegler, Harry, 43
Zigler, M. R., 115, 130, 186-187, 200-201, 206, 211
Zinzendorf, 28, 38, 81
Zollikon, 20
Zunkel, Wayne, *x*
Zwingli, Ulrich, 20